THE FUTURE OF OPEN DATA

THE FUTURE OF OPEN DATA

Edited by Pamela Robinson
and Teresa Scassa

University of Ottawa Press
2022

University of Ottawa **Press**
Les **Presses** de l'Université d'Ottawa

The University of Ottawa Press (UOP) is proud to be the oldest of the francophone university presses in Canada and the oldest bilingual university publisher in North America. Since 1936, UOP has been enriching intellectual and cultural discourse by producing peer-reviewed and award-winning books in the humanities and social sciences, in French and in English.

www.press.uottawa.ca

Library and Archives Canada Cataloguing in Publication

Title: The future of open data / Pamela Robinson and Teresa Scassa (eds.)
Names: Robinson, Pamela (Pamela J.), 1968- editor. | Scassa, Teresa, editor.
Series: Law, technology, and media.
Description: Series statement: Law, technology and media | Includes bibliographical references.
Identifiers: Canadiana (print) 20210296534 | Canadiana (ebook) 20210297042 | ISBN 9780776629742 (hardcover) | ISBN 9780776629735 (softcover) | ISBN 9780776629759 (PDF) | ISBN 9780776629766 (EPUB)
Subjects: LCSH: Electronic government information. | LCSH: Electronic public records. | LCSH: Geospatial data. | LCSH: Government information. | LCSH: Government information—Access control. | LCSH: Freedom of information. | LCSH: Transparency in government—Technological innovations.
Classification: LCC JF1525.A8 F88 2022 | DDC 352.3/8028557—dc23

Legal Deposit: Second Quarter 2022
Library and Archives Canada

Production Team

Copy editing	Robbie McCaw
Proofreading	Tanina Drvar
Typesetting	Nord compo

Cover design
Lefrançois Agence Marketing B2B

Cover Image
Data Binary Binary System Data Deluge Word Dataset. Max Pixel.

SSHRC CRSH

This book was published with the help of a grant from the Canadian Federation for the Humanities and Social Sciences, through the Awards to Scholarly Publications Program, using funds provided by the Social Sciences and Humanities Research Council of Canada.

The University of Ottawa Press gratefully acknowledges the support extended to its publishing list by the Government of Canada, the Canada Council for the Arts, the Ontario Arts Council, the Social Sciences and Humanities Research Council and the Canadian Federation for the Humanities and Social Sciences through the Awards to Scholarly Publications Program, and by the University of Ottawa.

ONTARIO ARTS COUNCIL
CONSEIL DES ARTS DE L'ONTARIO
an Ontario government agency
un organisme du gouvernement de l'Ontario

Canada Council for the Arts
Conseil des arts du Canada

Canada

uOttawa

Table of Contents

Part II: Pitfalls and Opportunities

Part III: New Landscapes for Open Data

Part IV: The Future of Open Data

Acknowledgements

This book is the result of a five-year multi-party research project funded by a partnership grant from the Social Sciences and Humanities Research Council of Canada: "How the geospatial web 2.0 is reshaping government-citizen interactions" (no. 895-2012-1023). The principal investigator for this grant was Dr. Renee Sieber, Associate Professor, McGill University. Partnership grants support collaboration across sectors and provide stable funding to mount ambitious, multi-year, and multifaceted projects. We are grateful for the support we received for a project that has built bridges across disciplines and sectors.

The contributors to this collection were either researchers or students under the grant, or were connected by close research ties with those who were part of the project. There were other researchers, collaborators, and partners on the project whose collaboration and collegiality across the span of the grant strengthened the work. We are also deeply appreciative of our grant partners—from public and private sectors alike. As a group, we learned much from one another, and these collaborations enriched our knowledge and insights.

The authors in this volume each acknowledge the assistance they received in preparing their contributions. We would here also like to acknowledge the support that we, the editors of this collective work, have received. Many thanks to Anthony Banks for his skilled and attentive assistance in preparing the manuscript for submission, and to Robbie McCaw for his excellent copy-editing. Thanks also to Maryse Cloutier, Marie-Hélène Lowe, Martin Llewellyn, and Mireille Piché of the University of Ottawa Press for carefully shepherding us through the process of producing this book. We gratefully acknowledge, too, the anonymous peer reviewers who read our manuscript and provided thoughtful and helpful feedback.

We are additionally grateful to the University of Ottawa for the funding that has permitted the publication of this book in open-access format. Given the topic of this book, open access was a priority.

The final stages of this book's writing and assembly were completed during the COVID-19 pandemic. Many of our authors were locked down, working from home. We very much appreciate their continued commitment to this project, and are grateful for the patience and good humour of our family members who put up with us as we finalized the manuscript.

Pamela Robinson
Teresa Scassa
March 29, 2022

Introduction

Teresa Scassa and Pamela Robinson

1. The Evolution of Open Data

The notions of "open government" and "open data" have both seen a marked uptake in global interest in the last decade. Many countries have issued open government and open data declarations—for example, New Zealand in 2011 and Australia in 2010. In May 2013, the Obama administration in the United States issued an executive order titled "Making Open and Machine Readable the New Default for Government Information." The multilateral Open Government Partnership (OGP), launched at the United Nations in 2011, requires its members to commit to its Open Government Declaration, which includes a commitment to open data. The OGP has grown from eight founding nations in 2011 to 78 countries, with 20 "local" members made up of subnational governments in both the Global North and South. OGP member states undertake to develop action plans and to address the objectives of the movement in their domestic policies. In 2013, the Group of Eight (G8) nations committed to the Open Data Charter, which set out five guiding principles that included a commitment to open data by default. The Open Data Charter is now subscribed to by over a hundred governments and organizations.

According to conventional views, open data consist of government data that are usually provided for free, in a machine-readable format, and with few, if any, restrictions on reuse (Janssen et al., 2012). Open data are made more accessible and usable by the infrastructure that accompanies them, including portals that facilitate searching for and finding relevant datasets. On the one hand, the provision of open data is closely linked to the open government movement. However, open data are different from other kinds of information provided in the open government context. Unlike information provided under access-to-information regimes, for example, open data are typically data rather than processed information. They are also provided proactively rather than per request. They may also be provided with regular updates. The scope of their reuse is also much broader—open data may be used in analytics by commercial or non-profit actors, they can be combined with other data, and they can be used for purposes that go beyond governmental transparency.

Canada launched its own open government policy, which included commitments to open data, in 2012. It joined the OGP in the same year. Since then, it has developed its open data program, including an open data portal, and an open government licence based on the UK government's. In 2018, Canada was co-national chair of the OGP. Many Canadian municipalities have been at the forefront of open data developments in the country, and most provincial governments have followed suit with open data programs of their own. The Government of Ontario was one of the first subnational governments to join the OGP.

Clearly, the global open data movement has evolved significantly in the course of the last decade. In that short period of time, it has been embraced by governments at all levels around the world, with varying degrees of enthusiasm. In Canada, open data commitments from federal, provincial, and municipal governments have snowballed, becoming increasingly sophisticated. In 2019, for example, Ontario became the first government in Canada to actually commit in legislation to open data (Simpler, Faster, Better Services Act, 2019). Concurrent with this evolution, our geospatial and open data research partnership, Geothink, which convened in 2013, set out to examine how the "geoweb"—the concept of a geospatial web—shapes government and citizen interactions. This Social Sciences and Humanities Research Council of Canada–funded partnership grant, led by Dr. Renee Sieber (of McGill University and a contributor to this volume), included 14 faculty members from Canadian universities, 12 international research collaborators, and 25 research partners from government (the federal, the provinces of Nova Scotia and Ontario, and nine Canadian municipalities). Over the life of the grant, we paid significant attention to the central role played by open data in the geoweb. We found that while there was considerable enthusiasm for open data and much literature that explored methods for opening data and applications for open government data, there was relatively little research that investigated the benefits and challenges of open data.

In the relatively short span of time in which opening data has become a commitment for so many national and subnational governments, other transformations in the digital and data economy have greatly impacted the value of data and their potential applications. The rise of big data analytics was just the beginning; currently, artificial intelligence (AI) and machine learning are driving technological innovation and, in doing so, are consuming vast quantities of data (Kitchin, 2014). Technological advancements are also increasing the volume, variety, and velocity of data collected by governments, thus changing the significance of open government data, and rendering its practice more complex from practical and policy perspectives (e.g., Scassa & Diebel, 2016; Johnson et al., 2017). Public–private partnerships in smart cities, to provide just one example, have also rendered open data more complex from a public-policy point of view (Scassa, 2020). Some of these complexities relate to who owns or controls the data generated in hybrid public–private partnerships. Some governments may also be increasingly tempted by the potential to license access to particular subsets of government data as a means of generating new revenue (Aggarwal, 2018; Pilon-Larose, 2020). As rapidly as open data has risen in importance, it has been swept into a period of technological change that challenges its foundations.

As we approached the end of our six-year research project, we found that we had already studied and explored the challenges and deployment of open data in the context of government–citizen interactions and had developed considerable expertise on a number of issues. Our researchers had explored hackathons (Robinson & Johnson, 2016), licensing (Scassa & Diebel, 2016), open data and privacy (Scassa & Conroy, 2016; Scassa, 2014a), and the use and uptake of open data (Sieber & Johnson, 2015; Johnson et. al., 2017). We had also begun to critically interrogate the merits of open data and some challenges thereof (Johnson et al., 2017). Nearing the end of the grant, and facing the technological transformations already underway, we considered it an opportune moment to ask: What is the future of open data? We issued a call to those involved in the grant—as researchers, collaborators, or partners—and invited them to reflect upon the future of open data and to contribute chapters addressing their reflections grounded in their disciplinary, interdisciplinary perspectives, or in their views from outside the academy. This book is the result of that call.

Looking back over the past seven years, we have taken stock of the fact that the landscape of the open data ecosystem has matured and changed, sometimes in unanticipated ways. Our unique vantage point allows us to look both back and forward in order to offer informed insights into what the future of open data may hold. A thread that runs through our work is that we have collectively taken a critical social science perspective, grounded in the imperative that our research should be relevant to our partners in the field, including our government, civil society, and private-sector partners. Accordingly, we anticipate that our insights into the future of open data will combine observations about what our research suggests will happen with a critical perspective on what should happen.

At the time we issued the call, it was not clear to us whether this collection of papers would be an epitaph for open data or a road map to the future. Perhaps ultimately, it is a bit of both. Most of our contributors have not given up on the potential for open data—yet most also acknowledge that it is time to look past the hype of open data, and time also to take stock of the dramatic changes in the evolving data economy and the impact such will have on open data.

2. Unravelling Open Data Assumptions

In the early days of the open data movement, advocates and activists were full of hope and optimism, particularly when the potential of open data was considered in contrast to the migration of government services online through e-government efforts. Open data was viewed as a new way of opening government, encouraging entrepreneurship, engaging citizens, and wiring new ways of working with government for the private sector and civil-society groups. In practical terms, what we find is a mixed record of success, functional rather than robust uptake of open data efforts, challenges, and middling potential being realized (Johnson, 2016; Lauriault et al., 2018).

The extent to which open data has led to governments being more open is rather varied. A review of open datasets on myriad government open data portals reveals a "mixed bag" of high-value, comprehensive, fragmented, quirky, and mundane datasets (Johnson et al., 2017). The desire to identify and release high-value datasets is such that the Government of Canada convened the Canada Open

Government Working Group (COGWG) to frame principles for prioritizing release (Government of Canada, n.d.). The Government of Ontario, which was the first substate actor in Canada to entrench open data in legislation, made efforts to demonstrate responsiveness to the open data community. It initiated a voting process by which people could request particular datasets; they would then prioritize the most popular 25. Public-salary disclosure, ministerial budgets and expenditures, the provincial staff directory, workforce statistics, and vehicle statistics ranked the highest. Substantively, this signals that there is public/entrepreneurial appetite for transparency- and accountability-related datasets.

The relationship between entrepreneurs and civic technology innovators around open data continues to evolve as well. In the early days of open data portals, government staff reported that they were sometimes asked to make a "business case" for opening datasets to the public (Robinson & Johnson, 2016). And it is now commonplace for open data portals to include examples of how the datasets have been used in practice. The City of Toronto's portal, for example, shows a range of applications, including garbage-collection schedules; SeeClickFix, a citizen-reporting platform tied to the city's 311 program; myriad transit apps; and a social well-being index (City of Toronto, 2020). This range shows the civic and private sector using open data for public good and potential profit.

Yet not all open data portals are full of opportunity; the richness, potential impact, usability, and range of data can vary widely. Open datasets of pet and baby names are commonplace across portals. In Brussels there is an open dataset showing where one can find murals of comics graphics and another with the hashtag #doesitfart that identifies which animals are flatulent (Open Data Institute, 2018). These kinds of datasets are fun but not necessarily impactful. Other open data portals look robustly populated with seemingly high numbers of datasets published, but it is important to look further into what these volume numbers suggest. One agonizing trend in open data portals arises when governments post datasets by sub-geographic unit (e.g., by municipal ward, by county) instead of at the most aggregated level, such as statistical units, health regions, or electoral districts. This fragmentation can frustrate users, and can also cynically be interpreted as a way to boost the numbers of datasets made open instead of having data that can be widely linked and compared.

Early open data advocates had the "if you build it they will come" mindset about open data portals. But in reality, these portals, along with other innovations like geoweb mapping tools, face the same barriers: their very existence does not guarantee impact or a natural user group (Sieber & Johnson, 2015). As more governments engaged in the processes of making data open, it quickly became apparent that there were and continue to be material, procedural, and political costs to doing the work (Johnson et al., 2017) of publishing the data people want and find useful. Open is neither cheap nor easy to achieve. In this sense, one of the lessons of the open data experience to date is that it is both a process and a commitment. It is not a problem solved by the creation of a portal stocked with datasets. Further, it requires ongoing engagement between those who supply open data and those who use them.

3. Changes in the Role and Value of Data

As noted above, the dramatic evolution of digital and data-based technologies has had a transformative impact on both the role and value of data. Open data policies were never uniquely about transparency. Many open data policies were implemented with a view to unlocking the economic power of data in the hands of government and making it available to the private sector for innovation purposes (Deloitte, 2012; Global Government Forum, 2020; Duus & Cooray, 2016). On a small scale, government data might be useful for the development of apps or other consumer-oriented services. On a larger scale, government data—particularly geospatial data—might be useful in populating maps or in feeding into data analytics. Big data analytics requires a high volume, variety, and velocity of data; not all open government data would be suitable for such analytics, but some might. Further, as the nature and variety of data collected by governments evolved, there began to be pressure to open not just static datasets but real-time data as well (Scassa & Diebel, 2016).

The rise of the "smart city" created new challenges for open data. In some cases, smart technologies involving sensors that collected significant volumes of data were adopted by cities under contracts that were not necessarily clear about who "owned" the collected data. This issue was relevant both as concerns the right to commercially exploit the data and to the ability of municipal governments to make such data available as open data to stimulate innovation

(Scassa, 2014b). As smart cities have evolved, public–private partnerships are increasingly common around digital infrastructure, and around sensors and related technologies. The role of the private sector in collecting and processing these municipal data raises thorny challenges in determining what data are available as open data. Such challenges turn on whether the data are public-sector data, private-sector data, or a novel combination of both, which calls for new governance mechanisms. Similar challenges are presented by the burgeoning artificial intelligence sector, which is hungry for a broad range of data from public and private sectors alike (Aggarwal, 2018; Kitchin, 2015). These developments are pushing governments to explore data-sharing frameworks other than open data—ones that might facilitate the sharing of data with complex origins or that might raise personal-data issues (Scassa & Vilain, 2019; Scassa, 2020).

Alongside smart city developments, the rapid evolution of AI and machine-learning technologies has also created a thirst for data. While more conventional open data in the form of static datasets might be of limited interest for developing AI, the more complex, live-streamed data from smart city and other sensor technologies deployed by governments are likely of more significant interest. Thus, the value of real-time government data is expanding, and questions are increasingly being raised as to whether "open" is the appropriate policy for valuable data, the licensing of which might offset the costs of collecting and maintaining them. In addition to issues of the cost of open data, data licensing as part of data-sharing frameworks is increasingly being contemplated as a means of protecting privacy and addressing ethical issues in the downstream uses of data (e.g., Dawson, 2020; Scassa & Vilain, 2019).

The changing value of data in a data-driven economy has also raised concerns over data sovereignty. Data sovereignty has both broad and narrow meanings. In the narrow sense, some have begun to advocate for policies of data localization—in other words, requiring that certain data (usually personal information) be stored within the physical boundaries of the state in which the data are collected (Brehmer, 2018). Data-localization advocates are motivated by concerns over privacy and security—fearing that offshore storage of personal data exposes individuals to unacceptable risks (Chander & Lê, 2015; Brehmer, 2018). Others are concerned about the cybersecurity implications of the offshore storage of crucial data (Brehmer, 2018; Baezner & Robin, 2018). Yet another view of data sovereignty includes the ability of state actors (including law enforcement) to access data through domestic legal channels rather than petitioning for access overseas, where they risk having domestic production orders rejected in a foreign jurisdiction (Daskal, 2016). The term "data sovereignty" is also used in a much broader sense by a growing number of Indigenous communities worldwide (Kukutai & Taylor, 2016; FNIGC, 2020). This view of data sovereignty is more robust and touches on sovereignty not just in storage and access to data but also in terms of being able to control decisions about what data are collected, according to what parameters, and for what purposes. Data-sovereignty concerns, both narrow and broad, go beyond open data concerns. However, they overlap with open data to the extent that data sovereignty requires a level of control that includes the ability to decide which data are to be made open. It certainly also includes the ability to place limits on access to and reuse of data.

Although big data analytics, smart cities, AI, and machine learning are all part of an ongoing digital revolution that has, in a relatively short space of time, changed the open data landscape, it is important to keep in mind that the economic value of open data has always been an element that has driven governments in their development of open data portals and programs. From the early days of open data, there has been an uneasy relationship between open data and open government. Democratic value alone has not been sufficient to drive the open data agenda; there is an intrinsic link between openness and economic value (Robinson & Johnson, 2016).

4. The Chapters in this Collection

It is within this context of, on the one hand, sober reflection on the "realities" rather than the promise of open data and, on the other, the rapidly evolving technological context that is shaping a new data-driven economy that the chapters in this collection are situated.

This book opens with a reflection on the origins of the practice of sharing data with a particular focus on Canada's engagement and efforts. Tracey Lauriault draws from her depth of experience as an early open-data advocate and her ongoing critical data studies research to evaluate the assemblage of ecosystems from which Canadian open data efforts emerged. She reminds us that open data has a rich and diverse genealogy, and that this genealogy may contain the DNA that will shape its future evolution. Her chapter concludes with reflections that bridge this past practice into current, and future, open data efforts, with a particular focus on the role of open data in smart-technology systems.

The second section of the book is titled "Pitfalls and Opportunities." As we move from early, optimistic thinking that open data was an innovative idea into a data-governance ecosystem that is more mature, the community of open-data users and researchers is well positioned to move beyond generic "open data is good" propositions to exploring more nuanced assessment.

In her chapter, "Open Data and Confidential Commercial Information," Teresa Scassa identifies this growing tension between public- and private-sector data as a part of the future of open data. She looks at access-to-information laws in Canada to show how the laws as they are currently framed place considerable restrictions on governments when it comes to sharing information that is identified as confidential commercial information or even "commercially sensitive" information. Just as open data regimes have had to find ways to balance privacy with open data, she suggests that similar balancing measures might be required to address the private-sector interests that are intertwined with an ever-growing volume of government data.

In "Reusability of Publicly Accessible User Data on Platform Websites," Haewon Chung explores a source of open data that is not governmental and that is "open" in a more contested sense. Platform websites host considerable volumes of data (not all of which is personal data) that are broadly publicly accessible, although they often use a variety of legal, technological, and contractual measures to limit the ability of others to harvest and use this data. Nevertheless, Chung argues that there are good reasons why much of this data should be considered open in the sense of being available for free and unrestricted access and use.

Both Scassa and Chung explore a future in which private-sector organizations contribute to the store of data available for reuse. In both cases, government policy/law/regulation play a role. Scassa argues for a reworking or reinterpretation of those laws limiting the disclosure of some types of data as open government data, while Chung suggests that changes in laws, or in their interpretations, should provide more liberal rights to reuse publicly accessible data. In this vision of the future of open data, the data sources are not just public sector, and openness is not necessarily entirely within the control of the party claiming rights in the data.

In their chapter, "Challenges to the Access of Government Open Data by Private Sector Companies," Peter Johnson and Christine Varga raise a question that is fundamental to the provision of open data: What does it mean to "access" data? By asking this question from a private-sector open data-user perspective, their research reveals that access for this user group is more dynamic and complex than might have been originally anticipated.

Elizabeth Judge and Tenille Brown's chapter on open data and government brings a new consideration for governments planning to launch, maintain, or enhance their open data efforts: liability. Again, building on the embryonic theme of "open data is good," the authors, both legal scholars, flag liability law as a prospective new challenge to open data. Through their assessment of the extent to which governments might be held liable for actions or omissions arising from government-provided open data, their work reinforces the tension between open data opportunities and obligations.

The third section of our book is titled "New Landscapes for Open Data." In their chapter, "Examining the Value of Geospatial Open Data," Sarah Greene and Claus Rinner examine a subset of Vancouver, Toronto, Edmonton, and Ottawa's open data provision. They focus on the types and distribution of geospatial open data and their relationship in helping local governments achieve their economic-development goals attached to broader open government initiatives.

In "Data for Development: Exploring Connections between Open Data, Big Data, and Data Privacy in the Global South," Teresa Scassa and Fernando Perini look at how open data is faring in less developed countries. In those contexts, the supply of open government data may be limited by the resource issues faced by governments that either lack the ability to collect the primary data at regular intervals or to fund and support open data programs, or both. Interestingly, in some contexts, governments have looked to the private sector as a source of open data.

Although rarely explicitly stated, open datasets are predominately gathered from urban and suburban settings. This predominance is not surprising given that populous areas lend themselves more naturally to the infrastructures that gather the data. Renee Sieber and Ian Parfitt, in their chapter "The Future of Open Data is Rural," argue that there are limits to conceptualizing open data as a rural phenomenon. As a result, more attention and research must focus on expanding the capacity of rurally based governments to be more active participants in open data efforts.

In the final chapter of this book, Pamela Robinson and Lisa Ward Mather draw links between the other chapters of the book and the future of open data in a world embroiled in rapid change and facing significant challenges. These include the COVID-19 global pandemic, the climate emergency, and our collective efforts to confront systemic racism. Many of our contemporary challenges have clear points of connection to data, as governments seek solutions in evidence-based decision-making, and as the private sector turns to data-driven technologies and analytics. These challenges, therefore, reinforce the pressing nature of the central question of this book: What is the future of open data?

Clearly, there is a growing demand for a greater volume and variety of high-quality open data. As many of our authors suggest, this demand may push the boundaries of what is understood as open data. As the demand for datasets expands, so too do demands for frequent updates and even real-time data. The costs of maintaining such systems of open data, combined with potentially greater concerns over privacy and ethical reuse, could spur a different approach to open government data, one that imposes more licensing restrictions to achieve certain ends, or one that requires some form of cost recovery. At the same time, some private sector actors might increasingly become sources of some form of open or freely shared data, and platforms will find themselves inadvertently a source of scraped, publicly accessible data. The legitimacy of modes of accessing and using these data will depend upon laws in place within jurisdictions. While not open data in its conventional sense, the ability to access and use these diverse sources of data will shape what data are open for access and development.

5. Signals about the Future of Open Data from our Contributors

In each chapter, the authors address the future of open data. The different visions presented reflect the complexity of the evolving data context. In her tracing of the history of open data in Canada, Tracey Lauriault argues that in order for the future of open data to remain open and to serve its originally democratic intent, actors in the open data ecosystem need to both know their history and also keep their attention broadly focused on changes in the technological assemblage. Her appeal for a governance framework that extends beyond open data advocates to include allied actors, including government staff and scientists from spatially oriented disciplines, is important, and it presents pragmatic challenges. With the accelerating trend toward smart city adoption, the momentum is moving toward datasets to be closed and proprietary rather than open in what she calls a "data-enclosure movement." Building on Sieber and Johnson's (2015) work showing that simply opening the data is not enough to ensure their use and uptake, Lauriault adds the further caveat that a history of open data does not ensure a future that is also open. New working relationships with new partners are needed if we want to make further progress with open data.

In their chapter about open data and government liability, Judge and Brown discuss the relevance of liability laws for government policies around open data and argue that, in order to realize the benefits of open data, a statutory framework should be created for all levels of government in Canada. This framework would outline the duties and responsibilities for governments and citizens, and would provide predictability and clarity for all members of the open data ecosystem. It would also incentivize the government to proactively release open data in the public interest.

The future of open data includes new challenges and opportunities for governments seeking to respond to private-sector interests in open data. In their study of private-sector interaction with government open data, Johnson and Varga suggest that governments work to improve data access in order to increase open data usage and, ultimately, demonstrate the value of open data. Analyzing the challenges of private-sector open data users, they conclude that, in the future, governments should provide improved access to linked open data, and implement and follow common open data standards. However, they qualify their discussion, stating that open data initiatives should not focus entirely on one type of user, lest other users be disadvantaged.

The Sieber and Parfit chapter is an important reminder that the future of open data needs to have a broader geographic reach beyond urban centres. The ability of rural areas to provide open data and realize the value from that data is affected by factors such as large spatial area, low population density, lack of government resources and technical skill, and, as a result, limited market incentive to develop open data or broadband Internet service. Building open data ecosystems in rural areas depends upon addressing key challenges, such as the lack of digital infrastructure, and the need to build capacity—including digital literacy and technical capacity. Promising approaches may include collaboration between rural communities to develop common standards and generate "a critical mass of interoperable data" that attracts business opportunities. The authors also suggest that rural areas engage in participatory and place-based rural economic development that can account for the community's specific characteristics.

Scassa and Perini's chapter firmly reminds the open data community that the open data ecosystem is established and growing in the Global South, thus further amplifying the calls for bigger open data geographies. As in the Global North, there are significant needs for building governance frameworks, and this chapter flags the importance of a human-rights-based approach to this work. Importantly, whether north or south, there is significant value in research about the emergence and delivery of open data efforts that must be shared. These kinds of case studies can help accelerate collaborative learning across continents, from south to north and vice versa.

In their evaluation of the value of geospatial open data, Greene and Rinner analyze the distribution and prevalence of GIS-ready data files, and conclude that a more strategic approach to opening data could help build support for open data programs. In particular, they advocate for releasing datasets that support the stated purpose of a municipality's open data initiative. Their study could help cities develop strategic guidelines to help direct data releases in response to user needs.

In her chapter, Teresa Scassa explores a possible future of open data in which increasing amounts of data in the hands of government are privately owned. She notes that governments that purchase confidential commercial data or commercially sensitive data may not legally be able to release those data as part of an open data catalogue. Such a situation could cause government open data offerings to be significantly reduced in time. She argues that in order to support open data in the future, governments must begin to attend to claims of confidential commercial information and assess these claims from the perspective of the public interest. There are proactive measures governments can implement in order to limit such claims if they are unreasonable.

Chung discusses technological and legal issues around the reuse of publicly accessible data hosted on private-sector platforms and concludes that legislation is required to support third-party use of public user data. Such legislation is necessary because these data are an important resource, and because the businesses that host these data will establish data-reuse policies that maximize profit. Such businesses cannot be expected to do what is in the public interest.

In sum, these chapters point to the durability and ongoing momentum of the open-data movement, and they signal directional changes if this movement is to carry on. It is clear from the research shared here that the future of open data is one in which the involvement of new actors is necessary to ensure that open data remain open; to make certain that the datasets that are shared are actually relevant and useful to civil society, government, and private-sector users; and to continue the efforts need to move the data out of portals and into users' hands. The future of open data must be guided by much-needed new legal and governance frameworks that protect privacy, ensure public-good outcomes emerge, and reduce risk and liability. And the future of open data needs to recognize that regardless of the pattern and form of communities, from rural to urban, the interconnectedness across this transect requires much broader thinking and engagement. The research casts an eye toward the future of open data, projecting a new time horizon with a long to-do list of how to advance the work.

Collectively, the chapters of this book push at the boundaries of both the nature and scope of open data. They reflect the changes wrought by the expanding role of data in the economy and in innovation. They also reflect the complicated relationships between government and the private sector, and between governments and citizens, when it comes to data.

Robinson and Ward Mather close the collection with a chapter that bridges the time in which this research was conducted with the current and future set of conditions to which open data needs to respond. Now, as much as before, there clearly remains a role for open government data. Government is a source of very particular types of data, the collection of which is not easily replicated elsewhere. While the future of open data may be an expanding and changing one, at its core will remain the importance of governments as a source of quality, accessible, and reusable data that can drive objectives of transparency and accountability, stimulate innovation, and increase citizen engagement.

References

Aggarwal, S. (2018). *The treasure of the commons: Global leadership through health data.* Centre for International Governance Innovation. https://www.cigionline.org/articles/treasure-commons-global-leadership-through-health-data

Baezner, M., & Robin, P. (2018). *Cyber sovereignty and data sovereignty.* ETH Zurich. https://doi.org/10.3929/ETHZ-B-000314613

Brehmer, H. J. (2018). Data localization: The unintended consequences of privacy litigation. *American University Law Review, 67*(3). http://digitalcommons.wcl.american.edu/aulr/vol67/iss3/6

Chander, A., & Lê, U. (2015). Data nationalism. *Emory Law Journal, 64,* 677–739.

City of Toronto. (2020). *Open data portal.* https://www.toronto.ca/city-government/data-research-maps/open-data/

Daskal, J. (2016). Law enforcement access to data across borders: The evolving security and rights issues. *Journal of National Security Law & Policy, 8,* 473–501.

Dawson, P. (2020, April 20). *COVID-19 tracking data should be managed the way data trusts are.* Policy Options. https://policyoptions.irpp.org/magazines/april-2020/covid-19-tracking-data-should-be-managed-the-way-data-trusts-are/

Deloitte. (2012). *Open data: Driving growth, ingenuity and innovation.* https://www2.deloitte.com/content/dam/Deloitte/uk/Documents/deloitte-analytics/open-data-driving-growth-ingenuity-and-innovation.pdf

Duus, R., & Cooray, M. (2016). *The future will be built on open data—here's why.* The Conversation. https://theconversation.com/the-future-will-be-built-on-open-data-heres-why-52785

First Nations Information Governance Centre (FNIGC). (2020). *The First Nations principles of OCAP.* https://fnigc.ca/ocap

Global Government Forum. (2020). *How governments can harness the power of open data.* https://www.globalgovernmentforum.com/how-governments-harness-power-open-data/

Government of Canada. (n.d.). *Open data across Canada.* https://open.canada.ca/en/maps/open-data-canada#cogwg

Janssen, K. (2012). Open government data and the right to information: Opportunities and obstacles. *Journal of Community Informatics, 8*(2). https://doi.org/10.15353/joci.v8i2.3042

Johnson, P. A., Sieber, R., Scassa, T., Stephens, M., & Robinson, P. (2017). The cost(s) of geospatial open data. *Transactions in GIS, 21*(3), 434–445. https://doi.org/10.1111/tgis.12283

Johnson, P. A. (2016). Reflecting on the success of open data: How municipal government evaluates their open data programs. *International Journal of E-Planning Research, 5*(3), 1–12.

Kitchin, R. (2014). *The data revolution: Big data, open data, data infrastructures and their consequences*. Sage.

Kukutai, T., & Taylor, J. (2016). Data sovereignty for Indigenous people: Current practice and future needs. In *Indigenous data sovereignty: Toward an agenda* (pp. 1–24). The Australian National University, Centre for Aboriginal Economic Policy Research.

Lauriault, T. P., Bloom, R., & Landry, J. (2018). *Open smart cities in Canada: Assessment report*. https://doi.org/10.31235/osf.io/qbyzj

Open Data Institute. (2018). *Open Data Day: Seven weird and wonderful open datasets*. https://theodi.org/article/the-open-data-olympics-seven-weird-and-wonderful-open-datasets/

Pilon-Larose, H. (2020, August 21). Données de la RAMQ : un « délire de businessman déconnecté ». *La Presse*. https://www.lapresse.ca/actualites/sante/2020-08-21/donnees-de-la-ramq-un-delire-de-businessman-deconnecte.php.

Robinson, P. J., & Johnson, P. A. (2016). Civic hackathons: New terrain for local government-citizen interaction? *Urban Planning, 1*(2), 65. https://doi.org/10.17645/up.v1i2.627

Scassa, T. (2014a). Privacy and open government. *Future Internet, 6*(2), 397–413. http://www.mdpi.com/1999-5903/6/2/397.

Scassa, T. (2014b). Public transit data through an intellectual property lens: Lessons about open data. *Fordham Urban Law Journal, 41*, 1759–1810.

Scassa, T. (2020). Designing data governance for data sharing: Lessons from Sidewalk Toronto. *Technology & Regulation*, 44–56. https://techreg.org/index.php/techreg/article/view/51.

Scassa, T., & Conroy, A. (2016). Strategies for protecting privacy in open data and proactive disclosure. *Canadian Journal of Law and Technology, 14*(2), 215–262.

Scassa, T., & Diebel, A. (2016). Open or closed? Open licensing of real-time public sector transit data. *Journal of e-Democracy, 8*(2), 1–20.

Scassa, T., & Vilain, M. (2019). *Governing smart data in the public interest: Lessons from Ontario's smart metering entity* (CIGI Paper No. 221). Centre for International Governance Innovation. https://www.cigionline.org/publications/governing-smart-data-public-interest-lessons-ontarios-smart-metering-entity.

Sieber, R. E., & Johnson, P. A. (2015). Civic open data at a crossroads: Dominant models and current challenges. *Government Information Quarterly, 32*(3), 308–315.

Simpler, Faster, Better Services Act, 2019, S.O. 2019, c. 7, Sched. 56.

PART I

Open Data Origins

CHAPTER 1

Looking Back toward a "Smarter" Open Data Future

TRACEY P. LAURIAULT

Abstract

Open data is a relatively new practice when compared to the history of data sharing. The idea of sharing government records may have started with the Domesday Book of 1086, or more officially with the 1766 Swedish Freedom of the Press Act (Government of Sweden, 1766), which argued for access to government records; or possibly with the data-sharing principles of the International Meteorological Organization (IMO) in 1873; or perhaps with one of the first international agreements on data sharing, the Antarctic Treaty of 1959 (Secretariat for the Antarctic Treaty, 1959). For Canada, the genealogy of data sharing has its own particularities. What is clear is that open data did not just appear out of the ether; it has a history, and I suggest that it starts with the natural and social sciences. This chapter tells a Canadian open data story from a critical data-studies approach. It conceptualizes open data as a social and technical data assemblage, and traces the genealogies of open access to data and open data in Canada. It argues that open data, and how it is technologically conceptualized, might be too narrow a focus, and instead calls for the adoption of a broader and more integrated openness approach, especially as open data are being subsumed by smart systems or digital twins. The chapter concludes by suggesting that the future of open data requires looking back at the epistemic groups involved in its creation, overcoming its technological legacy to ensure that when smart systems and digital twins come online, they do not suffer the same fate in terms of quality and a lack of systems thinking. It also suggests that a broader concept of openness be adopted, especially if there is to be an integrated and systems-based approach to smart systems, as seen in the case of the emerging open smart city.

Acknowledgements
This chapter is informed by work and research conducted at the Geomatics and Cartographic Research Centre at Carleton University, funded by the Social Sciences and Humanities Research Council (SSHRC) and the Canada Foundation for Innovation; the SSHRC-funded InterPARES 2 Project at the University of British Columbia; the European Research Council–funded Programmable City project at Maynooth University; and the Open Smart Cities project funded by the GeoConnections (2008, 2012) program of the Government of Canada.

In this chapter, I suggest that open data is a discursive regime, and to better understand it I apply a critical data studies perspective and frame the discourse within a socio-technological assemblage framework (Kitchin, 2014). I then proceed to briefly describe how open data in Canada evolved by tracing its genealogy (Cosgrove, 2001; Foucault, 2003) to demonstrate that epistemic groups, institutions, materialities, and legalities have uniquely shaped this discursive space. This is part of the social-shaping thesis to data and technology, whereby it is understood that data do not exist independently from the context within which they were created, and the systems and processes that produce them (Dalton & Thatcher, 2014; Kitchin & Lauriault, 2014; Iliadis & Russo, 2016). I then suggest that, as large "smart" social and technological systems (Hughes, 1987) are built, such as smart cities, smart grids, or digital twins, for data to remain open it is critical to move beyond the narrow technological conceptions of open data seen in most definitions. Also, I argue that greater attention should be paid to epistemic groups and their subjectivities so as to avoid the past mistakes made with open data, and I imagine the future of open data by situating it in the context of the emerging open smart city (Lauriault et al., 2019). I propose that if we want open data-driven decision making, we will have to think about openness more broadly; to govern data as more than simply technical objects and, instead, reconceptualize them as open social and technical processes. To conclude, I call for a more political form of citizen engagement, known as technological citizenship, to better govern open data systems (Barney, 2007; Feenberg, 2011). This, I suggest, is especially important to avoid data and technological colonialism (FNIGC, 1998 & 2019; Thatcher et al, 2016; Couldry & Mejias, 2018), which is increasingly being normalized within smart systems, digital twins, and is not addressed in digital strategies.

1. Open Data Social and Technological Assemblage

An assemblage is a theoretical framing of data as a constellation of co-functioning, loosely coupled, heterogeneous elements (DeLanda, 2016), as seen in Figure 1.1. Open data thought of as an assemblage implies that context frames how such data are socially understood in their environment, while technologies, processes, and materialities are the content that perform the tasks of making data open. Open data, because of the component parts of their assemblages, differ from place to place, but as an assemblage they are consistent and known. For example, open data is commonly understood by data formats, licences, standards, and dissemination portals but, it is argued here, should also be about systems and forms of thought. For example, open datasets are also part of new managerialism in government and efficiency discourses and practices, along with principles of transparency and accountability; and a political economy that includes the proactive disclosure of government contracts, procurement, and open corporate registries. Location also matters. For example, in Canada, the Personal Information Protection and Electronic Documents Act (OPC, 2021) regulates how personal data are shared with the private sector, while in the European Union the General Data Protection Regulation (European Union, 2021) governs data protection. Actors and their subjectivities also matter, as they bring different approaches, priorities, skills, and knowledge; for instance, open data are different for a scientist, an app developer, a chief data officer, a company, a government administrator, and an environmentalist.

By looking at open data as a discursive regime, and examining how its constitutive elements have evolved in different places across time, it becomes possible to imagine what this social and technological assemblage might look like in a smart context. This framing may lead to greater systems thinking, which, I argue, is required when it comes to smart cities, digital twins, and digital strategies.

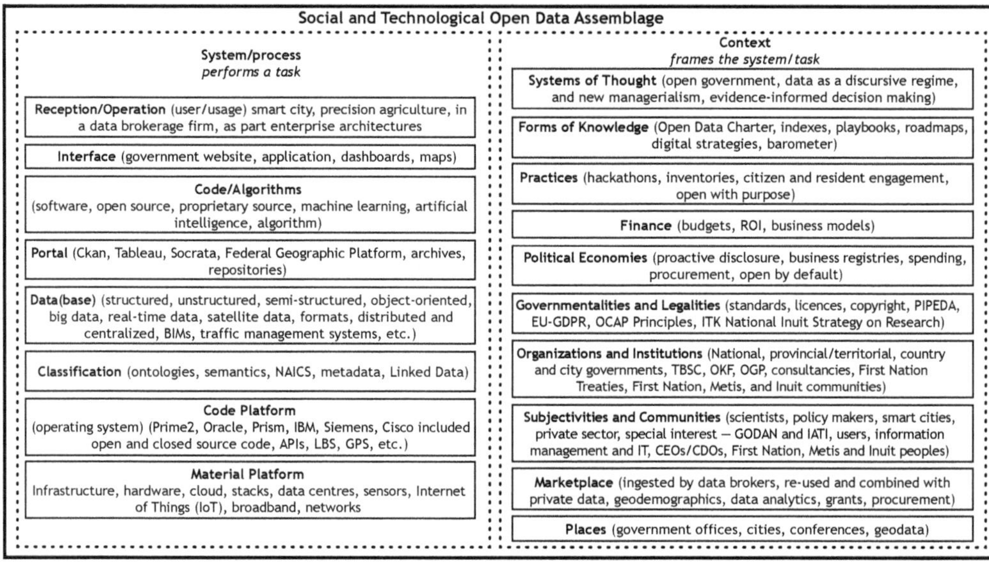

Figure 1.1. Open Data Social-Technological Data Assemblage for Canada. *Source*: Based on Kitchin's Framework 2014.

2. The Legacy of Technical Conceptualizations of Open Data

Critical data scholars, situated broadly in the domains of critical social science and science-and-technology studies, accept that the usual technological conceptualization of data as unbiased, objective, and neutral scientific facts about the world is limited and narrow. Unfortunately, for open data to be qualified as such, they are assessed against these types of criteria, and the legacies of those definitions persist within open data programs. For example, the foundational Open Definition (OKF 2005, 2016/17), a document stemming from the open source and free software movement, is also used to compare and assess open data in the Global Open Data Index (GODI), and was developed by the Open Knowledge Foundation, a global non-profit organization. Applying this definition has resulted in hundreds of thousands of datasets being made open, but without a critical assessment of whether these open data were of good quality or filled any knowledge gaps, such as equity and inclusion or disability and accessibility. As for data quality, the following elements ought to be considered: lineage or provenance, positional accuracy, attribute accuracy, completeness, logical consistency, semantic accuracy, and temporal information (Guptill & Morrison, 1995). Particularities about data quality vary according to the epistemologies of the domains a dataset stems from and the subjectivities of data authors (Lauriault et al., 2008). For instance, a biologist, astronomer, and spatial data or population health specialist will each have their own specific approach, yet they would most likely agree that knowing and reporting on the quality of the data they use and produce is a requirement of their practice. A lack of knowledge about data quality also precludes the possibility of scientific analysis, and affects the quality of the results; but also, a lack of geospatial or semantic interoperability, and basic standardized framework data, makes linking open data either a very laborious process or nearly impossible. Even though Canada ranked high according to GODI, a lack of data quality or a spatial referent means that important social and political analytical work, such as comparing the outcomes of national health programs or educational achievement, is not possible. Moreover, those kinds of data are rarely found in portals in the first place since these are not the data types listed as being important according to GODI's criteria. During the pandemic, the list of essential datasets a nation state ought to publish also proved to be lacking. In Canada, while data were published, there remained a distinct absence of foundational open data on retirement homes, residences for people with disabilities, and disaggregated equity and health data in general (Lauriault, 2020a). Technical conceptualizations of open data have resulted in many open datasets being available in open data portals, but we cannot create much evidence-informed policy with them because of a lack of quality, interoperability, and data gaps.

The fact that open data indices generally assess data at a national scale compounds the problem. In federations like Canada, where health, education, and cities are jurisdictions of the provinces, data are even less likely to be interoperable or standardized, as the GODI does not assess inter-jurisdictional cooperation or data from a systems perspective. This is unfortunate because there are mechanisms, beyond standardization, that support coordinated efforts. The Geomatics Accord, signed by Canada's provinces and territories and federal government in 2001, is one such example, and this has led to the promotion and development of trusted key national-framework datasets such as the road network file and a governance structure (CCOG, n.d.). While the Canadian Council on Geomatics is lauded for this collaboration, the focus remained in geomatics and not on framework data related to health regions or socio-economic data, as was seen during the pandemic in Canada. There are also models such as spatial data infrastructures, most notably the Canadian Geospatial Data Infrastructure (NRCan, 2020) and the Arctic Spatial Data Infrastructure (ASDI, 2021), national mapping strategies (OSI, 2017), and scientific-data-producing communities such as the Global Earth Observation System of Systems (GEOSS), among many others, that have well-developed data cultures and policies, practices, legalities, standards, and technologies from which to learn. Furthermore, Indigenous data considerations are also absent from these technical conceptualizations. For First Nation, Métis, and Inuit communities, cosmologies, ontologies, and epistemologies about what constitute Indigenous data, data models, and open data differ from conceptions found in Western notions of empiricism and science. These discourses can be read in works on Indigenous statistics, decolonizing research methodologies, and data sovereignty (Walter & Andersen, 2013; Tuhiwai-Smith, 1999; Kukutai & Taylor, 2016; FNIGC, 2021). For example, the First Nations Information Governance Centre (FNIGC, 2021) states that First Nations

> assert data sovereignty and support the development of information governance and management at the community level through regional and national partnerships. We adhere to free, prior and informed consent, respect nation-to-nation relationships, and recognize the distinct customs of nations.

This includes sovereignty over data in the possession of the Crown but that are considered to belong to First Nations in a post-colonial and reconciliation context. As just described, actors involved with open data in public administrations are different from actors in science, and both differ from Indigenous conceptions. Public administrators assess the qualities of their open data in terms of a set of technical and licence criteria; scientists consider data quality to be a primary concern, and often build interoperable data systems accordingly; while decolonization and data sovereignty, in addition to data quality, are concerns for First Nation, Métis, and Inuit communities.

Each of these actors operate in different contexts and have different subjectivities, resulting in different data practices and conceptualizations, which are often at odds. For example, an open by default approach is incommensurable with the FNIGC's (2021) principles of ownership, control, access, and possession (known as OCAP), since there are data about Indigenous people held by the Crown that should only be made open when there is agreement with the Indigenous communities or peoples they are about.

The Open Data Charter (2015), endorsed by members of the Open Government Partnership (OGP), of which Canada is a member, along with the provinces of Ontario and Quebec as local members, is somewhat better than the original Open Definition (see Chapter 1). The Charter includes six principles that state that data are to be (1) open by default, (2) timely and comprehensive, (3) accessible and usable, (4) comparable and interoperable, (5) for improved governance and citizen engagement, and (6) for inclusive development and innovation. It is a more nuanced approach to GODI and one that factors in institutional arrangements. The fourth principle, that data be comparable and interoperable, is an improvement, but the unfortunate legacy of earlier open data definitions and practices had already gained traction and momentum. The lag time between the adoption of the Open Data Charter and the legacy of institutional practices, combined with open data being administered in a non-systematic way, has resulted in lots of data that are open but which cannot be combined, linked, or compared semantically and spatially. Principles 5 and 6 of the Charter give purpose to the opening of data, and this is where issues of data governance in addition to data for governance ought to be considered. And with the ideals of inclusive development and innovation, values such as fairness, justice, equity, inclusion, and the identification of data gaps and things that are invisible in data ought to also be considered, such as police-shooting data, data on missing and murdered Aboriginal women, or, too, that there are no statistical programs in Canada about people with disabilities. Charter principles include transparency and proactive disclosure initiatives, originating from those involved in access to information, freedom of the press, open contracting, beneficial ownership, and international development. These principles are well suited to the governance of administrative data. The principle of open by default has, however, come under scrutiny of late, as in the context of Indigenous data, and also because it is a labour-intensive process for government administrators, who often struggle with prioritizing decision-making on what to publish first. The focus is shifting toward publishing with purpose (Open Data Charter, 2018) or, as in the case for a potentially new open government commitment in Canada, Open Data for Results,[1] which aims to mitigate data gaps and invisibilities.[2] Open data programs can also be informed by the experiences of international organizations like the Global Open Data for Agriculture and Nutrition (GODAN), comprised of experts who advocate for and publish data with purpose. GODAN is based in Montréal, and its expert members collaborate to make agricultural and nutritionally relevant data available, accessible, and usable for unrestricted use worldwide, ensuring that the "value chain for agriculture and nutrition is more efficient, innovative, equitable, and accountable" (GODAN 2016).

The Open Data Barometer is another important assessment system. Currently, it evaluates the programs of 30 countries that adopted the Open Data Charter and, for the G20 members, their governments are committed to the G20 Anti-Corruption Open Data Principles (G20, 2015). The Barometer applies the technical criteria of the Open Definition, the technical and policy principles of the Open Data Charter, and the G20 Anti-Corruption Open Data Principles to assess open data readiness in terms of the ability to deliver open data, how that delivery is done, and the political, social, and economic impacts of open data—and it does so quantitatively and qualitatively (Open Data Barometer, 2017). The Barometer is lauded for considering open data more broadly, even though the legacy of the technological criteria for open data persist, as does the lack of attention to data quality. Some organizations, like Open North in Canada, CiviTeo in France, and the City of Ottawa, recognize that technical conceptions of open data are limited, and instead focus on developing data-sharing cultures inside government, as there is also a need to make data

1 *Open Data for Results* is a new commitment as part of the Government of Canada Open Government, for which the public consultation has just been completed. There has been a general sense of dissatisfaction of the commitments from Government by civil society actors, since what was submitted does not resemble what went out to consultation but some progress has been made nonetheless. https://opengov.konveio.net/open-data-results.

2 As a member of Canada's Multi-Stakeholder Forum on Open Government, I am one of the proponents for this commitment, which form part of an open government plan for Canada. See https://open.canada.ca/en/multi-stakeholder-forum-open-government.

accessible and interoperable within organizations. This has become increasingly important as cross-organization data analytics teams are forming, in addition to existing geospatial data teams, resulting from the need for an integrated evidence-informed decision-making culture, and also because technical capabilities are increasing. We will see more data analytics teams in cities as more smart systems come online and as a new group of C-level executives (whose title begins with the word "chief") are appointed as a result of digital strategies. These cross-institutional teams are beginning to recognize that legacy administrative data systems in different business units preclude their ability to share data internally, and this is changing how new technologies are procured. For example, the City of Ottawa's Community and Social Services Department collects data in seven different information-management systems, some of which belong to other levels of government, and is now trying to reconcile how it will standardize the collection of equity and inclusion data across these to better inform service delivery, most notably the ongoing public-health response to the COVID-19 pandemic (City of Ottawa, 2021). Technical and data interoperability have been identified as a new priority in how data are produced, as has the need for semantic interoperability if processes are to be automated, such as in the case of artificial intelligence and machine learning (AI/ML). Although not a focus here, another constraint is accessibility, as there are requirements in North America that digital government systems be accessible, which is also the case for open data and their visualization. Currently, this form of accessibility is not assessed by GODI, the Open Data Charter, or the Open Data Barometer, as data about accessibility are not considered to be a key dataset to be published by any of these indicator systems nor is the notion of the accessibility of data for disabled people.

3. Global Data Sharing: A Genealogy

A genealogical approach to understanding the evolution of concepts and practices provides for a deeper analysis of the evolution of the power/knowledge of a discourse (Foucault, 2003). A genealogy historically situates discourse in a specific knowledge-production process. For example, access to data conceptually differs from open data, as it is more about data sharing between a set of specific actors, but it is from this social and technological practice of sharing data that an environment conducive for the emergence of open data exists. The subjectivities of the data-producing cultures of early actors developing data-sharing practices also differ from those of the open data communities we see today. The former were scientists and data authorities; the latter are the administrators of open data programs and may not necessarily be data authorities nor data owners. The early narrative on access to scientific and spatial data was grounded in systems and infrastructure thinking. Thus, data are part of technical as well as institutional, organizational, collaborative, research, and results-based systems, as data-sharing practices were purpose-driven (e.g., climate modelling). Data here might be in proprietary formats—and may be under a licensing regime, with some restrictions on use by the private sector. This would not be in keeping with open science, where data, methods, techniques, and technologies are open (Foster, n.d.). Nevertheless, data are shared. We need simply think of the multi-billion-dollar Earth observation (EO) community, with its hundreds of public- and private-sector satellite and radar systems circumnavigating the globe, and, within which, data production and sharing is standardized. EO data actors include states, the private sector, and scientific institutions collaborating to share and standardize data toward common goals and for specific purposes, and not simply for the sake of openness. EO principles are about sharing data for sustainable development, resource management, evidence-based decision-making in those areas, and the "benefit of humankind," in somewhat grandiose terms, but also economic viability (GEOSS, n.d.).

Open data, on the other hand, is part of the discursive regime of sharing publicly funded data in the absence of restrictions (OKF, 2005; G8, 2013; Berners-Lee, 2006), epistemically very different from data sharing in science and by Indigenous communities. Open data thinking also coincides with the development of techniques and technologies related to the spatial web and the launch of Google Maps, the advent of OpenStreetMap, and crowdsourcing, and to Web 2.0 platforms such as Facebook and Wikipedia, as well as mobile devices such as smartphones (Lauriault, 2017). The social web and mobile devices enabled people not only to be consumers of data but also to be content producers, creating a new set of data actors who were not necessarily scientists, data authorities, or producers in government but people skilled with coding, open source, APIs, and data science. The antecedents to open data are international natural- and social-science researchers, environmentalists, EO and geomatics communities, governments with spatial data infrastructures, librarians and archivists, sociologists, and transnational organizations such as the Organisation for Economic Co-operation and Development (OECD) and the United Nations engaged in international and sustainable development, or the European Union engaged with the facilitation of the regional integration of national data assets across borders. Data-sharing and open data actors differ.

Data-sharing has dynamically evolved across time and space for centuries, along with technological capabilities. For example, one of the first compendiums of statistics and maps was the Domesday Book of 1086, and 400 or so years later, data dissemination was accelerated with the invention and adoption of the printing press, in 1455. Governors were also pressured then, as they are today, into making the records of the state available, as exemplified by the 1766 Freedom of the Press Act in Sweden. The Enlightenment and the scientific revolution, with the formation of societies, also formalized and standardized data sharing, as seen in the founding principles of the IMO, articled by Buys Ballot, the organization's first president, in 1873: "It is elementary to have a worldwide network of meteorological observations, free exchange of observations between nations and international agreement on standardized observation methods and units in order to be able to compare these observations" (WMO, n.d.; Buys-Ballot, 1872).

Statistical, social-science, and scientific associations of the late Enlightenment period had similar principles, as was the case for the International Council of Scientific Unions (1931), which merged the International Association of Academies and the International Research Council, which inform the practices of granting councils such as the Canadian Tri-Agency of the Canadian Institutes of Health Research, the Natural Sciences and Engineering Research Council, and the Social Sciences and Humanities Research Council. The ethos of sharing was later codified into the CUDO-norms of science in 1942 by sociologist of science Robert K. Merton. CUDO stood for communism, universalism, disinterestedness, and organized skepticism, whereby scientists and scientific institutions were encouraged to share the results of their work for the common good, for the purpose of advancing the scientific enterprise, and to ensure that scientific claims were scrutinized before being accepted. As seen in these few examples, it is difficult to pinpoint when and how the practices of data sharing truly began; perhaps, then, as it is now, it was enabled by a social and technological assemblage of factors at different times, places, and contexts. Not least of these during the Enlightenment was patronage, secularism, literacy, and the means for information to be published, and for it to travel (Anderson, 1986).

Here, I choose to start with the Antarctic Treaty of 1959, which includes the following principles to govern how scientists involved in Antarctic research are to act:

> 1. In order to promote international cooperation in scientific investigation in Antarctica, as provided for in Article II of the present treaty, the Contracting Parties agree that, to the greatest extent feasible and practicable:
>   (a) information regarding plans for scientific programs in Antarctica shall be exchanged to permit maximum economy and efficiency of operations;
>   (b) scientific personnel shall be exchanged in Antarctica between expeditions and stations;
>   (c) scientific observations and results from Antarctica shall be exchanged and made freely available.

I start here because the impact of the treaty is easy to trace; for example, the International Polar Year of 1957 led to the formation of the Scientific Committee on Antarctic Research (SCAR) and, later, the Antarctic Treaty. SCAR scientists were and remain affiliated with global scientific institutions such as the World Data System, the International Science Council, GEOSS, the Committee on Data of the International Science Council (CODATA), the Research Data Alliance, and many others that have advocated for, institutionalized, and operationalized the sharing of data since. Furthermore, SCAR operationalized early data-sharing policies and created one of the first global, standardized, and interoperable scientific data portals (SCAR, 2020).

Making data accessible also became a key international policy at the UN Earth Summit of 1992, which mandated nations to collect and manage their data and information assets, and to build capacity and openly share them. Chapter 40 (UN, 1992) opens with the following statement:

> 40.1. In sustainable development, everyone is a user and provider of information considered in the broad sense. That includes

> data, information, appropriately packaged experience and knowledge. The need for information arises at all levels, from that of senior decision makers at the national and international levels to the grass-roots and individual levels. The following two programme areas need to be implemented to ensure that decisions are based increasingly on sound information:
> a. Bridging the data gap;
> b. Improving information availability.

Chapter 40 also featured a broad base of data actors, and not just scientists. Indigenous Peoples and regional communities were included because they possess important local knowledge, which comes in many forms, and translating that knowledge into digital data is vital to sustainable development. New governing structures have emerged to protect these data; one example is the FNIGC's OCAP principles, discussed above, which do not sit easily with open data by default. There are similar principles by Inuit in Canada, as seen in the Inuit Tapiriit Kanatami's National Inuit Strategy on Research (NISR) (ITK, 2018). The subjectivities of the FNIGC's (n.d.) OCAP and the ITK's NISR are situated in a post-colonial discourse that asserts sovereignty over the knowledge of First Nations and Inuit in Canada. This is important since private data about Indigenous communities are often possessed by the Crown but arguably should be owned by Indigenous Peoples and communities. Public access in this case would require a nation-to-nation form of negotiation and agreement. First Nation, Métis, and Inuit data should be governed differently, even though these data are often not in their communities' possession, such as archival data recorded by explorers, since for Indigenous Peoples these are considered private, are part of their story of colonialism, and might be about sacred sites or potentially sensitive from an ecological or biodiversity perspective. First Nations would argue that any data about them ought not to fall under an open-by-default policy, and that the sharing of these ought to be negotiated.

Access to data is also about capacity building, open science, and the restructuring of government institutions involved in science and statistics broadly, but also about building open data and data-sharing infrastructures such as GEOSS or spatial data infrastructures. In Figure 1.2, I illustrate how open data emerged as a concept and include some important global milestones.

Open data as an international concept is thought to have formally appeared in 2005–2006 with the Open Definition published by the OKF, and with the "Give us back our crown jewels" and Free Our Data campaign by *Guardian* journalists Charles Arthur and Michael Cross (2006 [March 6], 2006). Prior to that, scientific and geospatial communities and transnational organizations were developing organizations, data centres, practices, and protocols to share data for the advancement of science, better management of the environment, more efficient public administration, and generally for the betterment of society. Access to data and open data are also related to the open-source movement and the General Public Licence, the Open Source Initiative and the Creative Commons, open-access publishing, and the sharing of the results of publicly funded science, open science, and interoperability, as in the case of Global Map, the Open Geospatial Consortium, and national spatial data infrastructures (SDIs) built for the purpose of data sharing. Climate change and other environmental issues led to Agenda 21, followed by Rio+10 in 2002, where the EO community advocated SDIs in the *Down to Earth* report (2002) The EU project of integrating systems also developed directives to share public sector information, and the 2007 EU INSPIRE directive for SDI. For example, one of the first foundational datasets to be opened was the public use of the Global Positioning System, in 1983, upon which location-based services are built and are a key feature in mobile systems today, being part of every smartphone, wearable device, autonomous vehicle, the Internet of Things (IoT), smart cities, and digital twins. Open access for academic publications—called for in the Budapest Open Access Initiative (2002)—was also key, as journals were mandated to be not only accessible but also to publish data upon which results were based. This is promoted in Canada by the federal Tri-Agency, noted above, which funds the bulk of the research (GoC, 2016). Others were also involved in the sharing of data, notably scientific, transnational, and civil-society organizations like the Sunlight Foundation, OECD, CODATA, and W3C (the World Wide Web Consortium) for semantic interoperability, later followed by the G8, Open Government Partnership, and the Open Data Institute (ODI). Important agreements such as the Open Data Charter and indices like the Open Data Index and the Open Data Barometer also came online.

Open data as a discourse has normalized practices, and is becoming routinized and operationalized in governments, but it is disjointed as the focus is primarily on administrative data and, to a lesser extent, survey and science data. Although it is evolving, open data is not a systems-based approach, it is a policy, as it was in the sciences, where there was a purpose to sharing data within a community of practice or an epistemic community. This is in contrast with public-sector administrators who create data for the purpose of managing and operating government programs. New open data institutions are forming, but these are situated within a data-management and an information-technology (IT) context, informed by the management of government records and governed by what are known as C-level officers (chief technology, chief information, chief data, etc.), data-protection officers, and sometimes those who lead digital strategies and who manage data as objects in keeping with new managerialist forms of governing.

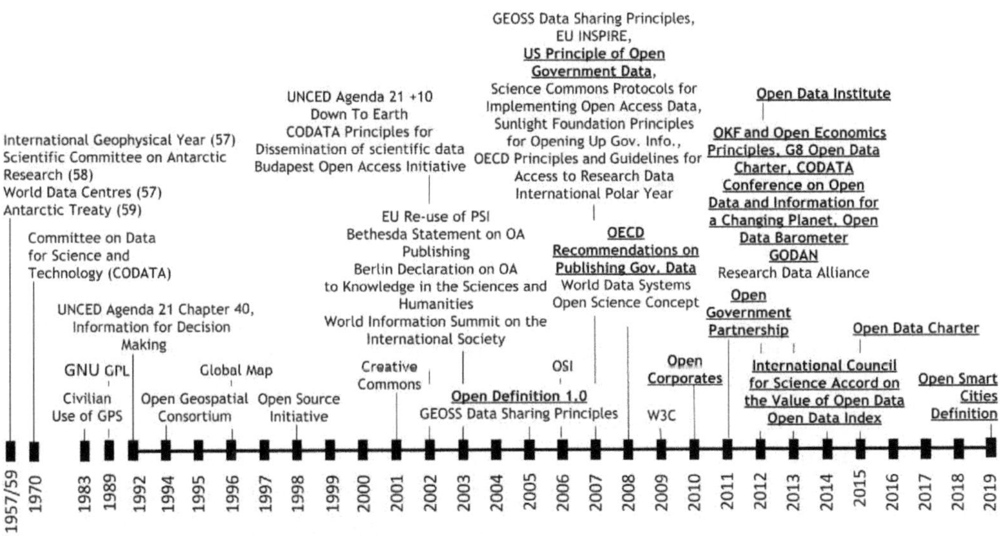

Figure 1.2. Genealogy of Global Milestones influencing Open Access and Open Data in Canada.
Source: Tracey P. Lauriault.

As seen in the genealogy in Figure 1.2, open data did not come from nowhere; it has a history and a provenance. This timeline includes only a selection of institutions, and is therefore partial as it does not include all related intellectual property initiatives, nor does it include a list of the global actors involved in the protection of Indigenous local and traditional data; it does, however, demonstrate that there are international actors that influence government administrations and civil-society actors. It is interesting to note the epistemological shift—access to data was situated in science, for open data it is new managerialism—and the subjectivities of these different approaches led to different outcomes. It is this shift in epistemologies and actors that, I suggest, has led to open data portals and the publishing of poor-quality data, and the lack of data about complex socio-economic issues such as homelessness, disability, and equity including framework or foundational data. The focus is more on administrative and public-sector data and less on the well-developed and scientific practices of government data such as statistics, mapping, and research data derived from publicly funded science. It is also the reason why data are published as discrete objects as opposed to being parts of sets of authoritative data, records sets, or systems such as open-science monitoring, and why there is a lack of standardization in terms of name space, tags, and spatial referents. These are important if different datasets are to be linked or joined for national scale and analytical purposes. Furthermore, data policies governing administrative data are neither as robust nor as integrative as the practices of the physical and social sciences, geospatial data infrastructures, statistical agencies, and research data, or of open science. This has implications for smart systems and digital twins: Will they be standardized, and will data quality be considered; will they be interoperable; and more importantly, how will these be governed? This will require systems thinking about data, AI/ML, sensors, and related infrastructures as social and technological assemblages.

The open data community also did not foresee the emergence of smart cities, digital twins, or big data analytics since this epistemic community was generally more attuned to e-government, digital strategies, and administrative data, not to the governance of cities, sectors like agriculture, or analytics beyond application development and application programming interfaces (APIs). This is changing, but integration is slow, while it is uncertain if the values of openness will be mapped onto the smart city or digital twin. The concern here is that smart systems may follow the same ahistorical and disconnected trajectory that open data has. For example, if we look to the collection of real-time data from sensors, data are inseparable from the systems that produce them, and these are often closed and proprietary; or, as Scassa and Diebel (2016) have demonstrated, they may start as open, but when value is discovered, they become closed. Also, if we look to the establishment of IoT and sensor-based approaches from science, as seen in the vast machines (Edwards, 2013) of seismology, EO, and meteorology, these later IoT systems most often practise open science and do not necessarily align with the intentions of corporate platform-based companies or city officials, where the priority is to manage city operations efficiently, innovatively, and economically. But there is no reason why there might not be a mutually beneficial arrangement between cities, the private sector, and civil society actors. It is out of this situated knowledge that the Open Smart Cities Definitions emerged (Lauriault et al., 2019), to develop a way to bridge sectors, and to build on good practices so that these systems are developed and governed with the public good in mind, and this is why looking to the discursive past of open data matters when it comes to managing the future of smart systems, especially since these will often be overseen by the same IT subcommittees that developed open data programs in a city, by the consultancies that advise them, and by platform companies.

4. Open Data in Canada: A Genealogy

As discussed, open data did not suddenly appear internationally as a fully formed concept, nor did it evolve in a consistent manner at the nation-state level. Open data has an international, national, and a local history. In this section, I provide an open data history for Canada as seen in the context of genealogy (Figure 1.3) and the materialities genealogy (Figure 1.4). The items that are in bold and underlined signify open data actors, while those not underlined are access to data actors. Table 1.1 provides a selection of elements related to the context components of a Canadian social and technological assemblage.

4.1 Open Data in Canada

This data-sharing origin story starts with the Canada Institute for Scientific and Technical Information (CISTI), created in 1974 at the National Research Council of Canada. CISTI was created to ensure that scientists had access to the data and information they need to do their work. These were disseminated with the CAN/OLE online catalogue system and the work of legal scholar and former politician Murray Rankin (1978), who argued that researchers should have access to government information. Librarians were also innovators as they developed data libraries with access, standards, policies, and user guides, as well as technological and user services in the days when data were only accessible on magnetic tape (Ruus, 1982). Furthermore, in 1986, the Canadian Association of Research Libraries created a research data consortium, and, in 1988, other researchers and librarians formed the Canadian Association of Public Data Users. Discourse on access to data also featured in government reports, most notably the mid-1980s Ministerial Task Force on Program Review, commonly known as the Nielsen Task Force. Led by Deputy Prime Minister Erik Nielsen (1984), it conducted an extensive inventory of data assets and concluded that these data should be made publicly available (1984). The Progressive Conservative government of Brian Mulroney, however, did not take this advice and instead created a cost-recovery regime for data, making government data cost prohibitive, especially statistical data. Some might say that this action spearheaded the movement to make data open and accessible in Canada (Humphrey, 1994). This also influenced the creation of data-purchasing consortia, whereby organizations pool their economic, technological, skill, and institutional resources to purchase and share data under a consortium licence (StatCan, 2019). In 1992, sociologist Paul Bernard (1992, p. 21) from the Université de Montréal argued that "knowledge is fundamental to economic development and democratic life in advanced societies; and the information gathered by statistical agencies is an important component of that knowledge. It is essential that such information be made available to researchers and to the public so that it can be used in debates and decision-making."

Sociologists in 1992 were also responsible for *Liberating the Data: A Proposal for a Joint Venture between Statistics Canada and Canadian Universities* (Watkins, 1992), which led to the creation of the federal Data Liberation Initiative (DLI) in 1994, and, for the first time, Statistics Canada disseminated data on the Internet via FTP (file transfer protocol). The DLI made data open to faculty and students but not to the public, as the Statistics Canada licence was restrictive. Outside the academy, statistical data were inaccessible as they were cost prohibitive. As a result, community-based social-planning councils in the mid-1990s also developed data-purchasing consortia, such as the Geographic and Numeric Information Systems (GANIS) and the Canadian Council on Social Development's (CCSD) Community Data Program. These groups coalesced hundreds of community-based organizations in urban and rural areas across Canada to co-purchase customized cross-tabulated data about socio-economic issues that were aggregated at local geographies, under a special consortium licence from Statistics Canada. In this case, hundreds of NGOs collaborated to gain access to data to study Canada's most marginalized communities.

There were other epistemic groups, such as the geospatial community. The *Atlas of Canada*, first published in 1905, started publishing maps online in the 1980s, and it launched the world's first Internet, open source, and web atlas in 1999. The geospatial community also launched the first open data portals with GeoGratis (1993) and GeoBase (1994), and formed the Canadian Geospatial Data Infrastructure in 1999. This was one of the world's first open-source, open-access, open-architecture, open-specifications, and standards-based data infrastructures. The geospatial community also spearheaded the first discussions to openly licence data under Crown copyright (2008). As seen in Figures 1.3 and 1.4, librarians, archivists, sociologists, and researchers were advocating for the release of social science and research data, while the geospatial community were disseminating their data in open spatial data infrastructures. The former group were working against cost recovery and outside the administration, while the latter were data producers within the administration who were developing systems very much in step with addressing specific issues, such as the environment and resource management. This required multisectoral and multi-jurisdictional collaboration, a workaround to cost recovery, and operationalizing technical, policy, and institutional interoperability.

As was the case internationally, open data in Canada emerged as a concept in 2005, with the How'd They Vote application enabling residents and citizens to see how elected officials voted, and to track what they said in the media with the Civicaccess.ca list and the DataLibre.ca blog (Lauriault & McGuire, 2010). The latter two were created by a group of individuals from community Wi-Fi, access-to-data advocacy, librarians, computer scientists, and many others.

They did not come together because of the Open Definition but instead out of a concern that government data such as statistics and elections data were not available. This was also a time when Web 2.0 tools such as Google Maps and mobile devices were coming online. These enabled mashups, and crowdsourcing projects like OpenStreetMap (2004). A new cohort of data users outside of research communities and government administrations, along with autonomous data producers not affiliated with organizations, emerged from social media, Web 2.0, and the proliferation of mobile devices enabled by location-based services (Kitchin et al., 2017). Open data in Canada was also the culmination of ideals, experience, research, practice, and the work of a number of actors, building on the pre-existing initiatives discussed above. It was also the result of a chance encounter between three people involved in community Wi-Fi, web accessibility, and access to data at the 2005 UNESCO World Summit on the Information Society (WSIS) II civil-society conference in Winnipeg. It was there that Lauriault, Lenczner, and Roy met on a panel to discuss open data, accessibility, and community technology initiatives. They were also invited to draft the "Canadian Civil Society Communiqué" that went to the Tunis World Information Society Summit, which included the following in the preamble: "We firmly maintain that democracy is reliant on an informed citizenry and civil society that has access to the data, information, knowledge and technology necessary to keep governments accountable" (UNESCO, 2005).

It was shortly thereafter that CivicAccess, DataLibre, and the G4+1[3] were formed, along with similar groups in Vancouver. The Open Data Summit and the BC Institute for Open Data were developed; along with actors in Toronto, the GO Open Data Conference, the Open Data Institute chapter, Open North, Ajah.ca, and Powered by Data were created. Individuals from these organizations are now part of the Multistakeholder Advisory Group on Open Government. Also, some of these open data actors were also involved in the creation of the Open Smart City Definition (Lauriault

[3] The G4+1 is an informal group of cities—Vancouver, Edmonton, Toronto, Ottawa—that had fledgling open-data programs, and Montréal is the +1 as it launched its open data program later. The group was founded by Lauriault in 2009–2010, at a GTEC Conference in Ottawa, to enable cities to work on common open-data issues. It continues to meet to discuss and resolve common issues.

et al., 2019), and some later went on to form open data civil-society groups, businesses, and new scholarly domains such as critical data studies.

In terms of operationalizing open data in Canada, cities were the early adopters and innovators, starting with the first open data portal coming online in Nanaimo, British Columbia, in 2009 (which included primarily geospatial data), and the creation of the G4+1 group that still meets monthly. This group pooled their resources to work on the first open licence with the Canadian Internet Public Policy Interest Clinic (2016), the standardization of open data metadata, the sharing of best practices, and promoting open data in cities. The federal government first mentions open data in the Standing Committee on Industry, Science and Technology (Lauriault, 2008), followed, in 2010, by the resolution of Canada's access-to-information and privacy commissioners under the leadership of Commissioner Suzanne Legault, in which open data, open government, and freedom of information are linked (see OPC 2010). In 2011, the Treasury Board Secretariat of Canada launched data.gc.ca, a comprehensive knowledge archive network (known as CKAN), data portal, and Canadian government officials attended the first Open Government Partnership meeting, in 2012 in Brazil, accompanied by civil-society actors from the Community Data Program, the Centre for Law and Democracy, and David Eaves, an open data advocate. And the rest, we might say, is history. Since that time, several provinces have launched open data programs (Hunter & Lauriault, 2020), and close to 90 cities and communities now have open data in one form or another.[4] Go Open Data in Ontario was created in 2014. The Open Data Charter has been adopted and is stewarded by Open North, there is the Multi-Stakeholder Forum on Open Government (2018), and Canada hosted the Open Government Partnership Global Summit 2019, in Ottawa, and the Canadian Open Data Society, incorporated in 2020. Dozens of other important civil-society organizations, such as Transparency International, have formed while open data is normalizing, including as seen in open data directives, road maps and proactive disclosure, open contracting, and beneficial ownership, to name a few.

[4] See the following sources for lists of open-data initiatives in Canada, none of which are complete or up to date: https://open.canada.ca/en/maps/open-data-canada, https://en.wikipedia.org/wiki/Open_data_in_Canada, and http://datalibre.ca/links-resources/.

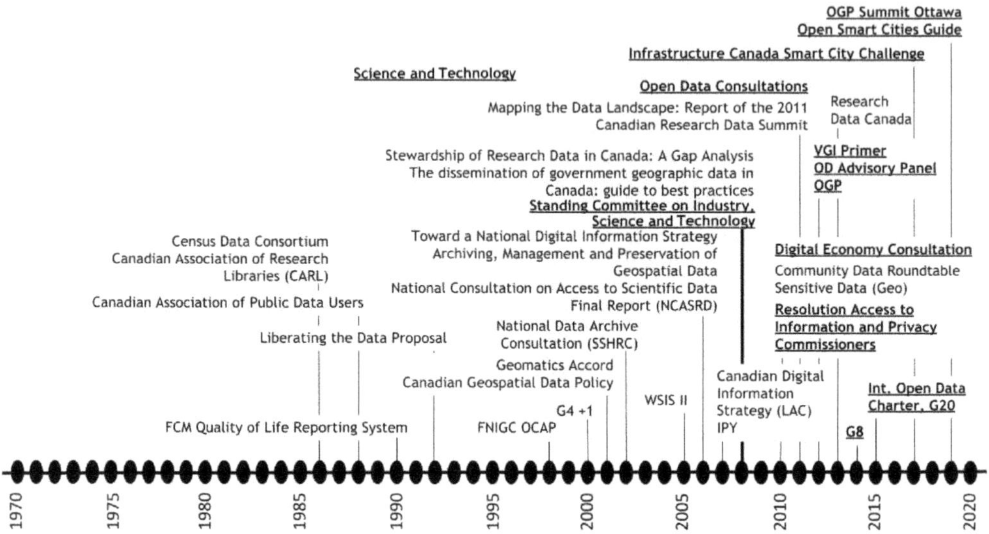

Figure 1.3 Genealogy of Open Access and Open Data Policies and Documents in Canada.
Source: Tracey P. Lauriault.

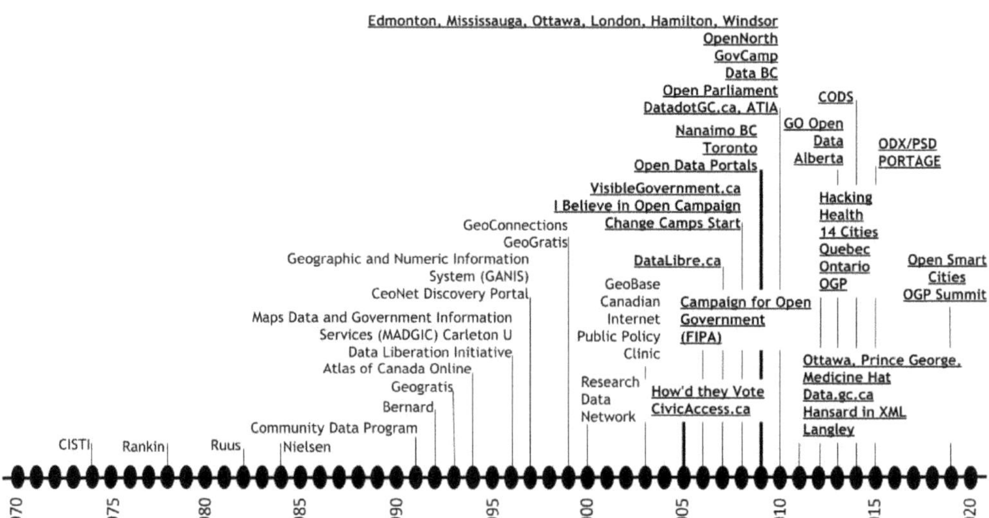

Figure 1.4 Genealogy of Open Access and Open Data Advocates and Initiatives in Canada.
Source: Tracey P. Lauriault.

5. Open Data in Smart Systems

Open data as discourse and practice dynamically evolves; it is not a stand-alone way of doing things, and it is now part of open government programming nationally, and in some provinces and many cities, as technologies and processes evolve, as new policy priorities emerge, and as public engagement and discussion about automated decision-making grow (GoC, 2021). As digital strategies and charters (GoC, 2019) take form, and as smart cities become a priority, open data have become less topical. In Canadian cities, open data programs are being subsumed as part of smart city initiatives; they are becoming a component of the smart city, while smart city data are not necessarily open data and technological systems are not being developed according to the practices of open science or spatial data infrastructures. The pandemic has also clearly demonstrated that open data has not become the norm in certain domains, most notably in public-health reporting (Hunter & Lauriault, 2020).

In 2017, a department of the federal government, Infrastructure Canada, launched a Smart Cities Challenge, where 225 large and small communities, including Aboriginal communities, submitted proposals: 130 were deemed eligible, 20 were short-listed, and four winners were announced on May 14, 2019 (Infrastructure Canada, 2019). This Challenge was interesting as the call made it clear that meaningful smart city outcomes included making data, decision-making, and technological processes open, transparent, and interoperable. The call also mandated that chosen technologies be transferable, and preferably open source and standards-based, for reuse by other communities; that communities have ownership over their data; and that technologies empower and enable communities large and small, as well as traditional and non-traditional partners, to collaborate and strengthen relationships between residents and public organizations, including gender-based analysis (known as GBA+) (Impact Canada, 2018). The procurement of technology and the ownership of data became part of the strategy, and cities had to define challenges to address with technology and also had to consult with their residents to do so. Prior to this, cities in Canada were developing smart city strategies and plans that looked more like a form of networked urbanism, whereby

> big data systems [prefigure and set] the urban agenda and are influencing and controlling how city systems respond and perform . . . cities are becoming ever more instrumented and networked, their systems interlinked and integrated, and the vast troves of data being generated used to manage and control urban life. Computation is now routinely being embedded into the fabric and infrastructure of cities producing a deluge of contextual and actionable data which can be processed and acted upon in real-time. (Kitchin, 2017, p. 43)

Yet, when Sidewalk Labs, a subsidiary of Google's parent company, Alphabet, announced its plans for the Toronto Quayside project at around the same time as Infrastructure Canada launched the Smart Cities Challenge, there was no data-governance strategy, and data were not going to be open. In May 2020, Sidewalk Labs (Carter & Rieti 2020) withdrew its participation from the Quayside project. Prior to these two big initiatives, cities across Canada had begun developing their own smart city programs, and as they were doing so, it became clear that these were innovation- and efficiency-driven, were being organized in the information-management and information-technology (IM/IT) division, and were part of data analytics plans. Citizens in these early smart city programs were not engaged, and open data programs were being subsumed as part of smart city units, while the data derived from smart city technologies were not necessarily going to be open (Lauriault et al., 2019). This is also in part related to the activities of corporate consultancies, technology alliances, and platform companies which have the ear of cities and advocate for closed proprietary systems (Lauriault et al., 2019). Many small, big, and real-time data are being generated by smart cities, and these may include administrative data from intake systems and big data and real-time data generated by sensors and cameras, some of which are private data or behavioural data, which are private and personal in nature. These smart city data bring forward issues related to algorithmic decision-making, and "open data" are no longer on the mainstage, and those data that can be open may be "locked up" into procurement agreements that impede sharing. In the case of smart cities, a new data-enclosure movement might be afoot, and perhaps we need to look at open science as a possible framework to ensure that data and technologies are open, procured, and deployed in the public interest. Open North's Open Smart City

Guide has advocated for this, and has since evolved into a city self-assessment instrument, education modules, several policy briefs, procurement plans, research, and a community solutions network, with several cities adopting these practices.[5] Will there be an open digital twin?

6. Conclusion

Canada has a unique open data social and technological assemblage (Figure 1.1, Table 1.1), and genealogy (Figures 1.3 and 1.4). And technical conceptualizations of open data persist, which limit the scope of open data. This chapter has framed open data as an assemblage to demonstrate how open data is a discursive regime that includes many content and context components that are both social and technical that, across time, space, and actors, constitute Canada's open data story. Also, Canada's open data story is situated in a global context, as seen in Figure 1.2. Open data, in reality, includes many interconnected yet disparate smaller assemblages found in many cities, provinces, and territories, and in the federal government and the international arena, and most often localized in IM/IT divisions. In Canada, open data as a discourse emerged from the efforts of separate and mostly distinct scientific, research, and geospatial communities that included granting councils, sociologists, librarians, archivists, and scientists. For example, the geospatial community created spatial data infrastructures; research-intensive universities developed their own social-science infrastructure, now coming together under the PORTAGE, a data preservation system by CARL and trusted digital repositories of data, the New Digital Research Infrastructure Organization (called the Alliance); the National Research Council focused on science; and community-based organizations created their own data-sharing consortia and portals (Figures 1.3 and 1.4). These access-to-data communities seeded the terrain. Open data in Canada was initiated by cities, first in GIS units and later in IM/IT departments, which are often disconnected from planning or social services, and it was new managerialist in tone, with data portals and indicators rendered in dashboards and maps. This

5 See, on the Open North website, https://opennorth.ca/publicationdetail?id=3Ptq7I6gVIfzBfl2ZAYoNs https://opennorth.ca/publications, and on the Future City Network website, https://futurecitiescanada.ca/programs/community-solutions-network/.

became evident with pandemic reporting by federal, provincial, and territorial governments, which made their data accessible in dashboards but not necessarily as open data (Hunter & Lauriault, 2020). Open data as operations and as a discourse has since become common at all levels of government. Open data, however, evolved separately from the early efforts of those involved in access to data; they constituted different actors and communities of practice in different sectors. Open data today still lacks much of the systems thinking of the access-to-data communities: there are fewer standards; the quality of the data and metadata is inconsistent; there is a lack of interoperability; there are few integrative framework datasets that stitch the country's assets together, although data linkage projects are emerging; and data discovery associated with metadata and tagging is poor. The corollary is that we have thousands of open datasets, and perhaps open-by-default practices might give way to publishing data with purpose, as was the case with the access-to-data communities, and this might improve data quality. And as discussed, there is also a tension between open data by default and Indigenous data that has yet to be resolved. And as seen during the ongoing pandemic, there are important datasets that just do not exist for some of Canada's most vulnerable communities, and there has been a lack of ethical and intersectional frameworks of equity and inclusion to inform the production of these data and the creation of important framework data (Linton & Lauriault, 2021; Hunter & Lauriault, 2020; Lauriault, 2020b).

Canada is now home to several fledgling smart cities, and although these may have subsumed open data programs, smart city technologies and the data they produce are by no means open. The winners of the Smart Cities Challenge were announced, their data will be open as per the requirement of the call, there will be public engagement about technological decisions, and here we may witness big and real-time open data coming from the short-listed and finalists (INFC, 2017). But what of all the other smart cities and digital twins: Will they be open? Open-smart city aspirations are becoming a reality; the definition counters the enclosure of data and technology, and it is becoming a made-in-Canada model. Of concern, however, is the lack of systems and infrastructural thinking overall in data and technology spaces; be they large social and technological systems such as smart cities, digital twins, or smart grids for utilities, we do not yet see data-governance plans that are systems-based, integrated, interoperable, standardized, and open. Will open data and open smart cities be included in digital strategies and become a core principle of data-governance plans?

It is also the hope that good and established practices from open science, open data, open source, open platforms, open government, and emerging engagement processes will be mapped onto them, but most importantly that there will be open smart cities, "where residents, civil society, academics, and the private sector collaborate with public officials to mobilize data and technologies when warranted in an ethical, accountable and transparent way to govern the city as a fair, viable and livable commons and balance economic development, social progress and environmental responsibility" (Lauriault et al., 2019).

It is important to learn from the history of open data to better understand its future and to steer a better course for smart systems. Here it is argued that open data will need to be governed as part of large social and technological systems; that its discourse ought to be about democratic deliberation and not just a new managerialist exercise; and that we move beyond narrow technological conceptions and include ethics, public good, and sustainability. Current smart city actors, in addition to public officials, data scientists, and software engineers, may want to look at established and experienced epistemic groups, such as those in the spatial-sciences and remote-sensing communities, and other scientific communities such as natural resources, meteorology, and oceanography or glaciology, where sensor-based open science has been practised for decades. There are many good practices to emulate, most especially when it comes to spatial data infrastructures. Open data in Canada evolved in the absence of the early actors who practised data sharing—scientists, early adopters in the spatial sciences, sociologists—and it is hoped here that open smart cities can steer the course away from more corporatist and closed smart cities and toward open smart systems. The future of open data, as it normalizes, will be subsumed as part of large and smart-technological systems, and we need to ensure that data and the systems that generate them remain open. Open data actors will need to work with open smart city and digital-twin actors to ensure that data remain open, and city actors need to think of smart cities and digital twins as more than operations, and to consider them to be part of urban plans and as part of public space that ought to be deliberated. Finally, for all, good governance includes, among other things, data and technological governance, and an inherent part of doing technological citizenship (Barney, 2004), since we do live in technological societies (Feenberg, 2011) after all.

Elements	Canada
Governments	Federated constitutional monarchy of provinces and territories with clear divisions of power between the Federal Government, Provincial / Territorial Governments and Cities. Population: 37+ Million
System of Thought	Open Government, Transparency, Accountability, Efficiency, Innovation, E-Government
Form of Knowledge	Open Government Charter Standards, WSF/WMS Metadata, ISO19115, Dublin Core Directives Policies Reports Political Platforms Indicators / Metrics Digital Strategies / Charters Enterprise Architecture Guides, Readiness Guides, Roadmaps, Theory of Change
Governmentalities and Legalities	Open Licences The Personal Information Protection and Electronic Documents Act (PIPEDA) Privacy Act P/T Privacy Legislation Municipal Freedom of Information and Protection of Privacy Freedom of Information Legislation Access to Information Legislation International Aid Transparency Initiative Proactive Disclosure Open Corporates AI Impact Assessment Data Trusts
Organizations and Institutions	*Government Open Data Programs* • Treasury Board Secretariat • Natural Resources Canada • Information and Privacy Commissioners • Provincial Governments • Municipalities and Regional governments • Most federal departments • Cities *Civil Society* • Multistakeholder Advisory Group • OpenNorth, Powered by Data, Data for Good, Open Data Institute • Centre for Law and Democracy • Open Corporates • Transparency International

Table 1.1. A Selection of the Attributes that form the Social and Technological Open Data Assemblage for Canada.
Source: Tracey P. Lauriault.

References

Anderson, B. (1983). Census, map, museum. In *Imagined communities: Reflections on the origin and spread of nationalism* (rev. ed., pp. 163–186). Verso.

Arctic Spatial Data Infrastructure (ASDI). (2021). *Home page*. Retrieved June 2, 2021, from https://arctic-sdi.org/

Arthur, C., & Cross, M. (2006, March 6). Give us back our crown jewels. *Guardian* [UK]. Retrieved July 9, 2019, from https://www.theguardian.com/technology/2006/mar/09/education.epublic

Arthur, C., & Cross, M. (2006). Free our data campaign. *Guardian* [UK]. Retrieved Aug. 18, 2021, from https://www.theguardian.com/technology/2006/mar/09/education.epublic

Barney, D. (2004). *The network society*. Polity Press.

Barney, D. (2007). *One nation under Google: Citizenship in the technological republic*. Hart House Lecture Committee. Retrieved May 10, 2019, from http://darinbarneyresearch.mcgill.ca/Work/One_Nation_Under_Google.pdf

Bernard, P. (1991). *Discussion paper on the issue of the pricing of Statistics Canada products*.

Bernard, P. (1992). Data and knowledge: Statistics Canada and the research community. *Society*, 21.

Berners-Lee, T. (2006). *5 star linked data*. Retrieved June 9, 2019, from https://www.w3.org/2011/gld/wiki/5_Star_Linked_Data

Budapest Open Access Initiative. (2002). Retrieved June 9, 2019, from https://www.budapestopenaccessinitiative.org/read

Buys-Ballot, C. H. D. (1872). *A sequel to the "Suggestions on a uniform system of meteorological observations."* Royal Dutch Meteorological Institute.

Canadian Association of Public Data Users. (n.d.). *About*. Retrieved May 11, 2019, from https://capdu.wordpress.com/about/

Canadian Association of Research Libraries. (n.d.). *About* CARL. Retrieved June 9, 2019, from http://www.carl-abrc.ca/about-carl/

Canadian Council on Geomatics (CCOG). (n.d.). *Canadian Geomatics Accord*. Retrieved May 11, 2019, from http://www.ccog-cocg.ca/en/accord

Canadian Internet Policy and Public Policy Interest Clinic. (2016). *CIPPIC proposal: An open licensing scheme for traditional knowledge*. Retrieved April 27, 2021, from https://cippic.ca/en/TK_Open_Licensing_Proposal

Carter, A., & Rieti, J. (2020, May 7). *Sidewalk Labs cancels plan to build high-tech neighbourhood in Toronto amid COVID-19*. CBC News. Retrieved May 7, from https://www.cbc.ca/news/canada/toronto/sidewalk-labs-cancels-project-1.5559370

City of Ottawa. (2021). Information shared in person as part of a presentation given as community partners with the Master Class in Critical Data Studies of 2021 at Carleton University, Ottawa.

Cosgrove, D. E. (2001). *Apollo's eye: A cartographic genealogy of the earth in the western imagination*. Johns Hopkins University Press.

Couldry, N., & Mejias, U. A. (2018). Data colonialism: Rethinking big data's relation to the contemporary subject. *Television and New Media, 20*(4), 336–349. Retrieved May 10, 2019, from https://journals-sagepub-com.proxy.library.carleton.ca/doi/10.1177/1527476418796632

Dalton, C., & Thatcher, J. (2014). What does a critical data studies look like, and why do we care? Seven points for a critical approach to "big data". *Society and Space*. Retrieved May 10, 2019, from https://societyandspace.org/2014/05/12/what-does-a-critical-data-studies-look-like-and-why-do-we-care-craig-dalton-and-jim-thatcher/

DeLanda, M. (2016). *Assemblage theory*. Edinburgh University Press.

Edwards, P. (2013). *A vast machine: Computer models, climate data, and the politics of global warming*. MIT Press.

European Union. (2021). *EU general data protection regulation*. GDPR.eu. Retrieved June 2, 2021, from https://gdpr.eu/

Feenberg, A. (2011). *Agency and citizenship in a technological society*. Lecture presented to the Course on Digital Citizenship, IT University of Copenhagen. Retrieved May 10, 2019, from https://www.sfu.ca/~andrewf/copen5-1.pdf

First Nations Information Governance Centre (FNIGC). (1998). *The First Nations principles of OCAP*. Retrieved May 10, 2019, from https://fnigc.ca/ocapr.html

First Nations Information Governance Centre (FNIGC). (2019). First Nations data sovereignty in Canada. *Statistical Journal of the IAOS, 35*(1), 47–69. https://doi.org/10.3233/SJI-180478.

First Nations Information Governance Centre (FNIGC). (2021). *Home page*. Retrieved May 24, 2021, from https://fnigc.ca/about-fnigc/

First Nations Information Governance Council (FNIGC). (n.d.). *OCAP principles*. Retrieved June 2, 2021, from https://fnigc.ca/ocap-training/

Foucault, M. (2003). *The essential Foucault: Selections from essential works of Foucault, 1954-1984*. The New Press.

Foster. (n.d.) *What is open science?* Retrieved June 2, 2021, from https://www.fosteropenscience.eu/node/2326

G8 (2013) *G8 Open Data Charter: UK Action Plan 2013*. Retrieved August 15, 2021, from https://www.gov.uk/government/publications/g8-open-data-charter-national-action-plan/g8-open-data-charter-uk-action-plan-2013

G20. (2015). *G20 Anti-Corruption Open Data Principles*. Retrieved May 11, 2019, from http://www.g20.utoronto.ca/2015/G20-Anti-Corruption-Open-Data-Principles.pdf

GeoBase. (2001). *About.* Retrieved July 9, 2019, from https://web.archive.org/web/20151125163309/http://ftp2.cits.rncan.gc.ca/pub/geobase/pdf/About.pdf

GeoConnections. (2008). *The dissemination of government geographic data in Canada: Guide to best practices.* GEOSCAN. Canadian Geospatial Data Infrastructure, Information Product 8, (ed. ver. 2). https://doi.org/10.4095/288853

GeoConnections. (2012). *Canadian geospatial data infrastructure vision, mission and roadmap—the way forward.* GEOSCAN. Canadian Geospatial Data Infrastructure, Information Product 28e. https://doi.org/10.4095/292417

GeoGratis. (n.d.). *Portal.* Retrieved July 9, 2019, from https://www.nrcan.gc.ca/science-and-data/science-and-research/earth-sciences/geography/topographic-information/10785

Global Earth Observation System of Systems (GEOSS). (n.d.). *Principles.* Retrieved June 9, 2019, from https://www.earthobservations.org/geo_community.php

Global Earth Observation Systems of Systems (GEOSS). (n.d.). *About.* Retrieved July 9, 2019, from https://www.earthobservations.org/geoss.php

Global Open Data for Agriculture and Nutrition (GODAN). (2016). *Agricultural open data package working group.* Retrieved May 10, 2019, from https://www.godan.info/working-groups/agriculture-open-data-package-working-group

Global Open Data Index. (2017). *About.* Retrieved July 9, 2019, from https://index.okfn.org/about/

Government of Canada (GoC). (2016). *Tri-agency open access policy on publications.* Retrieved June 2, 2021, from https://www.ic.gc.ca/eic/site/063.nsf/eng/h_F6765465.html

Government of Canada (GoC). (2019). *Canada's digital charter in action: A plan by Canadians, for Canadians.* Retrieved June 2, 2021, from https://www.ic.gc.ca/eic/site/062.nsf/eng/h_00109.html

Government of Canada (GoC). (2021). *Responsible use of artificial intelligence (AI).* Retrieved June 2, 2021, from https://www.canada.ca/en/government/system/digital-government/modern-emerging-technologies/responsible-use-ai.html

Government of Sweden. (1766). *Freedom of the Press Act.* Retrieved May 24, 2021, from https://sweden.se/society/20-milestones-of-swedish-press-freedom/#

Guptill, S., & Morrison, J. L. (1995). *Elements of spatial data quality.* International Cartographic Association Commission on Spatial Data Quality. Elsevier.

Hughes, T. P. (1987). The evolution of large technological systems. In W. Bijker, T. P. Hughes, & T. Pinch (Eds.), *The social construction of large technological systems: New directions in the sociology and history of technology* (pp. 45–77). MIT Press.

Humphrey, C. (1994). The case for a Canadian national social sciences data archive. *Government Information in Canada.* 1, No. 2.7. Retrieved June 26 from https://library2.usask.ca/gic/v1n2/humphrey/humphrey.html

Hunter, A., & Lauriault, T. P. (2020). *Tracing COVID-19 data: Open science and open data standards in Canada.* Retrieved May 24, 2020 from http://datalibre.ca/2020/10/13/tracing-covid-19-data-open-science-and-open-data-standards-in-canada/

Iliadis, A., & Russo, F. (Eds.), (2016). Critical data studies. Special Issue in *Big Data & Society.* Retrieved May 10, 2019, from https://journals-sagepub-com.proxy.library.carleton.ca/page/bds/collections/critical-data-studies

Impact Canada. (2018). *Impact Challenge finalist guide.* Retrieved February 14, 2020, from https://impact.canada.ca/en/challenges/smart-cities/finalist-guide

Infrastructure Canada. (2019). *Smart City Challenge.* Retrieved July 9, 2019, from https://www.infrastructure.gc.ca/cities-villes/index-eng.html

Inuit Tapiriit Kanatami (ITK). (2018). *ITK national strategy on research.* Retrieved June 2, 2021, from https://www.itk.ca/national-strategy-on-research/

Kitchin, R. (2014). *The data revolution: Big data, open data, data infrastructures and their consequences.* Sage.

Kitchin, R. (2017). Data-driven urbanism. In R. Kitchin, T. P. Lauriault, and G. McArdle (Eds.), *Data and the city* (pp. 44–56). Taylor & Francis.

Kitchin, R., & Lauriault, T. P. (2014). *Towards critical data studies: Charting and unpacking data assemblages and their work.* Retrieved May 10, 2019, from https://ssrn.com/abstract=2474112

Kitchin, R., Lauriault, T. P. & Wilson M. (Eds.). (2017), *Understanding Spatial Media,* Sage.

Kukutai, T., & Taylor, J. (Eds.), (2016). *Indigenous data sovereignty.* ANU Press.

Lauriault, T. P. (2008). *Open data.* INDU Standing Committee Submission, Government of Canada, House of Commons Standing Committee on Industry, Science and Technology Committees Directorate, Study on Canadian Science and Technology.

Lauriault, T. P. (2017). Open spatial media. In R. Kitchin, T. P. Lauriault, & M. Wilson (Eds.), *Understanding Spatial Media* (pp. 95–110). Sage.

Lauriault, T. P. (2020a). *Where is the national health region map of COVID-19 Cases?* Retrieved May 24, 2021, from http://datalibre.ca/2020/04/07/where-is-the-national-map-of-covid-19-data-by-public-health-units-in-canada/

Lauriault, T. P. (2020b). *COVID-19 data: Data and technological citizenship during the COVID-19 pandemic project description.* Retrieved June 2, 2021, from http://datalibre.ca/tracing-covid-19-data/.

Lauriault, T. P., Bloom, R., & Landry, J.-N. (2019). *The open smart cities guide.* Retrieved May 10, 2019, from https://opennorth.ca/publications/3ptq7i6gvifzbfl2zayons_en

Lauriault, T. P., & McGuire, H. (2010). Data access in Canada: civicaccess.ca. In B. Fitzgerald (Ed.), *Access to public sector information: Law, technology and policy: Vol. 1* (pp. 278–284). Sydney University Press.

Linton, M., Chokly, K., & Lauriault, T. P. (2021). *Invisible people and institutions: No data about custodial institutions for disabled people in Canada?* Retrieved May 24, 2021, from http://datalibre.ca/2021/02/18/invisible-people-and-institutions-no-data-about-custodial-institutions-for-disabled-people-in-canada/

National Research Council. (2002). *Down to earth: Geographic information for sustainable development in Africa.* The National Academies Press. https://doi.org/10.17226/10455

Natural Resources Canada (NRCan). (2020). *Canada geospatial data infrastructure (CGDI).* Retrieved June 2, 2021, from https://www.nrcan.gc.ca/earth-sciences/geomatics/canadas-spatial-data-infrastructure/10783.

Nielsen, E. (1984). *New management initiatives: Initial results from the ministerial task force on program review.* Government of Canada, Department of Finance.

Officer of the Privacy Commissioner of Canada (OPC). (2010). *Resolution of Canada's Access to Information and Privacy Commissioners.* Retrieved July 9, 2019, from https://www.priv.gc.ca/en/about-the-opc/what-we-do/provincial-and-territorial-collaboration/joint-resolutions-with-provinces-and-territories/res_100901/

Office of the Privacy Commissioner of Canada (OPC). (2021). The *Personal Information Protection and Electronic Documents Act* (PIPEDA). Retrieved June 2, 2021, from https://www.priv.gc.ca/en/privacy-topics/privacy-laws-in-canada/the-personal-information-protection-and-electronic-documents-act-pipeda/

Open Data Barometer. (2017) *Open data barometer–Leaders edition ODB methodology - v1.0 | 15 September 2017.* Retrieved May 11, 2019, from http://opendatabarometer.org/doc/leadersEdition/ODB-leadersEdition-Methodology.pdf

Open Data Barometer. (2019). Retrieved May 11, 2019, from https://opendatabarometer.org

Open Data Charter. (2015). *Principles.* Retrieved May 10, 2019, from https://opendatacharter.net/

Open Data Charter. (2018). *Publish with purpose.* Retrieved May 10, 2019, from https://drive.google.com/file/d/1hYmoTZTDgFe9E8CtxAW6qfbjfj5W93DL/view

Open Knowledge. (2015). *The open definition V 2.1.* Retrieved May 10, 2019, from https://opendefinition.org/od/2.1/en/

Open Knowledge Foundation (OKF). (2005). *History of the open definition.* Retrieved May 11, 2019, from https://opendefinition.org/history/

Open Knowledge Foundation (OKF). (2016/2017). *Global open index methodology.* Retrieved May 10, 2019, from https://index.okfn.org/methodology/

Ordnance Survey Ireland (OSI). (2017). *National mapping strategy.* Retrieved June 2, 2021, from https://www.osi.ie/services/national-mapping-agreement/

Rankin, M. (1978). *Access to information vital to researchers.* C.A.U.T. Bulletin.

Ruus, L. (1982). The University of British Columbia data library: An overview. *Library Trends, 30*(3), 397–406.

Scassa, T., & Diebel, A. (2016). Open or closed? Open licensing of real-time public sector transit data. *JeDEM–eJournal of eDemocracy and Open Government, 8*(2). https://doi.org/10.29379/jedem.v8i2.414.

Scientific Committee on Antarctic Research (SCAR). (2020). *Welcome to the Scientific Committee on Antarctic Research.* Retrieved June 2, 2021, from https://www.scar.org/data-products/data/

Secretariat for the Antarctic Treaty. (1959). *The Antarctic Treaty.* Retrieved May 12, 2019, from https://www.ats.aq/e/ats.htm

Statistics Canada (StatCan). (2019). *Data liberation initiative consortium licence.* Retrieved June 2, 2021, from https://www.statcan.gc.ca/eng/dli/caselaw/license

Thatcher, J., O'Sullivan, D., & Mahmoudi, D. (2016). Data colonialism through accumulation by dispossession: New metaphors for daily data. *Environment and Planning D: Society and Space, 34*(6), 990–1006. Retrieved May 10, 2019, from https://journals-sagepub-com.proxy.library.carleton.ca/doi/10.1177/0263775816633195

Tuhiwai-Smith, L. (1999). *Decolonizing methodologies: Research and Indigenous Peoples.* University of Otago Press.

UNESCO. (2005). *UNESCO, Paving the road to Tunis–WSIS II: The views of Canada's civil society on the Geneva plan of action and the prospects for phase II.* Retrieved July 9, 2019, from: https://www.mcgill.ca/channels/news/canadian-civil-society-communiqu%C3%A9-15735.

United Nations (UN). (1992). *Agenda 21, chapter 40, information for decision-making.* Retrieved May 12, 2019, from https://www.itu.int/net/wsis/docs2/pc3/contributions/Co13.pdfW3C

VanBuskirk, M. (2008). *The history of the NRC Canada Institute for Scientific and Technical Information 1924-2009.* National Research Council.

Walter, M., & Andersen, C. (2013). *Indigenous statistics: A quantitative research methodology.* Routledge.

Watkins, W. (1992). Liberating the data: A proposal for a joint venture between Statistics Canada and Canadian universities (unpublished).

Watkins, W., & Boyko, E. (1996). Data liberation and academic freedom. *Government Information in Canada, 3*(2) 2. Retrieved 26 June from http://www.usask.ca/library/gic/v3n2/watkins2/watkins2.html.

World Meteorological Organization (WMO). (n.d.). *History of the IMO.* Retrieved May 12, 2019, from https://public.wmo.int/en/about-us/who-we-are/history-IMO

About the Author

Tracey P. Lauriault is Associate Professor of Critical Media and Big Data, Communication and Media Studies, School of Journalism and Communication, cross-appointed to the master's program in Digital Humanities, and on the advisory board for the Institute for Data Science at Carleton University. She serves on the Multi-Stakeholder Forum for the Canadian Open Government Civil Society Network, and on the board for the Canadian Open Data Summit 2021, among other open data civil-society and government activities. She is Research Associate with the Maynooth University Social Science Institute in Ireland, the Geomatics and Cartographic Research Centre at Carleton University, the Institut national de la recherche scientifique in Montréal, and the Centre for Law, Technology and Society at the University of Ottawa. Lauriault is a citizen of the Algonquins of Pikwàkanagàn First Nation, the Republic of Ireland, and Canada.

PART II

Pitfalls and Opportunities

CHAPTER 2

Open Government Data and Confidential Commercial Information: Challenging the Future of Open Data

Teresa Scassa

Abstract

In a relatively short space of time, governments at all levels in Canada have committed to open data agendas and are making a growing volume of data available in reusable formats and under open licences. And yet even as open data advocates continue to pressure governments for greater access to more data, changes brought about by big data and artificial intelligence are affecting the open data environment. Data are a valuable commodity, and governments are increasingly entering into contracts with private-sector companies for technologies that collect, process, and analyze data. These changes raise important questions about data ownership and control. Public–private partnerships for smart cities and for algorithmic decision making by governments mean that a growing volume of data collected through public-sector activities and relied upon by governments may increasingly be in private-sector hands. This chapter considers the impact of rules that exclude confidential commercial data and commercially sensitive data from disclosure as open data. It asks: What is the future of open data where data about public activities and phenomena are increasingly privately owned?

Acknowledgements
The author gratefully acknowledges the support of the Social Sciences and Humanities Research Council of Canada for its support for the Geothink project, of which this research forms a part.

The open data movement in Canada is of relatively recent vintage, although the foundation for open government data was laid by Natural Resources Canada in its efforts to make Canadian geospatial data open in the early 2000s (Lauriault & Kitchin, 2014). In 2012, Canada signed on to the international multi-stakeholder Open Government Partnership, making open data part of its broader commitment to open government. While a few municipal governments had already taken some steps toward releasing open data, it was in the second decade of the twenty-first century that Canadians saw governments at all levels embrace a significant and more or less organized commitment to make government data open and accessible through co-ordinated open government programs. There have been important commitments to open data by provincial governments, and many of Canada's major cities now have significant collections of open data available through open data portals. The federal government has built its own open data portal and developed an open data licence (based on the UK Open Government Licence), which has been adopted in slightly modified form by some provincial governments.

The upshot of all this activity is a growing volume of government data that is available as open data through a variety of portals across the country. Accompanying the releases of data has been a mixture of hackathons, open data "book clubs," and other events designed to encourage the uptake and use of open data with a view to realizing its potential. While it is difficult to know exactly who is using open data, and to what extent, Johnson (2016, p. 4) has found that important users of open government data include "engineering consultants, property developers, post-secondary and graduate students, other government agencies and academics."

Open-data programs continue to evolve with new datasets being made available on a fairly steady basis. The future of open data could therefore be characterized as one in which, on an incremental basis, new datasets are made open, new uses are found for open data, and new user communities discover this important resource.

However, this vision may be subject to disruption by rapidly evolving information technologies that are changing both the nature and volume of data that can be collected by governments through public-sector services or activities. Such changes may also significantly impact the location of the ownership of these data. In this environment, data may be collected and processed by private-sector companies on behalf of government; alternatively, they may be collected by private-sector companies and licensed to a variety of users, which may include governments. In some cases, data about phenomena or activities once under the regulatory authority of government may be collected by private-sector companies which choose not to share these data with government, or to share only selected data under their own terms (e.g., short-term rental-economy platforms) (Scassa, 2017). Because governments generally cannot release private-sector data as open data, these changes may have a profound impact on the future of open data.

Our current context is one in which government's role as a collector (and therefore as a sharer) of data is altered and diminished by changes in technology, and by the growing role of the private sector as a source of data used by government. This chapter therefore queries the future of open data in an environment where a growing volume of data in the hands of government might not be available as open data. It begins with an introduction to open data, followed by a discussion of how two particular categories of data in the hands of government are excluded from release as open data. These categories are third-party proprietary data and confidential or commercially sensitive information. The chapter next considers how these categories may affect the availability of open data in a context in which governments increasingly contract for data, data analytics, and the hardware/software to collect and process data. Recent Canadian case law suggests that there may be an emerging role for government in managing third-party proprietary data in the public interest, which is addressed in the conclusion.

1. Opening Government Data

Ideally, open government data are made available in machine-readable formats and under open licences which impose minimal restrictions on reuse (Janssen et al., 2012). Open data have transparency and accountability value (Open Data Charter, 2015). There is also value in open data sharing between different departments or agencies of the same government or across governments (Johnson & Robinson, 2014). In addition to these uses, open-data policies are linked to goals of stimulating innovation by providing entrepreneurs with free access to important data assets (Manyika et al., 2013). In the big data and artificial intelligence (AI) context, open data may provide datasets useful to feed analytics or to drive machine learning.

While in theory any data may be made available as open data, in reality there are some important limits on what can be made open. Thus, for example, Janssen et al. (2012, p. 258) incorporate these limitations into their definition of open data as "non-privacy-restricted and non-confidential data which is produced with public money and is made available without any restrictions on its usage or distribution." Because of privacy laws, governments generally cannot release personal information as open data or as part of an open dataset. Since the statutory definition of personal information is quite broad (e.g., "information about an identifiable individual"), this can significantly limit the availability of some datasets for release (Scassa, 2010). Identifiability is assessed in terms of any other available data, and in an era of big data, reidentification risk can be high (Rocher et al., 2019; Ohm, 2010; Sweeney, 2010). Lest privacy concerns become an overwhelming barrier to open data, activists as well as governments have been working to develop guidance and strategies for opening data in ways that protect privacy rights and avoid privacy harms (Green et al., 2017; Simperl et al., 2016; Scassa & Conroy, 2016; Borgesius et al., 2015).

Governments are also obliged not to release as open data the proprietary data of third parties, as well as any confidential or commercially sensitive data. These two distinct grounds for non-disclosure are significant restraints. A government cannot release third-party proprietary data because it is not legally entitled to do so, nor may it license such data for reuse since it does not own the content. Governments are also barred from releasing confidential commercial information, since to do so would destroy the confidential character of the information, exposing governments to liability. Commercially sensitive data cannot be released because such may damage a government's relationships with those it regulates, and with those with whom it does business, by causing those entities commercial harm. These categories of data are considered below.

1.1 Proprietary Data

In order to release data under an open licence, which authorizes virtually unrestricted use of the data, the government must "own" the data in the sense of being the party legally entitled to license them. The Open Government Licence (Canada, 2017) thus specifically excludes from the terms of the licence "third party rights the Information Provider is not authorized to license." Data in the hands of governments may come from a variety of different sources. If such data are proprietary third-party data, they are excluded from release as open data.

The concept of proprietary data requires some consideration. Confidential information is considered to be a form of intellectual property, but its status as "property" was put in question by the Supreme Court of Canada in *R. v. Stewart* (1988). In any event, as noted below, open government data typically separately precludes the release of confidential commercial information, independent of proprietary issues. Proprietary data, therefore, may also include those data over which a company claims intellectual-property rights. Although copyright law does not protect facts, it will protect a compilation that amounts to an original selection or arrangement of facts (Scassa, 2018). Thus, datasets provided to government as part of regulatory processes, or shared with government under procurement contracts or other agreements, might constitute proprietary third-party data, whether or not they are also confidential.

Not every dataset is entitled to copyright protection, and thus it can be challenging to determine whether any given dataset in the hands of government is actually the "property" of a third party. Any claim to property rights in a dataset must be based on its being an original compilation of data. Originality depends on the existence of an original selection or arrangement of data; it is not a given that these elements will be present in every compilation of data (Judge & Scassa, 2010). While the threshold for protection is low, it must still be met. Further, the protection available is not for the underlying data; rather, it is only for their original selection or arrangement. The situation is made more complex by recent case law that distinguishes between "facts" (long held by copyright law to be in the public domain) and data (Scassa, 2018). Because facts themselves remain in the public domain, copyright in a compilation of facts is violated only if a substantial part of the selection or arrangement is taken. A "whole universe" set of facts (i.e., all the facts relating to a certain activity) may not demonstrate any original selection (Judge & Scassa, 2010). Similarly, an arrangement that is made according to an external standard will not be original. On the other hand, if data are qualitatively different from facts, datasets may be more likely to be found protectable under copyright law. Nevertheless, whether there is copyright in any given dataset is an open question. For example, the Federal Court of Appeal in *Toronto Real Estate Board v. Commissioner of Competition* (2017, para. 194) expressed the opinion that the board's compilation of data gathered from real-estate listings was not sufficiently original since its compilation amounted to a "mechanical exercise." By contrast, a compilation of seismic data was found to have copyright protection by the Alberta courts (*Geophysical*, 2017).

Notwithstanding that copyright in factual compilations is contingent, it is regularly asserted by those who create and maintain datasets. A decision not to release as open data datasets over which third-party proprietary rights have been asserted could involve some kind of process in order to assess whether proprietary rights exist, and if so, what their scope might be. The reality is, however, that where a third party has indicated to a government that their dataset is proprietary, the government will be unlikely to question this assertion. Governments' own claims to rights in their data are similarly accepted by industry. In cases where the government has contracted out for the collection or use of the data at issue, it is the contract with the third-party provider that may determine which of the parties has a proprietary claim to the data.

Claims by third parties to rights in data have clear implications for open government data. The number and importance of such claims may increase with the growth of smart cities, data analytics, and AI. Data and datasets are in high demand in the development of AI technologies. Smart cities are sensor-laden and lead to the collection of vast amounts of often very rich data that can have multiple applications, including in the AI context. Where governments have contracted with the private sector to supply the technology to collect, process, and analyze smart-cities data, or where they license data from app companies such as Waze or Strava, these data may be subject to intellectual-property rights claims by the private-sector company. If such rights exist and are located with the companies, or if the government accepts and accedes to the claims, then the data—even if they are about public infrastructure, programs, or spaces—cannot be released as open data. This would limit the ability of other developers, researchers, and governments themselves to access and use these data for a diverse range of purposes.

1.2 Confidential and Commercially Sensitive Data

Confidential information (of which trade secrets are a subset) is often treated as a kind of intellectual property, but it is different from other forms of intellectual property. Confidential information and trade secrets depend for their protection on their confidentiality; once that confidentiality is lost, so too is their protected nature. Hagen et al. (2017) argue that, unlike other areas of intellectual property, the public benefits much less directly from the protection of confidential commercial information. This is because, rather than support the publication and/or dissemination of the protected content (as is the case with patent and copyright law), the law of confidential information aids in keeping information secret. Hagen et al. (2017, p. 579) argue that the public interest in protecting confidential information lies in part in promoting fair competition and ethical behaviour, and in part in "promoting, protecting and enforcing relationships founded on trust and confidence." Where government has received confidential commercial information from companies in the course of their regulatory role, the protection of this information enhances trust in government and contributes to frank and honest compliance with regulatory disclosure requirements.

The protection of confidential information is a matter of domestic law, but it is also addressed in important trade treaties. The characteristics of confidential information are described in Article 39(2) of the *Agreement on Trade-Related Aspects of Intellectual Property Rights* (TRIPS). Information must be protected as confidential information if it:

> (a) is secret in the sense that it is not, as a body, or in the precise configuration and assembly of components, generally known among or readily accessible to persons within the circles that normally deal with the kind of information in question;
> (b) has commercial value because it is secret; and
> (c) has been subject to reasonable steps under the circumstances, by the person lawfully in control of the

> information, to keep it secret. (Agreement on Trade-Related Aspects of Intellectual Property Rights, 1994, Art. 39(2))

Article 20.72 of the *Canada–United States–Mexico Agreement* contains similar criteria. The protection of confidential information thus principally depends upon the control that is maintained over the information; this is usually achieved through physical and/or technological barriers that protect the information as well as by contracts that govern any necessary information sharing.

Governments are generally under obligations to protect from disclosure any confidential commercial information they receive from third parties. These obligations are found in domestic laws regarding access to information. For example, *Canada's Access to Information Act* (ATIA, 1985) contains a series of exceptions to the requirement to disclose information that relates specifically to third-party confidential information. Section 20 provides:

> 20 (1) Subject to this section, the head of a government institution shall refuse to disclose any record requested under this Act that contains
>
> (a) trade secrets of a third party;
>
> (b) financial, commercial, scientific or technical information that is confidential information supplied to a government institution by a third party and is treated consistently in a confidential manner by the third party;
>
> (b.1) information that is supplied in confidence to a government institution by a third party for the preparation, maintenance, testing or implementation by the government institution of emergency management plans within the meaning of section 2 of the Emergency Management Act and that concerns the vulnerability of the third party's buildings or other structures, its networks or systems, including its computer or communications networks or systems, or the methods used to protect any of those buildings, structures, networks or systems.

In addition to these exceptions to the disclosure of third-party confidential commercial information, the ATIA also carves out exceptions for another category of information that is excluded from disclosure: commercially sensitive information. A government may refuse to disclose such information where to do so would cause commercial harm to the party that supplied it. For example, paragraphs 20(1)(c) and (d) of the ATIA direct government institutions to refuse to disclose the following types of information:

> (c) information the disclosure of which could reasonably be expected to result in material financial loss or gain to, or could reasonably be expected to prejudice the competitive position of, a third party; or
> (d) information the disclosure of which could reasonably be expected to interfere with contractual or other negotiations of a third party.

Rosenblum and Maples (2009, p. 33) describe commercially sensitive information as "any information that has economic value or could cause economic harm if known." They observe that it is a widely used basis for claiming non-disclosure of information.

It should be noted that provincial access-to-information statutes also contain exceptions to disclosure for both confidential commercial information and commercially sensitive information, but the terms of these exceptions vary. Thus, for example, under section 17(1) of Ontario's *Freedom of Information and Protection of Privacy Act* (FOIPP, 1990), a government department or agency can refuse to release "a record that reveals a trade secret or scientific, technical, commercial, financial or labour relations information, supplied in confidence implicitly or explicitly" only where certain harms might arise. These harms are found to materialize where release of the information could reasonably be expected to:

> 17 (1) [...]
> (a) prejudice significantly the competitive position or interfere significantly with the contractual or other negotiations of a person, group of persons, or organization;
> (b) result in similar information no longer being supplied to the institution where it is in the public interest that similar information continue to be so supplied;
> (c) result in undue loss or gain to any person, group, committee or financial institution or agency.

Disclosure is the default position unless the applicability of one of the exceptions can be asserted. The emphasis is somewhat different in the federal statute where the default position is secrecy. Under the federal ATIA, the head of the government institution "shall" refuse to disclose trade secrets and confidential information of third parties, but it *may* disclose third-party confidential information and commercially sensitive information if:

> (a) the disclosure would be in the public interest as it relates to public health, public safety or protection of the environment; and
> (b) the public interest in disclosure clearly outweighs in importance any financial loss or gain to a third party, any prejudice to the security of its structures, networks or systems, any prejudice to its competitive position or any interference with its contractual or other negotiations. (ATIA, s. 20(6)).

This public interest override does not apply to third-party trade secrets. With the exception of Ontario (2019), there is no legislation at the provincial or federal levels that expressly addresses open data. Nevertheless, the principles relating to the release of open data track closely those found in access-to-information laws. In fact, the Ontario *Digital and Data Directive* creates an exception to the principle of open by default for: "Data that is subject to statutory confidentiality requirements, (i.e., exempt from publication under the *Freedom of Information and Protection of Privacy Act,* 1990, the *Personal Health Information Protection Act,* 2004 and/or other statutes)" (Government of Ontario, 2021). It then goes on to create a further exception for "[d]ata that should not be disclosed for legal, security, confidentiality, privacy or commercial sensitivity reasons."

The federal Directive on Open Government (Treasury Board Secretariat, 2014) describes those data that are required to be released as open data. The directive's definition of open data explicitly excludes confidential data or data owned by third parties:

> All data resources of business value held by Government of Canada departments are to be open by default and released as open data unless subject to valid exceptions, such as ownership, security, privacy, and confidentiality, as determined by the

> department. The Treasury Board of Canada Secretariat will support departments in the development of their decision-making and approval processes with regard to legal and policy issues by providing a release criteria checklist and other guidance tools. (Treasury Board Secretariat, 2014, Appendix B)

Confidential information may consist of information submitted directly by third-party companies for the purposes of regulatory compliance; or, for example, in the context of procurement or other bidding or application processes. In these contexts, the access-to-information regimes can provide guidelines about what information is public and what information is considered confidential. Companies may also draw to the attention of government specific information that is to be treated as confidential.

In the case of personal information, a combination of concerns for the public interest in privacy, as well as concerns that privacy should not unduly limit the availability of open data, have led to a considerable amount of work being done, both by governments and by those outside government, to develop tools for assessing when personal information is present in datasets and what techniques can be used to anonymize the data such that it might still be released. (see, e.g., Green et al., 2017; Simperl et al., 2016; Scassa & Conroy, 2016; Borgesius, 2015)

Interestingly, relatively little comparable work has been done in relation to confidential commercial information. Where guidance exists, it tends to be in fairly general terms (e.g., Information and Privacy Commissioner of Ontario, 2015). Certainly, the identification of confidential commercial information in a dataset is a different sort of undertaking from the identification of personal information. Whether something is confidential commercial information may well depend on the specific context and circumstances under which the information was shared with government, as well as the nature of the information and the nature of the third party's business. By contrast, with personal information, the question is more objective, even if it is sometimes challenging to answer. With personal information, the issue is whether information is about an identifiable individual. This may require an assessment of whether data can, by being linked with other available data, become information about an identifiable individual. Nevertheless, as is the case with personal information, excessive concerns over releasing confidential commercial information could lead to reluctance to release some data as open data. An overly cautious approach could work against the public interest. This is particularly the case where the allegedly confidential data are collected in the smart-cities context, for example, and are thus data about day-to-day operations and activities within the city in which the public has a clear interest.

Case law that has evolved under federal and provincial access-to-information regimes may be helpful in understanding when information supplied by third parties qualifies as confidential commercial information or commercially sensitive information for the purposes of the exceptions to release of data under open data directives. As noted above, under the ATIA, some grounds for refusal to disclose information are mandatory; others are discretionary. The head of a government institution must refuse to disclose confidential commercial information, whereas they have the discretion to disclose commercially sensitive information. The federal court has described it in these terms:

> With respect to mandatory exemptions, there is but one question to be considered; namely, the factual determination as to whether the material comes within the description of the exempting provision. If the contested information or record is found to fall within the description set out in the mandatory exemption provision, then the head of the government institution is obligated to refuse disclosure. In the case of discretionary exemptions, there are two decisions to be reviewed by the Court. First, as with mandatory exemptions, the Court must review the record to determine if the head of the government institution erred in making the factual decision as to whether or not the requested information falls within the exempting provision. If the information meets the criteria, the Court must then determine whether the head of the government institution exercised his or her discretion properly. (*Canadian Imperial Bank of Commerce v. Canada*, 2006, para. 28)

In either case, it is necessary first to determine if the information/data at issue falls within the boundaries of the exception. In the case of the mandatory exception for confidential commercial information, a finding of confidentiality is the end of the inquiry. With the discretionary exceptions, there is a second stage, which considers whether the discretion to refuse to disclose commercially sensitive data was properly exercised. By contrast, under Ontario's legislation, each inquiry has two steps, since even with confidential commercial information there is still discretion to disclose information in the public interest. The different approaches make it clear that, in Ontario, the protection of both confidential commercial information and commercially sensitive information can be treated as discretionary.

While, in general, courts and tribunals are responsive to the need to protect confidential or commercially sensitive information, where legislation requires third parties to establish with evidence the justification for non-disclosure, courts will critically assess whether the necessary evidence has been presented to support a claim of confidentiality (*Canadian Imperial Bank of Commerce v. Canada*, 2006; *Gartner Inc. v. Ontario*, 2017). It will not be enough for a party merely to assert that the information at issue is confidential and has always been treated as such. Courts have recognized that if the onus were not placed squarely on the third party to justify their claims to confidentiality, this "would surely undermine much of the purpose of this Act which in part is to make available to the public the information upon which government action is taken or refused" (*Ottawa Football Club v. Canada*, 1989, para. 487; *Canadian Imperial Bank of Commerce v. Canada*, 2006). In Ontario, where the confidential nature of the information is not the end of the inquiry, disclosure is refused only where the third party can demonstrate not just that the information is confidential or commercially sensitive, but also that its disclosure will create a "reasonable expectation of probable harm" (*Gartner Inc. v. Ontario*, 2017, para. 13).

In the case of the mandatory non-disclosure of confidential information under the federal ATIA, it is particularly important to ensure that claims to confidential information are carefully scrutinized. In *Air Atonabee Ltd. v. Canada* (1989, p. 272), the federal court made it clear that "whether information is confidential will depend upon its content, its purposes and the circumstances in which it is compiled and communicated." The court then went on to outline the criteria that would be considered, namely

> (a) that the content of the record be such that the information it contains is not available from sources otherwise accessible by the public or that could not be obtained by observation or independent study by a member of the public acting on his own ["not publicly available"],

> (b) that the information originate and be communicated in a reasonable expectation of confidence that it will not be disclosed ["reasonable expectation of non-disclosure"], and
>
> (c) that the information be communicated, whether required by law or supplied gratuitously, in a relationship between government and the party supplying it that is either a fiduciary relationship or one that is not contrary to the public interest, and which relationship will be fostered for public benefit by confidential communication ["public benefit"].

The access-to-information regime therefore establishes a balancing approach that considers the nature of the information, the relationship between the government and the party that provided it, and broader issues of public interest. It is important to note that while access-to-information regimes include both a balancing formula and checks and balances in terms of judicial review of decisions made about access, there is nothing equivalent for open data processes.

Access-to-information case law also makes it clear that it is conceivable that information or datasets may be composed of a combination of confidential and non-confidential information. Where it is possible to sever the confidential information from that which is non-confidential, it may be possible to release the non-confidential portion of the data (*Canadian Imperial Bank of Commerce v. Canada*, 2006). Thus, in the case of open data as well, it might be possible to strip proprietary or confidential commercial information from larger datasets, leaving data that are still meaningful enough to be released as open data. In general, confidential commercial information does not raise the same challenges as personal information when it comes to preparing datasets for release, since either the regulatory regime under which the information was shared or the party that shared the information will have identified that which is considered confidential. However, it is still possible for companies to be over-inclusive when it comes to identifying information as confidential commercial information. For example, in *Gartner Inc. v. Ontario* (2017), the applicant argued that the data, used in providing its benchmarking services, had commercial value that could be exploited by its competitors. The adjudicator, and later the reviewing court, found that the information at issue was not sufficiently detailed so as to cause commercial harm if disclosed, and ordered its release. This case, and many others like it, demonstrate that, as with privacy, there can be a delicate balance between the competing interests of protecting confidential commercial information on the one hand and providing an appropriate level of transparency on the other.

It has been argued that some data should be treated as confidential commercial information since their disclosure—alone or in combination with other data—could lead to the reverse engineering of the confidential proprietary decision-making processes or algorithms that were used in the creation of the datasets (see, e.g., Scassa, 2015; *Bertucci v. Royal Bank of Canada*, 2016). Such arguments may create interesting open data challenges for governments. For example, if the release by a city of datasets collected or processed according to proprietary algorithms could lead to the reverse engineering of those algorithms, the third-party company with rights over the algorithms might seek to have that data treated as confidential commercial information that is not subject to release as open data (or under access-to-information legislation). Thus, even where data are not proprietary to a third party, arguments still might be made that their release would lead to the disclosure of other confidential or commercially sensitive information.

2. Crown Copyright and Data Expropriation

Two Canadian court cases suggest that governments may have other tools at their disposal when it comes to balancing the public interest in the disclosure of data as open data with private-sector claims to ownership, confidentiality, or commercial sensitivity, at least in some contexts. In *Geophysical Service Incorporated v. Encana Corporation* (2017), for example, the Alberta Court of Appeal confirmed that a federal regulatory regime which required companies to submit data to a board as part of a licensing process for seismic exploration effectively meant that the federal government acquired the producer's copyright in the data by virtue of the provisions of the *Canada Petroleum Resources Act* (1985) and the related regulatory regimes. Under the legislation, the government was required to keep submitted data confidential for a period of years, after which point they would be published. Notably, the court accepted arguments that companies that used the published data without seeking a licence from Geophysical (the company which supplied it) did not violate that company's copyright in the data. The court referred to the legislative regime as having a "confiscatory nature" (*Geophysical Incorporated v. Encana Corporation*, 2017, para. 106). The decision confirms that governments, in creating regulatory regimes under statute, have the power to provide for the public interest in access to and use of the data not just by acquiring ownership of them, but by mandating the disclosure of the data, effectively as open data (Scassa, 2021).

In *Keatley Surveying Ltd. v. Teranet* (2019), the issue was whether land surveyors held copyright in their plans of survey, and if so, whether the company operating the provincial land-titles registry system owed them royalties when it charged fees for the reproduction of those plans of survey by users of the digital registry. While confirming that the plans were works protected by copyright law, the Supreme Court of Canada nevertheless ruled that the legislative scheme that governed both the deposit and the publication, through the registry, of the plans of survey resulted in the Government of Ontario acquiring Crown copyright in the documents. As such, it was entitled to control the terms of their dissemination and reproduction. The court ruled that section 12 of the *Copyright Act* (1985) gives the Crown rights in works that are "prepared *or published* by or under the direction or control of Her Majesty or any government department" (emphasis added).

In both *Keatley* and *Geophysical* there were complex legislative regimes in place. This is an important factor in each of these decisions. Although this suggests that a court will require firm legislative grounding before finding copyright to have been usurped by the Crown, the cases demonstrate that government may have latitude to create regimes under which it becomes entitled to publish data that are the subject of proprietary claims by others. This may be a useful tool to manage the public interest in access to some kinds of data.

3. Conclusion

That neither third-party confidential commercial information nor other proprietary third-party data can be released as open data is a limitation that takes on particular importance in the rapidly evolving big data and AI context. Governments may contract with private-sector suppliers for data (e.g., purchasing local cycling data from a fitness-app company; or traffic data from a driving-app company), for data analytics (e.g., software and systems that will analyze input data and produce analytics for use in predictive policing, or toward public transit arrival times), or for the sensors and systems used to collect and process smart city data. Unless close attention is paid to data ownership or to rights to publish data contracted for by governments, the pool of government data available for open data programs may shrink significantly.

In dealing with confidential commercial data and commercially sensitive data, governments have different options. Some of these are hard-coded in legislation, but it is evident that there are different models to follow. For example, access-to-information laws can create a bright-line rule that excludes confidential commercial information from disclosure, or they can provide latitude for discretionary release where disclosure is in the public interest. Even in the case of bright-line rules, it is possible to have an overarching public-interest override for exceptional cases. In the open data context, it is important to develop guidance and frameworks both for assessing the legitimacy of assertions of confidentiality or commercial sensitivity, but also for guiding discretionary decisions around release.

It is possible to draw lessons from the treatment of personal information in the open data context that can be applied to confidential commercial information or commercially sensitive information. First, governments have the authority to determine that the transparency value or other public interest in some data overrides any confidentiality considerations. There are many examples of where this occurs in the context of personal information. Regardless of its sensitivity, personal information is disclosed by government actors in published court and tribunal decisions, in public registries, in relation to certain activities such as consulting or political donations, and in sunshine laws, to give just a few examples. The Ontario Digital and Data Directive adopts a clear open-by-default approach, while maintaining exceptions for confidential or commercially sensitive data. In dealing with private-sector actors, governments must be more aware of what is being claimed as proprietary or confidential commercial information, and must assess these claims in light of the public interest. They can also implement proactive measures to limit claims that go beyond what is reasonable.

The privacy/open data context also demonstrates how datasets can be subject to anonymization or de-identification techniques in order to permit the release of valuable data without unduly impacting on privacy rights. Similar strategies might be available in the case of some kinds of confidential or commercially sensitive data. What is required is a process to determine which data within a dataset must remain confidential, and whether the remaining data have value for release as open data.

Recent case law also demonstrates that governments may have other options when it comes to data provided by private-sector actors. Legislative schemes can provide that data submitted to or shared with government are subject to disclosure. Such disclosure may be automatic and routine, or it may be subject to a confidentiality period to provide a kind of limited commercial advantage to offset the cost of creating or compiling the data. The *Keatley* and *Geophysical* cases show that such arrangements are possible, particularly where there is a compelling public interest served by providing access to the data at issue.

References

Borgesius, F. Z., Gray, J., & van Eeechoud, M. (2015). Open data, privacy, and fair information principles: Towards a balancing framework. *Berkeley Technology Law Journal, 30*(3), 2073–2130.

Government of Canada. (2017). *Open government licence–Canada, 2.0*. Retrieved April 9, 2018, from https://open.canada.ca/en/open-government-licence-canada

Government of Ontario. (2021). *Digital and data directive, 2021*. Retrieved May 21, 2021, from https://www.ontario.ca/page/ontarios-digital-and-data-directive-2021

Green, B., Cunningham, G., Ekblaw, A., Kominers, P., Linzer, A., & Crawford, S. (2017). *Open data privacy*. Berkman Klein Center for Internet & Society Research Publication. Retrieved April 9, 2018, from https://cyber.harvard.edu/publications/2017/02/opendataprivacyplaybook

Hagen, G., Hutchison, C., Lametti, D., Reynolds, G., Scassa, T., & Wilkinson, M. A. (2017). *Canadian intellectual property law: Cases, notes and materials* (2nd ed.). Emond Montgomery Publications.

Information and Privacy Commissioner of Ontario. (2015). *Proactive disclosure of procurement records*. Information and Privacy Commissioner of Ontario. Retrieved April 9, 2018, from https://www.ipc.on.ca/wp-content/uploads/Resources/open-contracting.pdf

Janssen, M., Charalabidis, Y., & Zuiderwijk, A. (2012). Benefits, adoption barriers and myths of open data and open government. *Information Systems Management, 29*(4), 258–268.

Johnson, P. A. (2016). Reflecting on the success of open data: How municipal government evaluates their open data programs. *International Journal of E-Planning Research, 5*(3), 1–12.

Judge, E. F., & Scassa, T. (2010). Intellectual property and the licensing of Canadian government geospatial data: An examination of GeoConnections' recommendations for best practices and template licences. *Canadian Geographer, 54*(3), 366–374.

Lauriault, T. P., & and Kitchin, R. (2014, April) *A genealogy of data assemblages: tracing the geospatial open access and open data movements in Canada* [Paper presentation]. Data-based Living—Peopling and Placing Big Data Session, Association of American Geographers (AAG) Annual Meeting, Tampa, Fla., United States. Retrieved April 9, 2018, from https://www.slideshare.net/TraceyLauriault/a-genealogy-of-data-assemblages-tracing-the-geospatial-open-access-and-open-data-movements-in-canada

Manyika, J., Chui, M., Groves, P., Farrell, D., Van Kuiken, S., & Doshi, E. A. (2013). *Open data: Unlocking innovation and performance with liquid information.* McKinsey Global Institute.

Maynard, C. (2021). *Observations and recommendations from the information commissioner on the government of Canada's review of the access to information regime.* Office of the Information Commissioner of Canada. Retrieved May 21, 2021, from https://www.oic-ci.gc.ca/en/resources/reports-publications/observations-and-recommendations-information-commissioner-review#1

Ohm, P. (2010). Broken promises of privacy: Responding to the surprising failure of anonymization. *UCLA Law Review, 57,* 1701.

Open Data Charter. (2015). *Open data charter.* Retrieved April 9, 2018, from https://opendatacharter.net/principles/

Robinson, P. J., & Johnson, P. A. (2016). Civic hackathons: New terrain for citizen-local government interaction? *Urban Planning, 1*(2), 65–74.

Rocher, L., Hendrickx, J. M., & de Montjoye, Y-A. (2019). Estimating the success of re-identifications in incomplete datasets using generative models. *Nature Communications* 10, 3069. https://doi.org/10.1038/s41467-019-10933-3

Rosenblum, P., & Maples, S. (2009). *Contracts confidential: Ending secret deals in the extractive industries.* Revenue Watch Institute. Retrieved April 9, 2018, from https://www.opensocietyfoundations.org/sites/default/files/contracts_20090915.pdf

Scassa, T. (2010). Geographic information as personal information. *Oxford University Commonwealth Law Journal, 10*(2), 185–214.

Scassa, T. (2015). Back to the future I: What past privacy findings tell us about the future of big data and privacy [Blog post]. Retrieved April 9, 2018, from http://www.teresascassa.ca/index.php?option=com_k2&view=item&id=180:back-to-the-future-i-what-past-privacy-findings-tell-us-about-the-future-of-big-data-and-privacy&Itemid=80

Scassa, T. (2017). Sharing data in the platform economy: A public interest argument for access to platform data. *University of British Columbia Law Review, 50*(4), 1017–1071.
Scassa, T. (2018). *Data ownership* (CIGI Paper No. 187). Centre for International Governance Innovation. https://www.cigionline.org/publications/data-ownership.
Scassa, T. (2021). Rights in data, the public interest and international trade law. In I. Bochert & L. A. Winters (Eds.), *Addressing Impediments to Digital Trade*. VoxEU/CEPR. https://voxeu.org/content/addressing-impediments-digital-trade
Scassa, T., & Conroy, A. (2016). Strategies for protecting privacy in open data and proactive disclosure. *Canadian Journal of Law and Technology, 14*, 215–262.
Simperl, E., O'Hara, K., & Gomer, R. (2016). *Analytical report 3: Open data and privacy*. European Data Portal. Retrieved April 9, 2018, from http://www.europeandataportal.eu/
Sweeney, L. (2010). k-Anonymity: A model for protecting privacy. *International Journal on Uncertainty, Fuzziness and Knowledge-Based Systems, 10*(5), 557–570.
Treasury Board Secretariat. (2014). *Directive on Open Government*. Retrieved April 9, 2018, from https://www.tbs-sct.gc.ca/pol/doc-eng.aspx?id=28108

Statutes and Case Law

Access to Information Act, RSC 1985, c A-1.
Agreement on Trade-Related Aspects of Intellectual Property Rights, 15 April 1994, 1869 U.N.T.S. 299. Retrieved April 9, 2018, from https://www.wto.org/english/docs_e/legal_e/27-trips_01_e.htm
Air Atonabee Ltd. v. Canada (Minister of Transport) (1989), 37 Admin. L.R. 245 (F.C.T.D.).
Bertucci v. Royal Bank of Canada (2016), FC 332 (CanLII). Retrieved April 9, 2018, from http://canlii.ca/t/gnzb2
Canada Petroleum Resources Act, RSC 1985, c 36 (2nd Supp.).
Canadian Imperial Bank of Commerce v. Canada (Canadian Human Rights Commission) (2006), FC 443. Retrieved April 9, 2018, from http://canlii.ca/t/1n3p4
Copyright Act, RSC 1985, c C-42.
Freedom of Information and Protection of Privacy Act, RSO 1990, c F.31.
Gartner Inc. v. Ontario (Information and Privacy Commissioner) (2017), ONSC 7181. Retrieved April 9, 2018, from http://canlii.ca/t/hpf5j
Geophysical Service Incorporated v. Encana Corporation (2017), ABCA 125 (CanLII). Retrieved April 9, 2018, from http://canlii.ca/t/h3jnp
Keatley Surveying Ltd. v. Teranet Inc. (2019), SCC 43 (CanLII). Retrieved May 21, 2021, from https://canlii.ca/t/j2kxw

Ottawa Football Club v. Canada (Minister of Fitness and Amateur Sports) (1989), 2 F.C. 480 (T.D.).
R. v. Stewart (1988), 1 SCR 963, 1988 CanLII 86 (SCC). Retrieved April 9, 2018, from http://canlii.ca/t/1ftdt
Simpler, Faster, Better Services Act, 2019, S.O. 2019, c. 7, Sched. 56.
Toronto Real Estate Board v. Commissioner of Competition, 2017 FCA 236 (CanLII), [2018] 3 FCR 563, <https://canlii.ca/t/hp34l>

About the Author

Teresa Scassa is Canada Research Chair in Information Law and Policy at the University of Ottawa, Faculty of Law. She is the author or co-author of several books, including *Digital Commerce in Canada* (LexisNexis, 2020), *Canadian Trademark Law* (LexisNexis, 2015, 2nd ed.), and *Law Beyond Borders* (Irwin Law, 2014); is co-editor of *Artificial Intelligence and the Law in Canada* (LexisNexis, 2021) and *Law and the Sharing Economy* (University of Ottawa Press, 2018); and has written widely in the areas of intellectual-property law, law and technology, and privacy. Scassa is a member of the Canadian Advisory Council on Artificial Intelligence and of the Geothink research partnership. She is also Senior Fellow with the Centre for International Governance Innovation.

CHAPTER 3

Reusability of Publicly Accessible User Data on Platform Websites

HAEWON CHUNG

Abstract

The open data movement has been concerned with increasing access to public sector data. In the future of open data, governments should also consider the reuse of user-generated data on popular online services and third-party use of automated programs to extract publicly accessible data from these platforms. Internet users increasingly rely on popular platforms, such as Facebook, Twitter, and LinkedIn, to access information and to communicate with others. This emerging structure of the virtual world allows platform companies to occupy an advantageous position over third parties seeking access to user-generated data. Platforms can deploy various legal and technological barriers against third-party access. Third-party use of publicly accessible data on the Internet can spur various commercial and non-commercial developments. Legal intervention is needed against platforms' proprietary management of such data for profit-maximization because their practice impedes the Internet as an open and generative technology and deters progress in society. Data are a valuable resource in today's knowledge-driven society. Institutions committed to the open data approach must also improve the reusability of web data.

Acknowledgements

I want to thank Dr. Teresa Scassa for providing valuable comments on this chapter. This research was carried out as part of the Geothink partnership, and the support of the Social Sciences and Humanities Research Council of Canada is gratefully acknowledged.

In the last decade, the global open data movement has largely focused on opening up third-party access to public sector data produced and collected by the government. Open government data policies and legislation increase government transparency (GoC, 2017). They also promote innovation, research, and competition by allowing others to access and use public sector data. Governments can also encourage economic growth and public benefit by improving third-party access to publicly accessible web data. Internet users upload and publicly share a massive amount of data and information through digital intermediaries, such as Facebook, Twitter, and Instagram (Constantine, 2012). However, platform companies' legal and technological access barriers discourage third-party data users. In the future of open data, governments should support the reuse of publicly shared data on online platforms with data policies and legislative measures that remove unnecessary barriers to third-party data use.

Third-party data users can access and gather data directly from platform websites manually or by using an automated program (i.e., a bot). This process is known as data scraping. Third parties can apply publicly accessible factual user data in various commercial and non-commercial endeavours, such as creating new products and services and conducting research on society and technology. On the other hand, platform companies, which often depend on advertising profits, can limit competition and maximize profit by tightly controlling user-generated content. Allowing platforms to turn publicly accessible user data into a private resource is not in the interest of the general public. Moreover, such tactics contradict the open nature of the Internet and its tremendous capacity to encourage innovation and knowledge.

Governments need to improve the regulation of web data. They should not leave it up to the oligopolistic market on the web to propertize valuable innovation resources such as web data. Relevant laws need to be modernized and legal uncertainties should be removed to promote fair and transparent third-party use of publicly accessible web data. Since Internet users share a variety of content over the Internet, I will limit the discussion in this chapter to the use of publicly shared factual data (e.g., user profiles and locational data). For the remainder of this chapter, I will refer to publicly shared factual data hosted on platform websites as "public user data." I will use the term "user-generated content" to refer to broader user contributions online that include factual data and copyright-protected works (e.g., original written expressions and images). It should be noted that not all user-generated content online is publicly accessible. Some platforms allow users to privately share data and information with one or more users, and such content is not publicly accessible. This chapter does not consider the use of private data.

This chapter is intended to encourage discussions among Internet users, scholars, and lawmakers about the Internet as an open network, automated data scraping, and web data regulation that can promote new technology and public benefit. The remainder of this chapter is organized as follows. Section one describes the role of platform services, possible uses of public user data, applicable laws on data access and use, and the platform businesses' possible motivation in user data regulation. Section two examines how new innovation policy in law supported the emergence of the Internet as an open network and a generative technology. Lawmakers need to take an ongoing and active role in protecting the Internet's open design as well as data and information freedom on the Internet. Following this, section three examines data scraping and anti-bot technologies. It then reviews contract law, tort law, copyright, and anti-circumvention law, which platform companies may rely on to prevent third-party data scraping. Section four discusses why it is inappropriate to rely on the market to create fair and adequate access to public user data on the Internet. Section five contains a conclusion and suggestions for the future.

1. Public User Data on Platform Websites

The World Wide Web consists of hyperlinked websites that display text, images, and other digital media and information on a web browser. As the Internet expanded, platform services grew rapidly to facilitate information exchange between Internet users. Platforms such as Facebook, Twitter, Instagram, LinkedIn, Google, Craigslist, Yelp, and Airbnb provide popular web services that allow people and businesses to create, upload, search, and/or share user-generated content. Platform services improve the usability of the Internet for ordinary users who lack programming skills. An ordinary Internet user can rely on platform services to share multimedia files, to search and exchange information, and to communicate with people globally without understanding technological details that enable activities on the Internet. A large portion of Internet users today rely on the tools and services offered by platforms to communicate and share information with others (Reyman, 2013, p. 513).

Depending on the nature of a platform's business, some or all of user-generated content hosted by the platform may be available for public access. Platform users can determine which user-generated content is made publicly accessible by examining a platform's policy, such as terms of service or user agreement, and also through their own interactions on and off a platform. Moreover, a platform may offer privacy settings for user-generated content, which allow users to specify how broadly their content may be shared. For example, according to Facebook's data policy, users' content is viewed by anyone if it is published under the "Public" setting, including "people off of Facebook and people who use different media . . . and other sites on the Internet".[1] It also notes that some information shared on Facebook is always made publicly available, such as some information under user profiles. Websites such as Yelp, TripAdvisor, Airbnb, and Kijiji that publish user reviews or user-created ads will make most of the user contributions freely accessible to the public to maximize traffic to their website and to facilitate business.

Public user data on platforms, such as user profiles, schedules, time stamps, preferences, locational data, or historical data, are valuable resources that can be used for various commercial and non-commercial endeavours. Third-party use of such data can contribute to economic growth and development in society. Possible third-party commercial applications include new services that create access to aggregated web data (e.g., price aggregators), analyze data (e.g., personalized ads), or offer new web tools (e.g., mapping locational data to create a visual display) (Scassa, 2017; Hirschey, 2014; Din, 2016; Gladstone, 2001). For example, in *hiQ Labs v. LinkedIn* (2017), hiQ Labs scraped publicly accessible user profiles on LinkedIn and sold the

[1] Consulted August 2021, from https://is-is.facebook.com/help/203805466323736.

statistical analysis of the data to businesses who wanted to learn more about their employees' skills.

Also, public user data could be used for various non-commercial purposes, such as research, lawmaking, and education. For example, public user data may be used to study human behaviour and societal issues (Landers et al., 2016). Governments may require access to public user data for regulation and planning purposes (Scassa, 2017). Moreover, web data can facilitate artificial intelligence and machine learning research (Mavridis, 2011; Pozzi et al., 2016; McClelland, 2017).

In spite of the many possible uses for public user data, there is considerable confusion in law about the accessibility of public user data on platform websites for third-party use and about what restrictions platform companies can impose on third-party data scraping. Third parties who seek to reuse public user data may need to bypass several technological access barriers, and they are subject to numerous laws which can vary by jurisdiction. Privacy laws, such as the *Privacy Act* of Canada, the *Personal Information Protection and Electronic Documents Act* (PIPEDA) of Canada, and the European Union's *General Data Protection Regulation* (GDPR), apply to the processing of personal information or information about an identifiable individual by government institutions and the private sector. Also, third parties cannot use copyright, trademark, and other intellectual property law-protected content without permission from intellectual property owners (subject to exceptions in law; see Section 3.2). Moreover, there are multiple laws, including contract law, tort law, copyright's anti-circumvention provisions, that platform companies can enforce against third parties accessing platform websites to collect data. The core discussion in this chapter will concern the relationship between platform companies and third-party data scrapers.

Privacy law issues are complex, and I will examine them briefly here. Privacy law addresses data regulation aimed at enhancing the digital economy while protecting individuals' right to their personal data. Both platform companies and commercial data scrapers are subject to numerous duties under the privacy laws of relevant jurisdictions to lawfully, fairly, and transparently use personal data, including the core requirement of obtaining meaningful consent of individuals where appropriate when commercial users collect, use, and disclose personal data (GDPR, Article 5(1)(a); PIPEDA, s. 6.1 and schedule 1; GoC, 2018, pp. 2–3). Privacy laws vary by jurisdiction on their treatment of publicly accessible data. For instance, Canada's PIPEDA includes exceptions to the requirement of obtaining meaningful consent when collecting, using, or disclosing some types of publicly available personal information, such as personal information that appears in a public telephone directory, in public business directories, and in printed or electronic publications (PIPEDA, s. 7; *Regulations Specifying Publicly Available Information*). However, data scrapers may not rely on a broad interpretation of such exceptions for consent to use personal web data because the Government of Canada has recently acknowledged that individual posting of personal information on a public website can attract privacy interests and there should not be unconstrained access to such data (ETHI, 2018, pp. 27–28; GoC, 2018, p. 3). On the other hand, the US district court in *hiQ Labs v. LinkedIn* (2017) noted that LinkedIn users' expectation of privacy on publicly posted user profiles is uncertain at best in light of LinkedIn's inadequate protection of its members' privacy interests, including allowing third-party access to such data without users' knowledge or consent. Canada and other countries are making efforts to update data protection laws to build a strong, coherent data protection regime in light of emerging information technology. These efforts are timely considering the recent privacy scandals relating to a popular social networking website (see Anderson, 2018).

There are various legal and technological measures that can discourage or bar third-party data scraping. These measures provide security against unauthorized access to a website. Platforms can also strategically use these measures for proprietary management of user-generated content and to maximize profits. For example, LinkedIn filed a lawsuit in 2016 in the United States against multiple anonymous data scrapers for automatically scraping LinkedIn user data. LinkedIn claimed that these unknown scrapers violated the US *Computer Fraud and Abuse Act* (CFAA), section 1201 of the *Digital Millennium Copyright Act* (DMCA), state criminal law on unauthorized computer access and fraud, breach of contract, trespass to chattel, and misappropriation (*LinkedIn Corporation v. Does*, 2016). Threats of litigation from platforms with multiple claims can create a chilling effect on third-party use of public user data.

Platform companies are commercially motivated; hence, the goal of profit maximization can overrule fair and transparent regulation of user-generated content. Platforms often generate revenues by including ads on their websites for human users and selling user data to their business partners and advertisers (Hirschey, 2014, pp. 898–899; DeNardis, 2014, p. 155; *Douez v. Facebook Inc.*, 2017). The business model based on advertising profit encourages platforms to tightly control third-party access to and use of the hosted user data because ad profits increase with more users and user-generated content on the website. It is commercially advantageous to establish themselves as the only access portal to the large user-generated content. By tightly controlling the hosted content, platforms can sustain users and limit competition. Hence, popular platform companies may be willing to use their large resources to discourage third-party data scraping that appears detrimental to business (e.g., *Facebook v. Power Ventures*, 2009). Such business tactics privatize user-generated content, including factual data, and cause the public to miss out on possible innovation and new knowledge in society.

Governments should expand their data regulation on the Internet to improve access to publicly accessible user data. In the regulation of public sector data and personal data, some governments have recognized data as "an innovation currency" and "the lifeblood of the knowledge economy" as it is vital to economic and social progress in an information society (EC, 2011, p. 3; GoC, 2018, pp. 1–2). Businesses are primarily driven to maximize profit (Lemley & Lessig, 2001, p. 11); they cannot be relied on to make fair choices about valuable resources such as public user data or to prioritize public interest over private commercial benefit. Third parties that fairly and transparently use public user data should not have to negotiate with platform companies to access such data. After all, search engines routinely access and collect data from publicly accessible areas of platforms and other websites (Christian, 2017). Lawmakers will need to examine laws in multiple areas to improve third-party use of publicly accessible facts on the Internet.

2. Legal Intervention in the Development of the Internet

Although technology is often solely credited for the World Wide Web, the law was also important for creating the Internet as a non-discriminating open network that facilitates information-sharing worldwide and permits anyone to freely contribute data and technology to it (Lemley & Lessig, 2001). The Internet's tremendous capacity to encourage economic and social benefit is closely tied to its underlying architecture reflecting open access ideology (Zittrain, 2008). Platform services that impose excessive and unfair restrictions on the use of public user data threaten the open nature of the Internet and the Internet as a generative technology. As this technology evolves, lawmakers must continue to play an important role in protecting the freedom of data and information online.

The earliest version of the Internet was built on top of existing telephone networks. Lemley & Lessig (2001, pp. 11–13) note that the Internet would not have evolved into a generative technology without the innovation policy that transformed the telephone networks from a monopolized resource to a general-purpose network (also see Zittrain, 2008, pp. 21–22). In the 1950s and 1960s in the United States, disputes over the use of third-party attachments on American Telephone & Telegraph (AT&T) networks led to decisions that opened up the telephone networks to work with third-party inventions. In *Hush-a-Phone Corporation v. U.S.* (1956), it was held that a user-invented cup-like device that attached onto a telephone receiver to allow a private conversation could not be barred by the telephone company because there was no evidence to support that its use impaired the telephone system or created public injury. The US Federal Communications Commission in *Use of the Carterfone* (1968) also rejected the telephone company's argument for absolute control over the telephone networks, and held in favour of allowing a third-party device of a two-way radio to be attached to the telephone system as long as the device did not adversely affect it (Wu, 2007). These decisions introduced a new innovation policy in law, turning the telephone networks in the United States into an open resource for inventors to build innovations that could address heterogeneous user needs. The inventors' freedom to access the physical layer of the telephone network at any point along the network (rather than access being granted at the discretion of the telephone company) made the physical layer generative. The decisions paved the way for inventions, such as fax machines, answering machines, and modems. Moreover, it became possible for academic researchers and amateurs to design and build the Internet on top of telephone networks. This attribute of the underlying network also influenced the development of the Internet as an open network and a generative technology that encourages users to contribute data and innovation without discrimination (Zittrain, 2008, pp. 22–35). Businesses generate profit by blocking potential competitors' access to the details of their products. However, the Internet was initially built by academics and amateurs who embraced open access and information sharing rather than being motivated by profit-seeking. Their decentralized collaboration led to the Internet as we know it today (i.e., the World Wide Web), which allows anyone to access and add data and services to the Internet from anywhere in the world, rather than a technology that is centrally located and controlled by a private entity (Saltzer et al., 1984; von Hippel, 2005, Chap. 3). This design allowed information and communications technology to advance rapidly.

Today, popular platform services improve users' access to information and communication over the Internet. Ordinary citizens often depend on these platforms for online communication (*Douez v. Facebook*, 2017; Reyman, 2013, p. 513). However, platform companies should not be allowed to privatize the massive amount of data and information contributed and generated by platform users. Popular platform websites can seriously challenge data and information freedom on the Internet and hinder technological progress. Instead, lawmakers must continue to play an important role in shaping the Internet, including the use of publicly accessible data to maximize public benefit.

Furthermore, third-party access to public user data will be necessary as the Internet evolution enters the next phase, which may be characterized by a proliferation of automated intelligent programs (i.e., bots) that deliver information and services to users (Berners-Lee et al., 2001). This next phase will depend on technology such as semantic web, artificial intelligence, and machine learning, which must process large amounts of data to extract new information or to create useful services (Mavridis, 2011; McClelland, 2017). Third parties need automated access to existing web data for these technologies to evolve.

3. Access Barriers to Public User Data on Platforms

Platform companies can use various technological and legal tools to bar unwanted third-party bots from accessing websites and gathering user-generated content. In this discussion, data-scraping bots are programs that enter target websites to collect publicly accessible data. Search engines widely use such programs to gather information about websites (e.g., Google's Googlebot). Bot users are individuals who use these programs to gather data from someone else's website. Data-scraping bots in this discussion are not malicious programs designed to purposefully harm websites or change or delete data from websites.

3.1 Technological Barriers

For Internet users, the main tool for accessing web content is a web browser. Nonetheless, browsers typically do not offer a means to reuse web data; they do not allow users to locate and save a large amount of web data into an easy-to-access format for future use (WebHarvy, n.d.). Users have three options for collecting web data: manual data scraping, downloading data from an application programming interface (API) if available on target websites, or automated data scraping.

To manually scrape data, users must locate and copy data on one or more web pages and then clean up, convert and save relevant portions into a particular format and/or a database for future use. This process can be extremely laborious if the user wants to extract frequently updated data or a large dataset from one or more websites. A website usually has multiple web pages. Manual data scraping is inefficient if the target website(s) is constantly updated and expanded.

Alternatively, some websites offer their data in a structured format for third-party use over an API. If so, data users can sign up to an API and download web data in an easy-to-use format. However, this method of data sharing may not be fair or transparent because it allows websites to control what data, when, and how much data are shared with third parties (Hirschey, 2014, p. 906). The data available through APIs may not match the latest data displayed or used on target websites, and some data may not be available at all via APIs when websites want to avoid third-party analysis.

Lastly, automated data scraping uses a bot (i.e., a program) to gather web data directly from target websites. A bot can access the latest data published on a website at the time of scraping, which is what a human user would see on a browser. As noted above, data scraping is a labour-intensive process. Automated data-scraping technology is an efficient tool because a bot can scrape publicly accessible web data significantly faster and more thoroughly than human users. However, automated data scraping may be difficult when bot users have not obtained permission to access a website that uses complex anti-bot technologies to stop bots from entering the website. Without firm, enforceable rules that regulate automated data scraping (and consequently, the use of automated data scraping and anti-bot technologies), public user data may have limited subsequent use.

The process of automated data scraping can be broken down into three steps (Peterson & Davie, 2000, pp. 640–645; ScrapeHero, 2014; Alhenshiri, 2012). First, a hypertext transfer protocol (HTTP) request is sent from the third party's machine to a platform website's web server. An HTTP request is a request to access the web page associated with a URL (i.e., website address). The web server sends the requested web page to the third party's machine in response to this request. This step occurs whether the request is made from a browser of a human user or a data-scraping bot. The fetched web page usually consists of hypertext markup language (HTML), codes, metadata (i.e., additional information about the web page), and contents displayed on the web page, such as images, texts, and web links. The second step involves parsing and cleaning up the fetched web page. This step is necessary because machines cannot interpret the contents of a web page like a human reader. Thus, a data-scraping program examines the fetched page, discards any unimportant parts, and keeps relevant data and web links to other web pages of the website. The third step involves storing the extracted data in a desired format and/or a database for future use. A bot will repeat these steps until there are no more web pages to visit on a website.

Unlike human users, bot users have to overcome the technological challenges of entering a website. A website is a black box to everyone but its owner. It is unclear from the outside how a website monitors and polices website users. Hence, a data-scraping bot usually needs to be programmed specifically to perform on a target website to fetch relevant data against the website's layout, structure, and technological access barriers. For this reason, one strategy to discourage third-party data scraping is to regularly change the website's layout and structure to throw off bots. A data-scraping bot that requests access to a website can encounter multiple anti-bot technological protection measures (TPMs) that discourage or stop automated access to a website, such as a login requirement, captcha tests, cookies, scripts, and IP blocking (Kerr, 2016, pp. 1161–1170). For example, some TPMs on a website operate inconspicuously for human users, such as session cookies, scripts, and networking tools that track and monitor visitors' browsing patterns. Websites can analyze this information to identify bots from human users and block only bot users. A website can refuse a bot's access, for instance, by blocking the IP address associated with the bot user and ignoring any HTTP requests from the blocked IP address (i.e., IP blocking). Thus, unlike human users, a bot may need to change its IP address multiple times or change its login information to visit publicly accessible areas of a website.

Bot users who want to examine data from a large website or multiple websites will likely need to overcome numerous technological barriers to access a website. Some TPMs are trivial (e.g., captcha and login requirements), and some are complex technology that can be difficult to bypass to enter a website. Increasingly sophisticated anti-bot technologies are significant access barriers to bot users (especially if Internet users have small resources to access bot technology) and deter third-party use of public web data (see Sawatzky, 2015). Popular platform companies with large resources can implement a combination of technological access barriers to discourage and block third parties from examining their web data. Circumventing TPMs, whether trivial or complex, can also raise legal consequences for bot users (*Facebook v. Power Ventures*, 2009; *Craigslist v. 3Taps*, 2013; also see the following section).

Third parties using data-scraping bots have two choices absent enforceable rules on using data-scraping technology: try to avoid detection by websites and data scrape discretely or convince the target websites to permit bot access for automated data gathering. Without enforceable rules to rely on, data scrapers may prefer to avoid detection by websites to avoid conflict. Risking detection of their bot can lead to punishment (e.g., website access denied) and lawsuits from target websites. Popular platforms have the financial resources to threaten lawsuits and engage in lengthy litigation with data scrapers. Avoiding detection may be more than a practical choice for a data scraper because it is difficult to predict how a website will react to third-party data scraping. If data scrapers communicate with platform services before collecting publicly accessible web data, platforms can identify bot users and selectively block their activities (see Scassa, 2018). For example, in exchange for granting bots' access, platforms can require data scrapers to agree not to publish critical or undesirable information about their business or non-participation in related business.

The robots exclusion protocol (REP) is a method that allows websites to specify the rules of automated access and use, and bot users voluntarily follow them (Lundblad, 2007). Websites can implement the REP by including a file called robots.txt in the root directory, which has a set of instructions for bots that request access. The file contains information, such as which bots are allowed to crawl the website, which portions of the website can be crawled, and how fast bots can fetch data from the website. A bot can be programmed to ignore the robots.txt file on a website, but programmers generally encourage each other to follow it out of good faith (Alhenshiri, 2012). However, websites can also include instructions that unfairly treat some third-party bots and refuse their automated access to content that is publicly accessible on a browser. The REP cannot prevent disruptive third-party access to websites or protect third parties' automated access to publicly accessible user data.

As noted above, the Internet, as an open network and a generative technology, has a tremendous potential to encourage innovation and progress. Nonetheless, a small number of companies (e.g., Google, Microsoft, and Facebook) dominate the big tech and Internet business. A few businesses or an oligopoly should not control valuable innovation resources, such as public user data. Moreover, the costs to sidestep anti-bot technologies will likely increase over time as technology evolves. Without proper regulation of data scraping, it can be quite inefficient and costly for third-party data scrapers to access publicly accessible data on large websites. When third-party data scraping is performed without causing harm to individuals or target websites (i.e., it is carried out politely by fetching public user data from publicly accessible web pages without significantly interfering with the website's operation), firm rules or law should support third-party access to data and deter platform companies' active interference.

3.2 Legal Barriers

Platform companies can also rely on multiple legal measures to deter third-party data scraping. Depending on the jurisdiction, platforms can bring lawsuits against unauthorized data scrapers for violating multiple laws, including contract law, tort law, copyright law and its anti-circumvention provisions, and criminal laws prohibiting access to a computer system (Snell, 2016; *LinkedIn Corporation v. Does*, 2016; Scassa, 2017, 2018). However, policy-makers can support open data and the open access ideology on the web by reviewing and modernizing appropriate areas of law to encourage third-party use of public user data. The discussion in this section will primarily be based on the laws of Canada.

Platform companies can bring a breach of contract claim against data scrapers. Platform users are bound by the website's terms of use or user agreement, which is enforced in contract law (*Century 21 v. Rogers*, 2011; *Trader v. CarGuru*, 2017). Some platform websites' user agreements may contain provisions that prohibit data scraping. Broad anti-data-scraping provisions protect platform companies' investment and future profits. However, such practice does not recognize the public's interest in third-party use of public user data. Furthermore, broad anti-data-scraping provisions contradict the Internet as a generative technology.

For example, according to Facebook's terms of service, Facebook does not allow automated data collection unless Facebook pre-authorizes it. Moreover, LinkedIn's user agreement does not allow users to "[d]evelop, support or use software, devices, scripts, robots, or any other means or processes (including crawlers, browser plugins and add-ons, or any other technology or manual work) to scrape the Services or otherwise copy profiles and other data from the Services." Platforms can discourage undesirable third-party data scraping by threatening lawsuits for violating the terms of use.

In contract law, online user agreements may become binding on a user when the user acknowledges the agreement by clicking on a box labelled "I agree" at login or website registration (i.e., a click-wrap agreement) (*Century 21 v. Rogers*, 2011; *Trader v. CarGuru*, 2017; *Douez v. Facebook*, 2017). In some cases, the act of using a website can bind website users to its user agreement (i.e., a browse-wrap agreement). When a bot enters a platform website to gather data, the person running the bot is likely bound by the website's user agreement because bot users typically need to visit the website before running the program to customize it to work against the target website's layout and structure. Contract law presumes that contracts are struck in a free market economy between parties freely entered into an agreement (McCamus, 2012). However, as noted above, when Internet users rely on popular platform services to access information and communicate with others, users cannot reject these platforms and their user agreements.

Platform owners motivated by advertising profit will protect and sometimes even expand their right to control user-generated content on platform websites. Therefore, platforms unilaterally modify user agreements from time to time to reflect any changes in law or business strategy. For example, Craigslist briefly unilaterally changed its terms of use in 2012 to stipulate that Craigslist had exclusive copyright licensing of user-submitted ads on the website, which would grant the company the right to block anyone from using the ads

(Carrier, 2013, p. 773; *Craigslist v. 3Taps*, 2013). Therefore, data scrapers who regularly collect data from a website also need to routinely examine the terms of use for any changes on data scraping. Third-party data scrapers should not presume that access to a website will be allowed on an ongoing basis.

Furthermore, platforms may bring a claim of tort of trespass to chattels against data scrapers (*Century 21v. Rogers*, 2011, para. 285). To make out this claim, platforms must show that a data scraper trespassed on personal property (i.e., web servers) within their possession. For example, there is no possession if a platform runs its website on a third-party server. Platforms must also show that data scraping interfered with their possession of the personal property; that is, they must have suffered some damage as a result of data scraping. Nonetheless, data scrapers need target websites to be functional and to be able to service users to generate user content (see Alhenshiri, 2012). They cannot scrape web data if their bots disrupt or damage the target websites' servers. Still, some US courts have adopted a flexible view on what is sufficient damage to allow this tort claim to be brought against a data scraper, such as data scraping that devalues a website's investment (Din, 2016, p. 438). While the availability of this claim in Canada is uncertain in the context of data scraping, it seems to be a viable claim against data scrapers in some American states (Scassa, 2018, pp. 47–49).

Moreover, platform companies can bring multiple claims against data scrapers under copyright law. Third parties collecting user-generated content from a platform website can infringe the platform's copyright in the collection or compilation of hosted user data or copyright in its website. Copyright law protects against unauthorized copying of original literary and artistic works fixed in a tangible medium, such as photos and written expressions (see *Copyright Act*, ss. 2 & 5(1)). Copyright law does not protect facts or mere ideas (*CCH v. LSUC*, 2004, para. 15). Therefore, third parties are free to use public user data that are facts. However, copyright law provides separate protection for a compilation of data (Vaver, 2011, p. 92; Scassa, 2017, p. 1050; Scassa, 2018, pp. 28–31). There is no separate database protection law in Canada like the European Union's *Database Directive*. Hence, factual data are unprotected, but an original selection or arrangement of facts is protected in copyright law as a compilation (*Feist Publications v. Rural Telephone*, 1991, para. 44). An original compilation can also consist of facts and other copyrighted works. Any substantial use of a compilation is a copyright infringement (Vaver, 2011, p. 185). A platform must establish that a compilation is "original" under copyright law, which may not be difficult in Canada (Vaver, 2011, p. 101; *CCH v. LSUC*, 2004, para. 34; Scassa, 2018, p. 28). On the other hand, the US Supreme Court in *Feist Publications v. Rural Telephone* (1991, paras. 17–18) stated that since facts are unprotected in copyright law, the protection of compilations of facts in copyright law is "thin."

Data scrapers can also infringe a platform's copyright in its web page (which is a compilation of data and other copyrighted works) when they make a temporary copy of a web page onto their computer to process and extract relevant data (Vaver, 2011, p. 163). Although this step is unavoidable in digital processing, some litigants in the United States have successfully argued that there is copyright infringement when a temporary cache copy of a web page is created on a third-party computer for the purpose of extracting data on the page (e.g., *Facebook v. Power Ventures*, 2009). On the other hand, several US courts have held that unauthorized copying of large amounts of copyrighted works for text- and data-mining analysis falls under the fair use exception and is not copyright infringement (Cox, 2015). When a temporary copy of a web page is made to digitally extract facts or ideas, copyright law should not interfere with third parties' right to use facts and ideas.

Bots must also create temporary copies of a web page to deliver automated services on the Internet (De Beer & Fewer, 2015, para. 5). The United Kingdom adopted a statutory exception in copyright law in 2014, which exempts copies made from lawfully accessed works for text and data analysis in non-commercial research (see UK *Copyright, Designs and Patents Act 1988*, s. 29A). However, this exception does not encourage a variety of third-party web data use described above because it requires data scrapers to obtain permission from target websites before accessing them, and it only exempts non-commercial research use.

There are provisions in copyright law that exempt some unauthorized copying from infringement, such as US fair use or Canadian fair dealing exceptions. Data scrapers making temporary copies of a web page for private study, research, commentary or review, news reporting, or education may rely on the fair use or fair dealing exception (see *Copyright Act*, ss. 29, 29.1, 29.2; Scassa, 2018, pp. 33–41; Aufderheide, 2011). Courts decide whether such uses are fair on a case-by-case basis by weighing several factors. It can be more difficult for commercial users than non-commercial users to argue fair use or fair dealing. A copyright user who directly competes in the market with the copyright owner will have a harder time arguing fair use or fair dealing (*CCH v. LSUC*, 2004, para. 59). Data scrapers cannot rely on this exception if they waive their fair use or fair dealing rights in a binding contract with a platform service (Cox, 2015, p. 1).

Anti-circumvention provisions in copyright law pose a serious threat to data scrapers. These provisions can bar data scrapers from gathering public user data regardless of the purpose of use if scrapers circumvent a TPM to access a website. The fair dealing exception does not extend to circumventing a TPM in Canada (Scassa, 2018, p. 42). Anticircumvention law is problematic in data scraping because it grants too much power to platform companies to restrict third-party access to web data, including publicly accessible user data. These provisions prohibit copyright users from circumventing TPMs that are intended to limit access to and use of copyright-protected works. Section 41.1 of the Canadian *Copyright Act* prohibits circumvention of a TPM (i.e., any effective technology, device, or component) that is placed to control access to a work. Copyright users cannot engage in actions such as "to descramble a scrambled work or decrypt an encrypted work or to otherwise avoid, bypass, remove, deactivate or impair the TPM, unless it is done with the authority of the copyright owner." A platform's copyright protection in its website allows the platform to enforce anti-circumvention provisions against data scrapers. A wide variety of anti-bot measures on a platform website may be deemed TPMs in Canada because the term "TPM" is broadly defined in Canadian law (*Nintendo America v. King*, 2017, paras. 81–84; Scassa, 2018, pp. 42–43). TPMs discussed in the previous section are likely protected in Canadian anti-circumvention law, and bypassing these measures without authorization can attract liability for data scrapers. For example, programming data scraping bots to change IP addresses to avoid the platform's IP blocking may be considered bypassing a TPM under anti-circumvention law (*Facebook v. Power Ventures*, 2009; *Craigslist v. 3Taps*, 2013).

Copyright law and its anti-circumvention provisions in Canada do not properly balance the rights of the public to benefit from third-party data use against the rights of platform companies. The law requires third-party data scrapers to explain their actions to powerful platform companies to get permission to access target websites. However, as noted above, these are businesses with no duty to maximize or prioritize the public's benefit from hosted user data. The law does not even allow data scrapers to defend bypassing TPMs as necessary for fair use or fair dealing. Moreover, since platform companies can unilaterally modify user agreements and technological measures on their website to enhance their control of user-generated content, copyright and anti-circumvention laws should not apply strictly against bot users who access a website to examine publicly accessible user data.

4. Discussion

There must be legal intervention to create better access to public user data shared on platform websites. Platform companies can discourage data scraping by increasing anti-bot measures that block automated access and data collection. The possibility of attracting multiple legal liabilities from data scraping can also discourage economically and socially beneficial uses of public user data. Moreover, in *hiQ Labs v. LinkedIn* (2017), the US Northern District Court of California acknowledged that "conferring on private entities such as LinkedIn, the blanket authority to block viewers from accessing information publicly available on its website for any reason [. . .] could pose an ominous threat to public discourse and the free flow of information promised by the Internet." Therefore, the rights of platform companies to create profit must be balanced against the public's right to benefit from third-party data use.

Clearly, both platform companies and data scrapers should be mindful of how their actions affect the general public and the functioning of the Internet. Both parties should exercise care in order to avoid causing harm to each other. One reason why a platform website may refuse an unfamiliar data-scraping bot from accessing and gathering public user data is because there is a possibility that a bot might interfere with the operation of the website. For instance, unlike human users who visit one web page at a time, bots can rapidly and concurrently send the request to visit a website's multiple web pages. Bots' rapid and concurrent access requests can tie up a website's servers, preventing the website from servicing other users. Thus, data scraping should never be done too rapidly to avoid exhausting a website's server resources and disabling the website (Alhenshiri, 2012). Such third-party access can be mistaken as a denial-of-service attack. Websites can use law and technology to block harmful uses of their resources. However, as noted above, when data scrapers need to gather public user data for commercial or non-commercial purposes, there is usually no incentive to harm or to interfere with the host platform's operations because data scrapers need to retain ongoing access to the website to collect the data.

Thus, it is generally recommended that programmers should develop a well-behaving and respectful bot that does not impose an excessive burden on a platform's web servers. For example, data scraping bots can request a web page from a web server at a similar rate to human users browsing a website (i.e., two to five seconds between each request for a web page) or mimic search engines that crawl the Internet (Sangaline, 2017). Data scrapers can also explain their bot use to target websites by attaching additional information in the HTTP request (Alhenshiri, 2012). If a bot politely enters publicly accessible portions of a platform website without imposing an excessive burden on its web servers, platforms should grant access.

On the other hand, platform companies may have strong incentives to privatize user-generated data and to block third-party data scraping, such as excluding competition and speech that can negatively impact their business. Hence, society cannot depend on platform companies to decide what kind of third-party data use is appropriate. Businesses cannot be expected to promote society's welfare before their other goals (Lemley & Lessig, 2001, p. 11). Businesses exist to generate profit, and can engage in selfish behaviours. After establishing themselves as industry leaders, popular platforms can use their market position and influence to control user-generated content more aggressively to maximize profit, reduce competition, and control speeches about their business. It also harms data and information freedom in cyberspace and the Internet as a generative technology when platform companies use technological and legal measures to discriminate against some third-party data users. For example, most websites welcome automated access by popular search engines, even when some of them commercially use scraped web data, because search engines benefit a website's business by directing more users to it. Google's automated program (i.e., the Googlebot) crawls most of the Internet to build an index for its search engine and uses the fetched content from various websites to provide services like Google News (Christian, 2017). Also, other large online companies may offer partnerships and other commercial incentives to gain access to a platform's user-generated content. However, platforms may be reluctant to provide access to third parties who do not offer a business advantage.

Lawmakers cannot expect the market to fix platform companies that behave badly. Online platforms should not have free rein over user-generated content because it can be difficult to replace the handful of popular services that control the digital environment. Popular platform companies may have the first-mover advantage (Burstein, 2012, p. 217) and the benefits of the network effects that accumulate over time (Helberger et al., 2015). These factors, coupled with many users' resistance to change and adapt to a new digital environment, allow popular platforms to maintain their positions of power in cyberspace. Allowing platform companies to determine who can use publicly accessible user data (i.e., by retaining laws that require third parties to seek prior permission from platforms to access data) can strengthen the existing oligopoly on the Internet and discourage new and disruptive innovation from other innovators.

5. Conclusion and Recommendations

Publicly accessible factual data on platform websites are a significant resource in a knowledge economy. Nonetheless, existing laws that regulate the relationship between platform data hosts and third-party data users may be outdated and uncertain in the context of data scraping. Popular platform companies have legal, technological, and perhaps financial advantages over data scrapers. Lawmakers should deter platform businesses from controlling third-party use of publicly shared user data. Undertaking this development in law is necessary to promote fair and transparent uses of public user data and to protect the Internet as an open and generative technology. Since Internet activities can occur across national borders, follow-on research can consider international guidelines for automated data scraping and web data use.

References

Alhenshiri, A. (2012). *Crawling the web: Creating data indices* [PowerPoint slides]. Dalhousie University. https://web.cs.dal.ca/~anwar/ir/lecturenotes/l13.pdf

Anderson, M. (2018, April 6). *Facebook privacy scandal explained.* CTV News. https://www.ctvnews.ca/sci-tech/facebook-privacy-scandal-explained-1.3874533

Aufderheide, P. (2011). Copyright, fair use, and social networks. In Z. Papacharissi (Ed.), *A networked self: Identity, community, and culture on social network sites* (pp. 274–299). Routledge.

Berners-Lee, T., Hendler J., & Lassila, O. (2001). The semantic web. *Scientific American, 284*(5), 34–43.

Burstein, M. J. (2012). Exchanging information without intellectual property. *Texas Law Review, 91*, 227–282.

Carrier, M. A. (2013). Only "scraping" the surface: The copyright hole in the FTC's Google settlement. *UBC Law Review, 46*(3), 759–790.

Christian, J. (2017, November 22). *We still don't know how Google News works.* The Outline. https://theoutline.com/post/2512/we-still-don-t-know-how-google-news-works?zd=1&zi=xdu635x6

Constantine, J. (2012, August 22). *How big is Facebook's data? 2.5 billion pieces of content and 500+ terabytes ingested every day.* TechCrunch. https://techcrunch.com/2012/08/22/how-big-is-facebooks-data-2-5-billion-pieces-of-content-and-500-terabytes-ingested-every-day/

Cox, K. L. (2015). *Issue brief: Text and data mining and fair use in the United States.* Association of Research Libraries. http://www.arl.org/storage/documents/TDM-5JUNE2015.pdf

Din, M. F. (2016). Breaching and entering: When data scraping should be a federal computer hacking crime. *Brooklyn Law Review, 81*(2), 405–440.

De Beer, J., & Fewer, D. (2015). *35918 CBC v. SODRAC: Factum of the intervener, Samuelson-Glushko Canadian Internet Policy & Public Interest Clinic (CIPPIC)* (SCC Court File No.: 35918). https://cippic.ca/sites/default/files/CIPPIC_Factum-CBC_v_SODRAC.pdf

DeNardis, L. (2014). *The global war for Internet governance.* Yale University Press.

European Commission (EC). (2011). *Open data: An engine for innovation, growth and transparent governance* [Communication]. https://eur-lex.europa.eu/legal-content/EN/TXT/?uri=celex%3A52011DC0882

Gladstone, J. A. (2001). Data mines and battlefields: Looking at financial aggregators to understand the legal boundaries and ownership rights in the use of personal data. *Journal of Computer & Information Law, 19*(2), 313–329.

Government of Canada (GoC). (2017). *Open Data 101.* https://open.canada.ca/en/open-data-principles#toc97

Government of Canada (GoC). (2018). *Government response to the twelfth report of the Standing Committee on Access to Information, Privacy and Ethics.* https://www.ourcommons.ca/DocumentViewer/en/42-1/ETHI/report-12/response-8512-421-344

Helberger, N., Kleinen-von Königslöw, K., & van der Noll, R. (2015). Regulating the new information intermediaries as gatekeepers of information diversity. *Info, 17*(6), 50–71.

Hirschey, J. K. (2014). Symbiotic relationships: Pragmatic acceptance of data scraping. *Berkeley Technology Law Journal, 29*(4), 897–927.

Kerr, O. S. (2016). Norms of computer trespass. *Columbia Law Review, 116*(4), 1143–1183.

Landers, R. N., Brusso, R. C., Cavanaugh, K. J., & Collmus, A. B. (2016). A primer on theory-driven web scraping: Automatic extraction of big data from the Internet for use in psychological research. *Psychological Methods, 21*(4), 475–492.

Lemley, M. A., & Lessig, L. (2001). The end of end-to-end: Preserving the architecture of the Internet in the broadband era. *UCLA Law Review, 48*, 925–972.

Lundblad, N. (2007). e-Exclusion and bot rights: Legal aspects of the robots exclusion standard for public agencies and other public sector bodies with Swedish examples. *First Monday, 12*(8). http://firstmonday.org/ojs/index.php/fm/article/view/1974/1849

Mavridis, N. (2011). Artificial agents entering social networks. In Z. Papacharissi (Ed.), *A networked self: Identity, community, and culture on social network sites* (pp. 291–303). Routledge.

McClelland, C. (2017, December 4). *The difference between artificial intelligence, machine learning, and deep learning.* Medium. https://medium.com/iotforall/the-difference-between-artificial-intelligence-machine-learning-and-deep-learning-3aa67bff5991

Peterson, L. L., & Davie, B. S. (2000). *Computer Networks: A System Approach* (2nd ed.). Morgan Kaufmann Publishers.

Pozzi, F. A., Fersini, E., Messina E., & Liu, B. (2016). *Sentiment Analysis in Social Networks.* Elsevier.

Reyman, J. (2013). User data on the social web: Authorship, agency, and appropriation. *College English, 75*(5), 513–533. http://www.ncte.org/library/NCTEFiles/Resources/Journals/CE/0755-may2013/CE0755User.pdf

Saltzer, J. H., Reed, D. P., & Clark, D. D. (1984). End-to-end arguments in system design. *ACM Transactions on Computer Systems, 2*(4), 277–288.

Sangaline, E. (2017). *Advanced web scraping: Bypassing "403 Forbidden," captchas, and more.* http://sangaline.com/post/advanced-web-scraping-tutorial/

Sawatzky, K. (2015). *Short-term consequences.* https://shorttermconsequences.wordpress.com/2015/06/20/airbnb-listings-in-vancouver-how-many-what-type-where/

ScrapeHero. (2014). *Webscraping using Python without using large frameworks like Scrapy.* https://www.scrapehero.com/webscraping-using-python-without-using-large-frameworks-like-scrapy/

Scassa, T. (2017). Sharing data in the platform economy: A public interest argument for access to platform data. *UBC Law Review, 50*(4), 1017–1071.

Scassa, T. (2018). Information law in the platform economy: Ownership, control and reuse of platform data. In D. McKee, F. Makela & T. Scassa (Eds.), *Law and the sharing economy: Regulating online market platforms* (pp. 149–194). University of Ottawa Press.

Snell, J. (2016). *Web scraping in an era of Big Data 2.0*. Bloomberg Law. https://news.bloomberglaw.com/tech-and-telecom-law/web-scraping-in-an-era-of-big-data-20

Standing Committee on Access to Information, Privacy and Ethics (ETHI). (2018). *Towards privacy by design: Review of the Personal Information Protection and Electronic Documents Act* [Report]. House of Commons. http://publications.gc.ca/site/eng/9.852663/publication.html

Vaver, D. (2011). *Intellectual property: Copyright, patents, trademarks*. (2nd ed). Irwin Law.

von Hippel, E. (2005). *Democratizing innovation*. MIT Press.

WebHarvy. (n.d.). *What is web scraping?* https://www.webharvy.com/articles/what-is-web-scraping.html

Wu, T. (2007). Wireless Carterfone. *International Journal of Communication, 1*, 389–426.

Zittrain, J. (2008). *The future of the Internet*. Yale University Press.

Statutes

Copyright Act, RS C 1985, c C-42.

Personal Information Protection and Electronic Documents Act, S.C. 2000, c. 5 [PIPEDA].

Regulation (EU) 2016/679 of the European Parliament and of the Council of 27 April 2016 on the protection of natural persons with regard to the processing of personal data and on the free movement of such data, and repealing Directive 95/46/EC (General Data Protection Regulation), [2016] OJ, L119/1 [GDPR].

Regulations Specifying Publicly Available Information, SOR/2001-7.

Case Law

CCH Canadian Ltd. v. Law Society of Upper Canada, 2004 SCC 13, (2004) 1 SCR 339.

Century 21 Canada Ltd. Partnership v. Rogers Communications Inc., 2011 BCSC 1196, (2011) BCJ No 1679.

Craigslist Inc. v. 3Taps Inc., 942 F. Supp. 2d 962 (N.D. Cal. 2013).

Douez v. Facebook Inc., 2017 SCC 33, (2017) SCR 751.

Facebook v. Power Ventures, 91 U.S.P.Q. 2d 1430 (2009).

Feist Publications, Inc. v. Rural Telephone Service Co., 499 U.S. 340 (1991).

hiQ Labs Inc. v. LinkedIn Corp., No. 3:17-cv-03301 (N.D. Cal. 2017).

Hush-a-Phone Corporation v. U.S., 238 F2d 266 (D.C. Cir. 1956).
LinkedIn Corporation v. Does, Case No. 5:16-cv-4463 (N.D. Cal. 2016).
Nintendo America v. King, (2017) FCJ No 253, 2017 FC 246.
Trader Corporation v. CarGurus, Inc., 2017 ONSC 184.
Use of the Carterfone in Message Toll Serv., 13 FCC 2d 420 (1968).

About the Author

Haewon Chung is a computer scientist and a legal scholar. Her doctoral thesis at the University of Ottawa examined patentable knowledge management in the context of amateur-driven, open, and collaborative do-it-yourself biotechnology. She has written about decision-support systems in healthcare, open access to knowledge and science, software patents, and intellectual property law.

CHAPTER 4

Challenges to the Access of Government Open Data by Private Sector Companies

PETER A. JOHNSON AND CHRISTINE VARGA

Abstract

Many governments around the world are releasing open data, yet an understanding of how diverse stakeholders access this data is only just emerging. To understand how the private sector accesses and uses open data, interviews were conducted with Canadian information technology (IT) companies in the Kitchener-Waterloo to Toronto, Canada, high-tech corridor. Questions regarding how open data is accessed and used reveal what "access" to open data means for the private sector—seamless access across jurisdictions, access to a full catalogue of data, and access to accurate and current data. For governments that deliver open data, this nuanced reading of "access" can provide key feedback to improve current open data programs, and conceptualize the future of open data provision as an "ecosystem" of roles that governments could potentially fill, including as data creator, custodian, and provider.

Acknowledgements

We would like to thank the Geothink.ca partnership grant, led by Dr. Renee Sieber, for supporting this research. Funding for Geothink was provided by the Social Sciences and Humanities

Research Council of Canada (SSHRC). We would also like to thank Kevin Tuer, Communitech, and the Canadian Open Data Exchange (codx.ca) for facilitating connections with research participants.

Open data, though a relatively new concept, has rapidly become a dominant topic in the fields of IT, civic technology, and government information (Gurstein, 2011; Janssen et al., 2012; Sieber & Johnson, 2015). Typically provided by governments at all levels (municipal, provincial/state, federal), open data are made freely available through online portals, in machine-readable formats, and are shared under terms of a generous usage licence (Sieber & Johnson, 2015). Open data is considered to be one of the key ways in which governments can deliver on the transparency and collaboration principles of open government plans or strategies (Ruvalcaba-Gomez et al., 2018). As the provision of open data expands, questions about its value and use are posed, particularly concerning the value of open data to specific user communities (Janssen & Zuiderwijk, 2014; Johnson, 2016). The private sector—that is, profit-maximizing companies, that are either from sole proprietorships or to publicly traded entities—is frequently identified as one of the major user communities for government open data (Deloitte, 2012a; Bonina, 2013; Ruppert, 2015). Despite this, there is little direct research on how the private sector interacts with government open data, and what barriers may exist to access. As part of the rapidly developing open data "ecosystem" (Heimstädt et al., 2014; Sangiambut & Sieber, 2017), it is important to address the differential needs and preferences of diverse user communities. This research aims to fill this gap, using interviews with key stakeholders at a variety of private-sector companies in the Waterloo–Toronto, Canada, IT corridor to better understand how open data, typically provided by municipal governments, are accessed and used, identifying key challenges that restrict this use. We use these empirical findings to frame a discussion of strategies that government open data providers can employ to develop an open data ecosystem that is more responsive to the needs of the private sector. In this instance, the future of open data is one where data-producing governments can better connect their data with the specific needs of an identified non-government user base. The simple provision of open data was an early challenge, and moving forward, the future of open data should begin to tackle the challenge of facilitating use.

We conclude with a discussion of the roles that governments can play within this open data ecosystem, including as data creator, data custodian, and data provider, and the potential opening up of these roles to non-government actors.

1. Measuring the Use and Value of Open Data

It has traditionally been challenging to track how users access and work with open data. The very nature of open data as free from access restrictions can make it difficult for open data provisioning governments to gather metrics of use (Johnson, 2016; Johnson & Greene, 2017). When considering quantitative approaches to measuring the value of open data for private sector use, studies note that value cannot be determined through correlations with factors regarding the provision of, or access to, the data. Fumega (2014, p. 29) refers to attempts to count the number of website visits, published datasets, or downloads as "flimsy metrics," and notes that conclusions based on these measures are unlikely to be robust. Harrison, Pardo, Cresswell, & Cook et al. (2011) explain that metrics which attempt to quantify the number of datasets or the opportunities for participation and collaboration do not always indicate value. Similarly, Deloitte (2012a) notes that the number of downloads, or "clicks," on a dataset cannot be directly equated to economic benefit. They explain that when using the number of downloads as a proxy for demand, "detailed quantitative estimates of economic impact can then only be established if such demand can be positively correlated and causally linked to conventional measures of economic output per sector" (Deloitte, 2012a, p. 8). These estimates cannot always be established, however, due to the challenges of tracing use of open data once they are downloaded from a government open data portal. Simply put, there are few tools that governments have at their disposal to trace the use and impact of open data by a broad range of end users (Johnson, 2017).

Existing studies have highlighted a variety of challenges to the use of open data by the private sector. For example, in a study by the Open Data 500, an international network of organizations that studies the use and impact of open data, the most significant challenges found for users of open data were access, accuracy, and level of detail (Australian Government, 2015). In Fumega's (2014) case studies, common obstacles for open data users included overemphasis on technical aspects and lack of usability for non-technical users. Other issues found with the data include lack of standardization, information that is not up to date, and too much "noise" in the data (Latif et al., 2009; Manyika et al., 2013). Zuiderwijk, Janssen, Choenni, Meijer, and Alibaks et al. (2012) take analysis of these and other issues further, by identifying 118 impediments to open data use. Their findings are divided into 10 impediment categories: availability and access, findability, usability, understandability, quality, linking and combining data, comparability and compatibility, metadata, interaction with the data provider, and opening and uploading. Not only are there many possible issues with the data, but these issues are proven to be present in many cases. In the study by Sayogo et al. (2014), it was found that only 66% of the existing open data portals provide the ability to manipulate the data, and that only 49% of the existing data portals provide data in formats that support linked data. These statistics, as well as the long list of potential obstacles to reuse of the data, demonstrate major areas for improvement in easily accessing the data and using it to capture value.

Davies et al. (2013) see two possible future paths for open data impact research. The first is analysis at the macro-level, observing statistical correlations between open data implementation efforts and outcomes that imply some expected impacts of open data. They give the relationship between economic growth and levels of open data publication as an example, with governments that publish large open data catalogues spurring economic growth and innovation, typically in the IT sector. Jetzek, Avital, and Bjørn-Andersen et al. (2013), have conducted this type of macro-level analysis, searching for correlations between four enabling factors (exogenous variables) and four value-generation mechanisms (endogenous variables). The exogenous variables are openness, data governance, capabilities, and technical connectivity, while the endogenous variables are efficiency, innovation, participation, and transparency. As a result of the analysis, all relationships between exogenous and endogenous variables were supported except for the openness-to-transparency relationship, for which a slight negative correlation was found. Jetzek et al. (2013) find results that provide some merit for their efforts, yet it should be noted that these correlations encompass a broad definition of value that is not limited to the private sector.

A common quantitative approach to measuring the value of open data is the attempt to estimate value in terms of currency (Carrara et al., 2015; Gruen et al., 2014). Two of the most extensive and most commonly cited efforts to estimate the economic impact of open data are a 2011 report from the European Commission, and a 2013 report by McKinsey & Company (Manyika et al. 2013). These and similar studies and other similar efforts review previous work on estimating open data's value, or explore research from multiple sectors and attempt to aggregate the findings. The European Commission's paper report (see Vickery, 2011) concludes that if current public sector information was available for free or at marginal cost, data-use activities could increase by up to €40 billion each year, as compared to the case where the data is not open (Vickery, 2011). McKinsey & Company find $3 trillion in annual economic potential globally through the release of open data. This value is not the result of an extensive study of all sectors (Manyika et al., 2013). Similar to efforts to determine value through correlations, these estimates of value are not limited to the private sector. Despite these findings produced by this quantitative approach to measuring the impact of open data, there is a level of nuance missing. Rather than an instrumentalist focus on connecting data provision to outcome via quantitative measures, we propose to build on Johnson and Greene's (2017) work that conducted qualitative interviews with public sector open data providers to better understand their process of data provision and use tracking. This qualitative approach matches with the second path proposed by Davies et al. (2013) for open data impact research, a micro-level analysis of the processes through which open data is used. This research places a focus on understanding how private sector start-up IT companies access and use open data, and the challenges to their access and use.

2. Interviews with Private Sector Open Data Users in the Kitchener/Waterloo–Toronto Corridor

To refine our understanding of how private sector companies access open data, individuals from 11 Ontario-based companies were interviewed, representing finance, logistics, mobile-app development, data provision, and IT consulting. These companies are based in the Kitchener-Waterloo to Toronto corridor, Canada's most significant cluster of IT companies. Interviewees were from a combination of start-ups and established companies, with study respondents recruited through connections with the Canadian Open Data Exchange (www.codx.ca), a public–private partnership agency founded to support the use of open data in private sector companies. The interviews took approximately 30 minutes, and were conducted either in person or by telephone. Interviews were audio-recorded, transcribed, and coded for main themes, including benefits of open data and challenges faced in accessing and using open data. The results of these interviews are presented in two sections. The first is a descriptive section that details the classification of users, sources of open data accessed, and description of the benefits of using open data. The second section presents responses from the respondents, including on the challenges to using open data, including access to data across jurisdictions, access to the full data catalogue, and data accuracy and currency.

2.1 Classification of Users

Using the open data user classification developed by Deloitte (2012b), which divides private sector open data users into five categories, we found that respondents included three categories of users who employ open data to support their operations: aggregators, developers, and enrichers. Of the companies surveyed, six are providers of new products or applications built using open data. One company acts as an aggregator, providing processed open data to clients, while the other five companies are considered developers of new applications based on open data. There is overlap between these latter two categories of user, with some respondents displaying characteristics that point to both the aggregator and developer user definitions, given their diverse product lines. Unlike these new product and service providers, five individuals identified their organizations as enrichers, because of their use of open data as an input into existing products and services. As one respondent said, "the product is what people are interested in, not the fact that it's just a bit of open data." All three user types noted the need to generate a value-added component to their product, compared to simply replicating the raw data available directly from the government open data catalogue. In this way, the respondent pool was largely working with open data as a base material that would be used to create or combine with other data and services to form a saleable product.

2.2 Sources and Types of Open Data Accessed

Private sector open data users that were interviewed accessed open data from a wide variety of sources from Canada, the US, and around the world. The specific sources of open data accessed were closely related to a particular project or client of the company. One respondent noted, "our big focus is in Canada and the US, primarily because that's where we are and that's where the market is ripest and richest." Open data sources varied based on the application area. Examples of open data sources given included government-owned or affiliated sources like Statistics Canada (www.statcan.gc.ca), openNASA (open.nasa.gov), World Bank (www.worldbank.org), Land Information Ontario (www.ontario.ca/page/land-information-ontario), Environment Canada (weather.gc.ca), and various provincial ministries or local municipalities, and other non-government associated open data sources like OpenStreetMap (www.openstreetmap.org). Some of the specific datasets being accessed by these companies include geospatial data, like flood data, terrain, aerial photography, land use, building footprint, building heights, zoning, surficial geology, groundwater data, forest cover, woodlots, and weather data. This is consistent with findings from other studies that note geographic or geospatial data to be the most heavily used open data in the private sector (Australian Government, 2015; Greene & Rinner, 2021 this volume). Other examples given include demographic sources like poverty indexes, macroeconomic indexes, population and housing projections, or financial data, business registry data, licence data, and government procurement information. These examples are consistent with findings from previous studies. At the local level, sources being assessed included transit data, traffic collision data, local points of interest, event information, and polling data. Given the wide range of open data topics available across many different levels of government, the respondent pool indicated that data sources and topics were selected on a case-by-case basis, dependent on the needs of a particular client or project.

2.3 The Benefits of Using Open Data

Past literature identifies methods of generating value through private-sector open data use, including combining open and proprietary data, integrating open data into a particular analysis, and the development of novel applications (Johnson, 2016; Australian Government, 2015; Granickas, 2013; Kassen, 2013; Manyika et al., 2013). By interviewing private-sector users of open data, we aimed to determine the benefits, challenges, and constraints to the use of open data. When asked about the benefits of open data use for private sector companies, financial benefit was often mentioned first by respondents. Respondents also noted that the ability to charge for their products and services is based on the value-added customization provided in addition to, or "over top" of government open data. One company indicated that being able to access open data from various jurisdictions allows them to vend a similar product to many clients, explaining that "the idea would be, we can provide the application, scale it to as many clients as we would want and [our customers] would have a more straightforward means of populating our application with their data sources." In this sense, as open data becomes easier to access and use, the company will be able to support more clients in using open data within their analysis ecosystem.

For companies who identify as enrichers, open data was seen to add value to existing analytical products at minimal cost, allowing the company to receive some of the same data for free that it would otherwise typically need to purchase. The use of free open data effectively reduced costs to the company, and allowed for a more cost-competitive product to be offered to the end consumer. This also allowed companies to create prototype or "test" models and products more quickly, adding a free or low-cost tier to their product offerings allowing companies to test out a number of different strategies without needing to commit to expensive proprietary data sources. As one respondent noted, "it's a great way to start a business where your supply chain is a free product." In some cases, data these companies rely on are only provided by governments, thus the provision of these data as "free" is a significant way in which government and taxpayer funds were seen to support the expansion and profitability of the private sector.

Specific types of open datasets were seen as more valuable than others. Given the range of open data provided by many governments, that there are certain "key" datasets of interest to private companies is not surprising. As is consistent with the past literature, respondents noted that market-related data were most valuable (Granickas, 2013). As one respondent pointed out, "you can just imagine what it would do for the real-estate market to have access to business directories, locations of parks, things like that." Demographic data were also of interest, with one respondent noting, "governments tend to have the best demographic data. The only companies that can really compete with that are some of the very large retailers like Walmart and Google." Data from these companies are expensive to acquire, so open data accessed at no cost to the users is often a better investment, despite its potential limitations.

Another benefit of open data identified by private sector open data users is the combination of multiple datasets, especially the aggregation of government data and other types of non-governmental data. This aggregation across scales of government and geography is widely identified as one of the potential benefits of a broad ecosystem of government open data (Janssen et al., 2012). One research respondent explained how this aggregation of data could be valuable to their organization, particularly when compared to proprietary data sources: "We have to have hundreds of sources merged together in order to have a compelling counter argument to the closed data that people are used to because it's comfortable." Many respondents noted that they always use more than one data source, and in some cases used up to 25 unique data sources for certain projects. Most respondents also noted that they engaged in some aggregation of public sector open data with private sector data from other sources. These sources could include data from marketing companies, data provided by clients, or data found by scraping other websites. One respondent also noted that they were seeing companies aggregate open data with data generated internally by the company itself, a process of "accenting big data with open data." Some companies are also engaged in the process of combining multiple open data sources across jurisdictions to derive insights that cross geographic areas. Across the private sector respondents interviewed, the value of this aggregation of open data and its combination with proprietary sources was seen as a key benefit of the provision of open data.

3. The Challenges of Using Open Data

Despite several benefits identified by respondents about the use of open data to support their business, there was significant commentary on the challenges of accessing and using open data, including data format, standards, quality, and technical constraints. Many of the respondents were also concerned with the relative lack of strategies to overcome these open data access and use challenges. This lack of existing knowledge on overcoming challenges is likely due to the emerging state of open data use by the private sector, as well as the lack of data provision standards between data-delivering governments. This section of results presents three key dimensions of "access" identified by research respondents as challenging: access across jurisdictions, access to the full catalogue, and access to accurate and current data.

3.1 Access across Jurisdictions

Respondents frequently mentioned issues with access and availability of data across jurisdictions. For example, a significant issue was found with respondents needing to access many different government open data catalogues to piece together sufficient data to meet client or project requirements. This need to access data that crosses jurisdictions was further aggravated by the different approaches used by each government to collect and deliver similar data types. One respondent explained: "Federal information is not often comparable to provincial information . . . I'm stuck working at cross-purposes, where I'm kind of extracting bits and pieces of various datasets at the federal level and various datasets at the provincial level to get comparable data, and it gets even worse when I start looking country to country." Respondents noted that it is difficult to go to many different government catalogues to get all the data they need. This time-consuming searching for data was augmented by additional post-processing and data formatting required to create a blended dataset. Overall, the lack of seamless access across varying levels of government and jurisdictions led to fragmentation of projects and difficulty in developing business models at the required scale to be profitable.

3.2 Access to the Full Catalogue

Respondents often noted that not all data that businesses would like to access are actually available through an open data catalogue. One respondent explains, "I know there are datasets that I would like to be able to access, but there hasn't been a consistent and coordinated effort on the part of the government agencies to provide it." Another respondent echoed this, stating, "I'm not sure governments are completely open to releasing all the data that they should be releasing." Given the significant repositories of data collected by governments (particularly provincial or federal), making or prioritizing specific data releases can be challenging. Recent efforts on the part of governments to publish comprehensive lists or inventories of all data that could possibly be made open are a significant step towards improving on this issue of access, facilitating more targeted data requests by end users. Similarly, government-open-by-default policies, where data produced are considered open when created, and only protected by specific request or through a privacy assessment, will also serve to reduce gaps in open data catalogues that can impede open data access.

3.3 Access to Accurate and Current Data

The accuracy of data obtained through open data portals was an issue impeding use by the private sector. Most respondents had noted some issues with datasets that may not be "ground truthed" or verified with actual locations or features. This issue stems from the high cost of checking datasets for quality before they are used in a paid product. One respondent explained that they would need to retreat to using paid data to be confident enough to use the data as part of a paid commercial product. Another respondent commented that since their company would need to take responsibility for inaccuracies, "a lack of data, in my opinion, is better and something I'll accept over wrong data." An opinion expressed by one respondent was that private sector companies need to demonstrate the value of the data to governments before they will commit to improving quality. They explained: "The city could go through the trouble of creating an open dataset, adhering to the standard and checking that set for completeness because they anticipate that it's going to be used in something, or they know it's being used in something that's returning value to them in some way, shape or form, then they are incented to make sure at least it's good." Some respondents gave an alternate opinion, claiming that governments must ensure data are accurate before they are published, and that this series of checks creates unnecessary delays in data release: "I think governments are good at making sure the numbers are correct, which is a really good thing that they are doing. The problem is I think that's actually slowing down update frequency, so there needs to be a better balance between the two." This lack of timeliness in publishing updates was a major issue noted by nearly all respondents.

Timeliness, or data currency, was mentioned as an issue by several respondents. In regard to demographic data, such as a census, a respondent explained: "Many countries do it once every five years. That is not sufficient for our clients. We still have to add commercial data to it, to make sure that it is updated every year." Nevertheless, most respondents agreed that improvements to future publishing timelines would be a positive development. A respondent explained, "in a perfect world, you would have real-time data of everything, allowing an infinite number of use cases. Whatever your imagination is in terms of a way to extract value from that data, you're not limited because it is data that can be called through an API [application programming interface] and it is relatively real-time streaming of that data, so that you can do everything." Overall, given access to more current and accurate data, respondents felt that open data could be reliable as an integral component of new commercial applications.

4. Discussion: Improved Linking and Standardization of Datasets to Support Private Sector Use

The findings from this research indicate that there are select openings for governments to support the use of open data by the private sector. When considering the future of open data provision by governments, there is a strong case to be made in improving data access as a way to increase usage. Specifically, we aim to answer the question of how a government that provides open data can also support the access and use of these data with private sector users in mind. Moving forward with the maturation of government open data, there are key actions that can support more than the simple provision of open data (the "data over the wall" approach, according to Sieber & Johnson, 2015), creating an open data ecosystem (Heimstädt et al., 2014). This more fully developed open data ecosystem brings together data providers and end users to consider how to best deliver open data to satisfy the various needs of constituent end user communities. Through the results of our research with private sector open data users, we propose two core actions that governments can take in the near future to support the development of an open data ecosystem. These are: (1) development and support for linked open data, and (2) improved adoption of common open data standards whenever possible.

4.1 Linked Open Data

A first notable opportunity for improving open data published by the government is the development of linked open data. Linked open data are both human and machine readable, and adhere to uniform conventions of naming and linking, allowing data to be easily connected, queried, and even integrated. For example, by offering linked open data, governments may be able to partially solve the jurisdictional variation issues, creating a link in metadata that allows similar datasets to be connected across jurisdictions. While a recent study finds that only four European countries officially support linked data (Carrara et al., 2015), it is also clear that linked data are an important element of data provision and functions to make data more accessible and usable. In discussing what he calls the "linked value chain," Granickas (2013) sees linked data as a cost saver, as information can be easily found, and connected, moving from data simply provided, to data embedded in a linked network of data sources, much like the Internet exists as a collection of connected documents. Ubaldi (2013) also notes that linked data are required for more sophisticated queries, particularly those that cross geographic scales, or connected themes.

Current work on developing linked open data builds on early development of the "semantic" (or machine-readable) web (Berners-Lee, 2009). Currently, the World Wide Web Consortium (W3C) Linked Open Data community project aims to develop a global data commons of open datasets linked through the use of resource description framework (RDF) links that make machine-readable connections between data. From a government perspective, as a data creator, custodian, and publisher, adding RDF metadata to a given dataset would enable these types of connections based on geography, topic, content, and other data characteristics (Ruback et al., 2016). Taking existing government data and creating linked open data is not necessarily a trivial step, necessitating changes in the way that data are created and shared. Additional resources, including staff time and an advanced knowledge base, are required for municipal staff to not only provide data, but to link them and maintain those links. The adoption of linked open data from a data provider perspective hinges on continued support of and investment in the broader role of government as a key open data provider. This future, though optimistic, is not a given, as governments continually must respond to varying levels of political will to invest in open government and transparency initiatives, as well as the often slow pace of government IT projects. Though potentially valuable as a contributor to private-sector use of open data, the broad adoption of linked open data is still ongoing, presenting a notable area of future attention for data-providing governments.

4.2 Greater Standardization of Datasets

Implementing and following data standards is a significant way that governments can support improvements to the open data provision ecosystem, particularly private sector users of open data. According to Davies et al. (2013), the development and enforcement of standards between different open datasets can simplify data sharing and use. Ensuring that data are produced and structured according to commonly held standards improves data coverage over many jurisdictions, and also allows for common analysis and development tools to be used. As revealed by the respondents, and mirrored in open data literature, from a private sector user perspective, a lack of data standardization leads to greater challenges in bringing together datasets from different jurisdictions, or replicating tools and analyses from one area in another area (Janssen et al., 2012). A lack of use of data standards can create a situation where data from one jurisdiction are not structured in the same way as data from another jurisdiction, necessitating multiple pre-processing steps to create a common frame for analysis and development. From a private sector perspective, this lack of standards between different datasets can prevent the generation of economies of scale that would be required to create profitable services (Zuiderwijk et al., 2012).

The implementation of data standards is a challenging process, requiring time, effort, resources, and coordination between different data producers and standard developers or proponents (Plu & Scharffe, 2012; Zuiderwijk et al., 2012). A handful of open data standards have been successfully adopted, most notably the General Transit Feed Specification (GTFS), which sets standards for how real-time transit data are stored and shared (McHugh, 2013). Given the additional value to be derived from increased standardization, not only for private sector users but for all open data users, the continued development, promotion, and adoption of standards are critical areas of ongoing work. Current work on developing an open data standards directory (see http://datastandards.directory) is an important step towards sharing information about available standards, a key precursor to enabling standard adoption. As referenced by our respondents, to truly support an innovation ecosystem and provide service to private sector users, government, in its role as data creator, custodian, and provider, should increasingly look to adopt existing open data standards, and work across government jurisdictions and with the data user community to increase the use of standards in open data provision.

5. Conclusions

When considering the future of private sector use of open data, it is important to note the critical role that governments play as data creator, custodian, and provider. Governments may play all three of these roles or potentially only one or two, offloading specific roles to the private sector or other entities. How each of these roles that governments play can be managed, affects private sector use of open data, and the ability for open data to fulfill even partially the much-hyped "innovation" agenda that often drives data release (Bates, 2014; Zuiderwijk et al., 2014). For example, data creation roles involve adherence or non-adherence to standards (where they exist), data-custodian roles can restrict certain aspects of a dataset or entire datasets, depending on privacy and data quality concerns, and the data provider role can serve data to end users in a variety of formats and frequencies, which may or may not fill the needs and preferences of varied end user communities. When governments look to provide data through an open data platform, many factors come into play, including ease of publishing, perceived demand for a specific dataset, overall value of data, as well as other dataset-specific issues, such as quality and completeness. The results of this research support existing literature that shows the challenges of open data provision (Janssen et al., 2012; Sieber & Johnson, 2015; Johnson et al., 2017), but frames these challenges from a private sector use perspective, informing the current state of knowledge with their unique needs as an important user community. From the perspective of our respondents, there is a notable lack of consistency between government open data providers in what a data user could expect to find in an open data catalogue, both in terms of dataset availability and in the relative quality of any given dataset. These factors serve as a damper on the possible use of government open data in a private sector context, restricting the generation of value from the provision of government data. Additionally, there is risk that governments be removed or replaced as a provider of certain types of specialty data, as private sector organizations seek to overcome access challenges implemented by laggard governments (Johnson, 2019).

To rectify these shortcomings, our sample suggested several possible strategies. Of these, there are straightforward suggestions, such as ensuring that data released are of the highest quality and completeness possible, and are released in a timely manner. Pushing governments, particularly at the municipal level, towards releasing a common suite of datasets that represent those most common or critical datasets, would help to provide better coverage across areas. This research supports existing work on understanding and promoting the concept of "linked open data" (Ubaldi, 2013), as a way to improve access to open data, creating a valuable part of an open data ecosystem. Linked open data are structured so that metadata provide links with other related datasets. From a private sector perspective, a linked dataset eases discoverability of other related datasets, saving time and money (Granickas, 2013; Janssen et al., 2017). Lastly, open data standards also have a strong role to play in supporting access to open data and enabling reuse, allowing users to scale up projects more quickly and seamlessly transfer work from one jurisdiction to another. Many of the respondents noted that they want governments to work towards these initiatives, including developing an open data ecosystem that crosses jurisdictions, linking open data, and increasing the standardization of datasets. Despite this interest from the private sector in having governments lead these challenges, it remains to be seen who may be driving these types of initiatives. An example would be the development of a third-party open data catalogue that crosses many jurisdictions, or federates a number of municipal catalogues into a higher-order regional or provincial data catalogue (Johnson, 2019; Wang & Shepherd, 2020). Similarly, there is potential for private business to assume the role of data enricher and re-seller, taking government data and repackaging them for other audiences. Given this encroachment on government open data provision, future work in this area needs to address not only the constraints to data access that may challenge a particular user community, but also the potentially changing role of government to that of the data custodian, abdicating the role of data provider to the private sector.

Despite the existing opportunities for governments to better meet the needs of private sector open data users, there remains a potential risk that in shifting from the simple provision of open data towards tailoring to the needs of one specific user community, governments may create areas of disadvantage for other user groups (Yang & Wu, 2021). For example, government data-provision resources may become exhausted through meeting the technical requests from private sector or large-scale users, reducing government capacity to invest in the provision of other, less commercially relevant datasets (Johnson et al., 2017). Additionally, this shifting focus towards the private sector can also create an open data ecosystem where all users, including from civil society, or the public sector, would need to make a business case or demonstrate economic value for data to be opened or provisioned in a specific way. Though data-providing governments can better meet the needs of specific user groups, this should not come at the expense of service to other user groups, or the development of unequal or selective pathways for data access.

Given the potential for government priorities to change, particularly when it comes to open government policies and open data programs, there remains the possibility that data will cease to be open, disrupting private sector use of open data (Johnson et al., 2017). Though there is a tendency to view open data as a permanent resource that will continue to be provided by governments, there is a possibility for the existence of open data to contract rather than expand. Advocates of open data need to demonstrate returns in order to secure more support and financing. This "impermanence" of open data could be driven by government reaction to any number of local or global trends, as well as a further retrenchment of government as a direct service provider to citizens and the development of a consultative layer (Brabham & Guth, 2017) that enters to mediate connections between government and data end user. Government policies and actions change over time, and if open data is not deemed beneficial, it may cease to exist. This permanence, or "online stickiness," of data is a key foundation in governing open data (Sunlight Foundation, 2010). Absent the expectation that data are consistently available, use from all sectors, whether private, public, or not-for-profit, will be restricted. As such, open data becomes less "open" and less valuable if they are not permanent.

References

Australian Government. (2015). *Private sector use of open government data: Results from the Open Data 500 Australia.* https://www.communications.gov.au/publications/open-data-500-report

Bates, J. (2014). The strategic importance of information policy for the contemporary neoliberal state: The case of open government data in the United Kingdom. *Government Information Quarterly, 31*(3), 388–395.

Berners-Lee, T. (2009). *Linked data*. https://www.w3.org/DesignIssues/LinkedData.html

Bonina, C. M. (2013). *New business models and the value of open data: Definitions, challenges and opportunities.* Department of Management, London School of Economics and Political Science. http://www.nemode.ac.uk/wp-content/uploads/2013/11/Bonina-Opendata-Report-FINAL.pdf

Brabham, D. C., & Guth, K. L. (2017). The deliberative politics of the consultative layer: Participation hopes and communication as design values of civic tech founders. *Journal of Communication, 67*(4), 445–475.

Carrara, W., Fischer, S., & van Steenbergen, E. (2015). *Open data maturity in Europe 2015: Insights into the European state of play.* Capgemini Consulting. https://www.capgemini-consulting.com/open-data-maturity

Davies, T., & Fernando, P., & Alonso, J. M. (2013). *Researching the emerging impacts of open data: ODDC conceptual framework.* World Wide Web Foundation. http://www.opendataresearch.org/sites/default/files/posts/Researching%20the%20emerging%20impacts%20of%20open%20data.pdf

Deloitte. (2012a). *Open data: Driving growth, ingenuity and innovation.* https://www2.deloitte.com/content/dam/Deloitte/uk/Documents/deloitte-analytics/open-data-driving-growth-ingenuity-and-innovation.pdf

Deloitte. (2012b). *Open growth stimulating demand for open data in the UK: A briefing note from Deloitte Analytics.* http://www2.deloitte.com/content/dam/Deloitte/uk/Documents/deloitte-analytics/open-growth.pdf

Fumega, S. (2014). *Opening cities: Open data in Buenos Aires, Montevideo and Sao Paulo: A report for the City of Buenos Aires Open Government Data Initiative.* World Wide Web Foundation. http://opendataresearch.org/sites/default/files/publications/Final-Opening%20Cities%20-%20Buenos%20Aires%20final%20report.pdf

Granickas, K. (2013). *Understanding the impact of releasing and re-using open government data.* European Public Sector Information Platform. http://www.epsi-platform.eu/sites/default/files/2013-08-Open_Data_Impact.pdf

Gruen, N., Houghton, J., & Tooth, R. (2014). *Open for business: How open data can help achieve the G20 growth target.* https://www.omidyar.com/sites/default/files/file_archive/insights/ON%20Report_061114_FNL.pdf

Gurstein, M. B. (2011). Open data: Empowering the empowered or effective data use for everyone? *First Monday, 16*(2).

Harrison, T., Pardo, T., Cresswell, A., & Cook, M. (2011). *Delivering public value through open government.* The Research Foundation of State University of New York. http://www.ctg.albany.edu/publications/issuebriefs/opengov_pubvalue.pdf

Heimstädt, M., Saunderson, F., Heath, T. (2014). From toddler to teen: growth of an open data ecosystem. *JeDEM-eJournal of eDemocracy and Open Government, 6*(2), 123–135.

Janssen, M., Charalabidis, Y., & Zuiderwijk, A. (2012). Benefits, adoption barriers and myths of open data and open government. *Information Systems Management, 29*(4), 258–268.

Janssen, M., & Zuiderwijk, A. (2014). Infomediary business models for connecting open data providers and users. *Social Science Computer Review, 32*(5), 694–711.

Janssen, M., Konopnicki, D., Snowdon, J. L., & Ojo, A. (2017). Driving public sector innovation using big and open linked data (BOLD). *Information Systems Frontiers, 19*(2), 189–195.

Jetzek, T., Avital, M., & Bjørn-Andersen, N. (2013). Generating value from open government data. *Proceedings of the 34th International Conference on Information Systems (ICIS).* https://aisel.aisnet.org/icis2013/proceedings/GeneralISTopics/5/

Johnson, P. A., & Greene, S. (2017). Who are government Open Data infomediaries? A preliminary scan and classification of open data users and products. *Journal of the Urban & Regional Information Systems Association, 28*(1), 9–18.

Johnson, P. A., Sieber, R., Scassa, T., Stephens, M., & Robinson, P. (2017). The cost(s) of geospatial open data. *Transactions in GIS, 21*(3), 434–445.

Johnson, P. A. (2016). Reflecting on the success of open data: How municipal government evaluates their open data programs. *International Journal of E-Planning Research, 5*(3), 1–13.

Johnson, P. A., (2017). Models of direct editing of government spatial data: Challenges and constraints to the acceptance of contributed data. *Cartography and Geographic Information Science, 44*(2), 128–38.

Johnson, P. A. (2019). Disintermediating government: The role of open data and smart infrastructure. *Proceedings of the 52nd Hawaii International Conference on System Sciences.* https://doi.org/10.24251/HICSS.2019.346

Kassen, M. (2013). A promising phenomenon of open data: A case study of the Chicago open data project. *Government Information Quarterly, 30*(4), 508–513. http://www.sciencedirect.com/science/article/pii/S0740624X13000683

Latif, A., Saeed, A. U., Hoefler, P., Stocker, A., & Wagner, C. (2009). *The linked data value chain: A lightweight model for business engineers.* http://citeseerx.ist.psu.edu/viewdoc/download?doi=10.1.1.181.950&rep=rep1&type=pdf

Manyika, J., Chui, M., Groves, P., Farrell, D., Van Kuiken, S., & Doshi, E.A. (2013). *Open data: Unlocking innovation and performance with liquid information.* McKinsey & Company. http://www.mckinsey.com/insights/business_technology/open_data_unlocking_innovation_and_performance_with_liquid_information

McHugh, B. (2013). Pioneering open data standards: The GTFS story. In B. Goldstein & L. Dyson (Eds.), *Beyond transparency: Open data and the future of civic innovation,* (pp. 125–135). Code for America Press.

Plu, J., & Scharffe, F. (2012). Publishing and linking transport data on the web: Extended version. *Proceedings of the First International Workshop on Open Data*, (pp. 62–69). ACM Press.

Ruback, L., Casanova, M. A., Raffaetà, A., Renso, C., & Vidal, V. (2016). Enriching mobility data with linked open data. *Proceedings of the 20th International Database Engineering & Applications Symposium*, (pp. 173–182). ACM Press.

Ruppert, E. (2015). Doing the transparent state: Open government data as performance indicators. In R. Rottenburg, S. E. Merry, S.-J. Park, & J. Mugler (Eds.), *The World of Indicators* (pp. 127–150). Cambridge University Press.

Ruvalcaba-Gomez, E. A., Criado, J. I., & Gil-Garcia, J. R. (2018). Discussing open government as a concept: A comparison between the perceptions of public managers and current academic debate. ACM Press.

Sangiambut, S., & Sieber, R. (2017). The civic open data and crowdsourcing app ecosystem: Actors, materials, and interventions. *Journal of the Urban & Regional Information Systems Association, 28*(1).

Sayogo, D. S., Pardo, T. A., & Cook, M. (2014). A framework for benchmarking open government data efforts. *47th Hawaii International Conference on System Science.* http://ieeexplore.ieee.org/stamp/stamp.jsp?arnumber=6758838

Sieber, R. E., & Johnson, P. A. (2015). Civic open data at a crossroads: Dominant models and current challenges. *Government Information Quarterly, 32*(3), 308–315.

Sunlight Foundation. (2010). *Ten principles for opening up government information.* http://sunlightfoundation.com/policy/documents/ten-open-data-principles/

Ubaldi, B. (2013). Open government data: Towards empirical analysis of open government data initiatives. *OECD Working Papers on Public Governance, 22*, 1–61. http://dx.doi.org/10.1787/5k46bj4f03s7-en

Vickery, G. (2011). *Review of recent studies on PSI reuse and related market developments.* European Commission. http://ec.europa.eu/newsroom/document.cfm?doc_id=1093

Wang, V., & Shepherd, D. (2020). Exploring the extent of openness of open government data–A critique of open government datasets in the UK. *Government Information Quarterly, 37*(1), 101405.

Yang, T. M., & Wu, Y. J. (2021). Looking for datasets to open: An exploration of government officials' information behaviors in open data policy implementation. *Government Information Quarterly, 38*(2), 101574.

Zuiderwijk, A., Janssen, M., Choenni, S., Meijer, R., & Alibaks, R. S. (2012). Socio-technical impediments of open data. *Electronic Journal of e-Government, 10*(2), 156–172.

Zuiderwijk, A., Helbig, N., Gil-García, J. R., & Janssen, M. (2014). Special issue on innovation through open data: Guest editors' introduction. *Journal of Theoretical and Applied Electronic Commerce Research*, 9(2), 1–13.

About the Authors

Peter A. Johnson is Associate Professor in the Department of Geography and Environmental Management at the University of Waterloo. His research expertise is in the application and evaluation of geospatial technologies within government, including open data, the geospatial web, mobile devices, crowdsourcing, participatory geomatics, and volunteered geographic information.

Christine Varga is a recent graduate from the Economics program at the University of Waterloo. This work presents the findings of her co-operative work term with the Canadian Open Data Exchange (www.codx.ca).

CHAPTER 5

Open Data and Government Liability

ELIZABETH F. JUDGE AND TENILLE E. BROWN

Abstract

This chapter introduces different aspects of liability laws as they relate to government policies on releasing open data through open data portals. The chapter reviews potential liability that the government could incur from open data actions and omissions. We consider liability issues from a range of perspectives: governments that want to reduce their liability risks with respect to open data, open data advocates who are looking for strategies to spur open data release, and the general public who would like more useful open data and open data that do not infringe individual rights such as privacy. A better appreciation of how liability law intersects with open data will strengthen frameworks for the management of open data, as it will provide clarity in rights and obligations for users of open data, creators of open datasets, managers of open data portals, and advocates of open data. We explain how negligence liability will apply to government actions and omissions arising from open data. We then argue that, rather than the incremental development of common law negligence to set open data principles, the enactment of a specific statutory framework for open data would address government concerns over liability and would be in the public interest. We conclude by recommending that open data statutes be enacted for each level of government, with clear open data duties by the government, clear scope for liability, and clear rights of action for individuals to litigate when governments fail to comply with these duties.

Acknowledgements

The authors thank the Social Sciences and Humanities Research Council of Canada for research support through the Geothink partnership grant, and principal investigator Renee Sieber. We are grateful for insights from the editors and reviewers of this volume and from panelists and audience members at the open data panels at the Boston (2017), Chicago (2015), and Tampa (2014) meetings of the American Association of Geographers conference, where early versions of this research were presented.

In the current environment of data-driven government, and in citizen and industry activities alike, the importance of "open" data as a public good has grown. The role of datasets as they are held and generated by government, and in turn released to citizens through open data portals, reflect principles of good governance and capture added value for the public. Open data, which are generated by government processes, facilitates transparency and accountability, and encourage citizen-government interaction (Johnson & Sieber, 2012). Open data also promises economic and social benefits, as open data represents existing publicly funded value that can fuel innovation and new markets.

Although interest in open data has grown, there is also a growing critique of the utility of the open data that have been made available and the slow speed with which open data initiatives have been implemented. Government collects data across a wide variety of sectors. However, the type and number of datasets made available so far have been disappointing. Few open datasets have been made available relative to the volume of public-sector data held by the government, and those that have often concern subjects that garner little public interest. The release of a given dataset or type of data is not guaranteed. Further, once a dataset is released, the completeness, accuracy, and continuing availability of a given dataset in an open data portal are not certain. Open data advocates have called for the release of open datasets that are of wider interest and more comprehensive. From the perspective of civil society, there are valuable datasets that could be used to improve citizen-centric government processes or to support advocacy efforts that are not currently released through open data portals.

The democratic principles at the heart of the open data movement are important, and to succeed they require a clearer allocation of rights and responsibilities to ensure the release of meaningful data. To implement a detailed public-interest strategy in the management of open data, liability issues should be considered as a central part of open data planning. Perhaps counterintuitively, a better appreciation of how liability law intersects with open data will strengthen frameworks for the management of open data, as it will provide clarity in rights and obligations for users of open data, creators of open datasets, managers of open data portals, and civil-society advocates for open data. In order to fully and correctly consider rights and responsibilities in the use of open data, we recommend that each level of government enact a statute in order to provide clarity and predictability on liability and to provide incentives for open data release. An open data statute should detail clear open data duties by the government, the scope for liability, and clear rights of action for individuals to litigate when governments fail to comply with these duties. Our recommendation of a specific open data statute, as opposed to waiting for the incremental development of negligence principles to be applied to open data, addresses both ongoing liability uncertainty and imposes a positive obligation to release open data so that open data avoidance as a risk-mitigation strategy is no longer a rational response. The enactment of an open data statute would provide better clarity and predictability to government on liability for both acts and omissions related to open data. An open data statute would also set out administrative oversight, judicial enforcement, and remedies for the public. Accordingly, such a statute would provide incentives for governments to proactively release open data in the public interest.

In Section 1, we describe the public demand for open data and governmental support for open data policies. Section 2 examines the deterrents to open data, including limited resources and fear of infringing rights such as privacy and intellectual property. Section 3 presents reasons why faster and more complete open data could be feasible despite these obstacles. Section 4 highlights that government's real and perceived liability risk remains an obstacle to a more complete release of open data. Although liability is often portrayed in obstructionist terms, we explain how the efficient allocation of responsibilities could support rather than deter the release of open data in the public interest. Section 5 describes the legal tests for applying negligence law to government activities around open data, but stresses that many legal uncertainties remain which make negligence liability unpredictable for governments and the public alike. Section 6 examines ways that governments shield themselves from open data liability, such as waivers and disclaimers, and Section 7 outlines how open data advocates might use liability as a sword to spur open data initiatives. In Section 8, we argue that a specific statutory framework for open data that specifies duties and responsibilities for government and citizens would provide more clarity and predictability than common law negligence, and we highlight what a model open data statute should include. We conclude in Section 9 with the recommendation that governments at all levels in Canada enact an open data statute to provide incentives for government to release open data proactively and in the public interest.

1. The Demand for Open Data

As interest in open data as a governance and accountability tool has gained traction and developed in government systems, the requirements for open data have increased. The advent of data-driven processes in government and industry requires that available data be robust, meaningful, and of good quality. In order to create strong open data processes and to balance what are sometimes competing interests in open data, the objectives for open data need to be defined in advance. For the most effective utilization of open data with the greatest added value, the objective should not simply be the release of any data in the most expeditious manner; rather, the objective should be to release data in the public interest (Sunlight Foundation, n.d.b). This entails the meaningful release of good-quality data that will satisfy public objectives and reduce liability risks.

Open data has support from many different perspectives. This includes government bodies who have shared their support for open data by establishing open data policies and portals. Ontario, for example, legislatively created a data-officer position to promote the availability of government data in "useful forms" and to create a provincial data-action plan (*Simpler, Faster, Better Services Act*, 2019), and the province has issued the *Digital and Data Directive* (Government of Ontario, 2021) to support transparency and access to government data. Canadian municipal governments, in particular, have embraced the principles of open government, which are so closely tied to open data processes. By illustration of the datasets held by each level of government that would be relevant to citizen engagement, federal government data include information about national museums, memorials, and national parks;[1] provincial and territorial governments have data about water quality, education, and roadways;[2] and municipal governments have highly localized data such as lighting in public spaces, the management of potholes, waste removal, pet licences, and transit.[3] Access to the scope and variety of data collected by government, however, is partial and varied.[4] For example, in 2016, when the authors sought to receive open data access to the City of Ottawa's traffic cameras through the city's open data portal, access required registration and submission of a form with an email address in order to receive an access certificate. Currently, registration is required in order to access live updated information on related traffic-map content, including construction work, special events, and incidents (City of Ottawa, n.d.). There are, of course, many

1 The federal Open Government Portal contains a variety of datasets, such as an "inventory of Canadian Military Memorials," "National Historic Sites of Canada," "Bankruptcy and Insolvency Records," "Postal Code Database," and "Outdoor Recreational Spaces"; see https://open.canada.ca/data/en/dataset?portal_type=dataset.

2 The Ontario Data Catalogue (https://www.ontario.ca/search/data-catalogue) contains open datasets related to education, including "college enrolment," "average OSAP debt," and "enrolment by grade in elementary schools." The BC Data Catalogue (https://data.gov.bc.ca) contains open datasets on topics such as motor vehicle accidents and hospitalizations by road-user type: "BC HighwayCams," "Ministry of Transportation Safety Features."

3 For examples in municipal open data portals, the City of Edmonton's contains datasets on "potholes filled" (https://data.edmonton.ca/browse), the City of Toronto's contains datasets on "TTC Ridership Analysis" (https://open.toronto.ca/dataset/ttc-ridership-analysis/), and the City of Halifax's contains datasets on "solid waste collection areas" (http://catalogue-hrm.opendata.arcgis.com).

4 For example, the Edmonton open data portal contains information on potholes, but those datasets begin with the year 2012. In addition, there is information about the amount of monthly payments made by the city ("Risk Management – Pothole Payout Claims") going back to 2010, and information about the amount of potholes filled by the city going back to 2007. This is indicative of the lack of uniformity across these datasets in terms of years that they cover. It is also important to note that users do not know what available data on potholes have not been shared in open data format.

examples of datasets that can be downloaded without registering, as is the requisite standard for open data format (McKinney et al., n.d., s. 1.2). But open data may be included in portals with other types of data that make them harder to find. For example, some data portals mix different data types in their catalogues, use other terminology such as "open information" (GoC, n.d.a), place data "under review" or include "restricted data" (Province of Ontario, n.d.), where the user must filter results in order to locate data that are in open data format.

2. Slow Down, Don't Move Too Fast: Deterrents to Open Data

Despite the positive support on all sides for open data, there are lingering concerns by government, which have impeded a full implementation. From the government perspective, while there may be strong internal support for creating open data portals, there are also a host of competing considerations that may explain the slow and partial implementation of open data initiatives in Canada. The slow adoption of open data has been attributed to governmental organization culture, which emphasizes conservative action (Sangiambut et al., n.d., pp. 9–10). Governments are concerned that open data initiatives are too expensive, too risky, and unnecessary because there are other legal mechanisms for the public to obtain the data. According to these concerns, open data initiatives require too much technical expertise, are too labour intensive, duplicate existing laws for access to information, and may incur litigation costs if the "wrong" data are released.

From a resource perspective, open data portals require technical and financial resources to create the portals and identify and manage datasets. With the vagaries of government budgeting, open data may not be a priority and may not have continuing budgets to support maintenance, which could result in poor data quality and incomplete datasets. Qualified staff with the required technical and policy skill sets may not be available. There may be a lack of continuity and institutional memory as personnel are transferred (who may or may not be replaced), making it difficult for governments to build and maintain open data expertise. Historic datasets that were not created digitally originally need to be identified, scanned, and converted to machine-readable formats, which is resource intensive. Further, data pertaining to a particular topic may be spread across government departments and may need to be classified and integrated.

From the legal perspective, governments are concerned that the release of open data could subject the government to liability. This perception of liability, regardless of whether it is fully accurate or not, may result in the slow and partial implementation of open data releases even where technical and staff resources exist. First, governments are concerned that data releases could violate intellectual property rights if data initially categorized as "open" are actually protected by intellectual property rights (e.g., copyright) held by third parties. Relatedly, the release of data could inadvertently include proprietary corporate information that is protected from disclosure by confidential information rights. Second, the release of data could infringe individual privacy rights if data are insufficiently de-identified or contain sensitive personal information. Third, the release of data could be a cyber-security risk if they contain information that could be used for identity theft, hacking, or disinformation. Fourth, the release of data could be defamatory where data could harm someone's reputation. Fifth, the release of data could lead to injuries arising from poor spatial data quality. "Open data" is not a pre-existing category that simply needs to be uploaded to an open data portal; rather, whether there are third-party claims and whether other rights would be infringed must be evaluated for the information that is created or held by the government, and these decisions require legal and technical expertise.

The liability concerns regarding intellectual property, privacy, cybersecurity, defamation, and spatial quality are valid from the government, and it is also in the public's interest to ensure that data in open data portals do not infringe other rights and are of good quality. It is in the public interest to ensure that publicly held data are made available expeditiously and completely, *and* in a manner that does not infringe other rights. However, identifying which data are actually "open" and not infringing other rights may be time consuming and costly for the government. Excessive caution may also unnecessarily delay this objective due to potentially exaggerated fears of liability, as well as a failure to recognize that *not* releasing data can also potentially incur liability for the government.

Governments may also refrain from creating open data portals under a mistaken belief that open data initiatives are redundant because the public already has an established way to access the same data by requesting them through existing access-to-information laws. Governments could argue that they do not need to expend the effort to proactively post comprehensive open datasets because if the public is interested in a particular dataset they can simply use access-to-information mechanisms to get it.

3. Hurry Up, Open It Up: Rebuttals for Open Data

Increasingly, open data constitutes an important element of open-governance movements (Cerrillo-i-Martinez, 2012; Yu & Robinson, 2011; Peixoto, 2012), which call for greater transparency by government through the release of government information.[5] In Canada, open data advocates call for open data as a means to promote openness, accountability, and responsiveness from the government (Open Government Partnership, 2019). For advocates, the existence of open data is a touchstone requirement for modern forms of governance, although open data in itself does not equate to or constitute open government (Yu & Robinson, 2011). In order to promote good governance, advocates argue for government that is "open by default," which entails the proactive release of all public-sector information.[6] Civil society advocates argue that open data are essential to citizens as they promote citizen engagement, increase opportunity for innovation, and promote accountability. As the network of interested parties who work in and with open data is growing, public access to good-quality data is increasingly important (Verhulst, 2017). Civil society advocates argue that without continued efforts to develop open data, broaden the variety of data, and maintain oversight over the quality of data released, the good-governance aspects of open data are undermined (Powered by Data, 2015; Furnas, 2013; Bhusan and Bond, 2013). Thus, it is important to acknowledge and address government concerns that impede the release of open data.

With respect to the resource costs associated with open data, these costs may decrease over time as expertise can be shared

[5] See "The Open Government Partnership" (http://www.opengovpartnership.org), a multinational network of NGOs that advocate for public-sector transparency and accountability. See also the work of Open North (http://www.opennorth.ca), a leading Canadian NGO in the field of data and technology, and member of the implementation working group of the International Open Data Charter.

[6] See, for example, an open-data proponent objecting to any limitation: http://gijn.org/2014/09/22/open-data-is-not-open-for-business/.

intra-governmentally and technical requirements can be standardized. Liability risks exist but can be mitigated through mechanisms such as licences, waivers, and disclaimers. Furthermore, liability can also arise from a failure to act, and hence the government likewise has risk if it does not post open data. Inaction does not necessarily mean that the government is free from liability. Finally, while it is true that open data by definition are public information, and as such would also be subject to access-to-information mechanisms, in practice this is not an efficient framework and has multiple and often repetitive transaction costs associated with it. Access-to-information procedures require significant time and costs both for requestors of information, who prepare the requests and submit them, and for government staff who search, compile, and prepare information for release to comply with access-to-information obligations. As such, proactively posting open datasets could actually reduce the labour, time, and material costs associated with individual access-to-information requests.

4. Liability and Efficient Allocation of Duties

Government's real and perceived liability concerns are perhaps the most significant obstacle to a more complete embrace of open data by government. Open data advocates, scholars, and government alike have recognized that liability concerns by government are partly to blame for the slow and partial release of open data. Liability refers to the legal responsibility for an activity. Laws imposing liability assign rights and responsibilities, and they are used to remedy people against harm caused by another party. Laws that impose liability provide mechanisms for individual parties, or for large groups of people through a class action, to seek compensation from another person or entity that is at fault. The most common remedy imposed by courts is monetary damages, but courts can also order the defendant to stop the activity or require the defendant to take specific actions to remedy the injury.

Legal research focused on the management of open data processes has identified multiple ways in which government handling of open data could raise legal issues. Areas of concern include privacy, particularly concerning the reidentification of personal data (Conroy & Scassa, 2015; Borgesius et al., 2015; Finch & Tene, 2014); intellectual property infringements, most commonly copyright and confidential information, which conflict with the sharing of data in a publicly accessible and open format (Judge, 2010); defamation if data containing personal information have not been verified or lack veracity and where they are damaging to a person's reputation (Judge, 2005); product liability if inaccurate data, particularly for spatial data, render downstream products unfit for purpose (Chandler & Levitt, 2011); contract if data do not satisfy warranties for use;[7] and cybersecurity if data lead to hacking, identity theft, or the spread of disinformation (Kesan & Hayes, 2019). In addition to these, there is also the possibility of actions based on general negligence principles if the release of open data does not meet standards of reasonable care.

The Sunlight Foundation, an early advocate for the adoption of open data, recognizes that liability concerns could be a deterrent and provides several recommendations to allay government fears through various measures to limit liability. They recommend that governments limit the scope of open data by tautologically and restrictively defining it as data that will not cause liability. Hence, according to Sunlight, governments should begin "by defining 'data to be released' as referring only to information that's under the authority of their jurisdiction and as not including information otherwise protected by law, including local right-to-know law exemptions, privacy, security, and accessibility laws and otherwise legally privileged information" (Sunlight Foundation, n.d.a). Second, they recommend that multiple and layered disclaimers be included in an open data policy and terms of use, with "exclusions of any express or implied warranties, relieving governments of responsibility for consequential damages, and indemnity clauses." They note that "[i]deally the disclaimers are not overbroad," should "include a right to access (save for narrowly defined emergencies)," and "are coupled with a policy that also has a strong process to ensure data quality." Third, Sunlight recommends governments build in "multiple opportunities to review data," and add legal checks into the procedures for release (Sunlight Foundation, n.d.a). These recommendations are pragmatic and rational given the context that governments face of uncertain liability. Yet their effect is

7 Some advocates recommend that governments make no warranty in the data at all; see, for example, Open Knowledge International's blanket disclaimer against creating a warranty for the use of the "open data commons licence" (Open Knowledge International, n.d.a).

to delegate concerns about liability and data quality to the public. Multiple layers of checks can slow the release of open data. Further, the value-added benefits of open data may not be realized if downstream users are concerned that the "as is" nature of the data makes it hard to rely upon or potentially subjects them to liability.

A European Commission report on "Open Data and Liability" similarly recognizes that liability has been "an open data showstopper" (de Vries, 2012, p. 4). The report observes that public-sector bodies get "bogged down by (perceived) lurking risks of liability" and attributes this to overly cautious government lawyers, who "tend to warn of risks that may occur when data are opened up, arguing that (a) the data may not be public or (b) it may be incorrect or (c) free use may create unfair competition" (de Vries, 2012, p. 4).

The report, however, nonetheless concludes that the liability risks around open data can be managed. It offers pragmatic responses that third-party infringements are no different than when data are released by individual request, that risks related to incorrect data can be handled by releasing them "as is" with "proclaimers" that keep end-user expectations in mind, and that risks related to unfair competition are limited unless there are contracts in place or other expectations. Again, as with Sunlight's advice, the report tries to allay government concerns about releasing data by promoting the use of broad disclaimers, which may limit subsequent uses. It is also important to note that the report arises in a context of reassuring EU member states who are required by an EU directive to release public-sector information (EU, 2003).

In the United States, the 2019 *Open, Public, Electronic, and Necessary (OPEN) Government Data Act* mandates federal agencies to publish government information in open format by default and to establish and maintain comprehensive data inventories. Further, half of the states in the US have open data mandates through legislation or executive orders (National Conference of State Legislatures, 2021) that apply to executive agencies. By contrast, in Canada, there is policy support but no legislative mandate for the government to release open data, apart from limited statutory requirements in Ontario (*Simpler, Faster, Better Services Act*, 2019). Without a comprehensive statutory framework for open data, governments lack regulatory directives to provide clarity on the rights and responsibilities around open data efforts.

The threat of liability, real or perceived, on the development of open data processes and activities is an important factor for successful implementation of open data initiatives, but disclaimers and defining open data narrowly are at best partial solutions and at worst counterproductive. One objective of tort law is the idea that the possibility of liability changes behaviour (Linden, 1973, 1995).[8] Although the risk of liability can be negatively characterized as something that obstructs or aborts good ideas, it can also be characterized as a societal benefit because it spurs proactive measures, so harmful behaviours are avoided. The tort system is designed to balance risks and benefits so that activities are carried out safely and so that the entity best placed to shoulder responsibility for avoiding bad behaviour or for adding safety features does so. Economic analysis is commonly used in tort law to determine who should bear the risk of liability by determining who best can bear the costs and whether it is efficient to take steps to prevent an injury (Posner, 1972). The classic negligence calculus considers the possibility of risk versus the utility of a given action, by balancing the probability of injury, the gravity of any injury that occurs, and the burden of having adopted adequate precautions to prevent the injury (*U.S. v. Carroll Towing*, 1947). Under an economic analysis, to determine what level of precautions should be taken, the cost of the precaution is weighed against the benefit that the precaution will provide (Chayes et al., n.d.).

The impact of tort processes is not solely focused on litigation losses and monetary damages. Instead, there can also be a deterrent effect in the negative public perception of actions in liability being filed, the costs involved in defending liability actions, and the increased government oversight that can result from liability actions (Linden, 1973). Public choice theory is the application of economics to explain and predict decisions by collectives or groups (Ostrom, 1975). Applying public choice theory to government decision-making suggests that governments faced with unpredictable or unquantifiable liability risk for actions will make what they perceive to be an economically efficient decision to forego that action. In the context of open data, that would support the view that liability concerns could delay or derail open data initiatives by government; by corollary, clarifying and simplifying liability could invigorate them.

[8] Tort experts extensively debate whether tort law is based on a normative/moral or instrumental/utilitarian foundation.

Tort scholar Allen M. Linden (1973, p. 156) recognized this potential re-balancing of power through tort liability, stating "[t]he law of torts may still serve in the years ahead as an instrument of social pressure upon centres of governmental, financial and intellectual power." Accordingly, under an instrumentalist view of tort law (as opposed to normative views), tort law serves the objectives of compensation, punishment, and deterrence. Deterrence is a particularly salient motivation for groups who are aware in advance of the possibility of tortious action against them and who accordingly take proactive steps to avoid it (Osborne, 2015, pp. 13–16). Government is an example of such a knowing party who is acutely aware of and sensitive to the potential liability that could arise from government action (Johnson & Sieber, 2012). Applied to government activity, the theory is that the possibility of liability can act as an incentive for governments to implement actions at the outset that are in the public interest and to do so safely; liability can also act as a deterrent to prevent unsafe activities from going forward; finally, it can act as a punishment after the fact, enabling citizens to address harms caused by government behaviours and to reduce the likelihood of such harms reoccurring (Foong, 2010; Phegan, 1976; Hardcastle, 2012; Rosenthal, 2007).

5. Negligence and Public Authority Liability

A tort is a "private or civil wrong or injury, other than breach of contract, for which the court will provide a remedy in the form of damages," or, more generally, "a violation of a duty imposed by general law" (*Black's Law Dictionary*, 1979).[9] Actions in tort law include both intentional torts, which are based on an intentional act, and negligence, which is based on a failure to exercise reasonable care.[10] When negligence is applied to government bodies, it is called "public authority liability." Public authority liability is the subset of negligence

9 While this is a conventional definition, "it is perhaps impossible to give an exact definition of 'a tort,' or 'the law of tort' or 'tortious liability,' and as a corollary, it is certainly impossible to give a definition [that] will satisfy every theorist who has taken any interest in the topic" (TE Lewis, *Winfield on Tort* 1, 6th ed 1954, as cited in Garner, 1995).

10 Examples of intentional torts include stalking, harassment, discrimination, assault, battery, and trespass.

actions brought by private citizens against the government. The term "public authority" is used to refer to the Crown and any other public governmental bodies, including municipal governments.[11]

The categories of negligence-based torts are neither fixed nor closed, and hence are flexible enough to adapt to harms from new types of activities (Linden & Feldthusen, 2011, p. 113; *Donoghue v. Stevenson*, 1932, p. 619). Indeed, there is a long history of arguments for using negligence to address harms arising from new technologies, particularly in transitional periods when the activity has begun but before legislatures have implemented specific legislation to regulate it (Judge, 2005; Rustad & Koenig, 2004). New technologies to which negligence has been applied range from injuries resulting from the industrial age, such as the deployment of trains and cars, up to the more inchoate harms resulting from information technologies (Warner, 1919; Morris, 1967; Kaczorowski, 1990; Schultz, 2014; Strachan, 2011; Blackman, 2009; Blagg, 2008). General principles of negligence thus may be used to address harms arising from digital activities, including open data.

For a negligence action related to open data, a plaintiff must show the government had a duty of care, a subsequent breach of that duty, and resulting damage (*Cooper v. Hobart*, 2001). The test for a duty of care has three elements. First, there must be foreseeable harm to the plaintiff and proximity between the parties to establish a prima facie duty of care (*Cooper v. Hobart*, 2001, paras. 30–31). If this first part is established, then, second, the court will undertake a consideration of residual policy concerns that may prevent the creation of a duty of care between the parties (*Cooper v. Hobart*, 2001, para. 37). Once a duty of care has been found to exist from the defendant to the plaintiff, the court then considers whether the activity complained of amounts to negligence. According to the Supreme Court of Canada, "conduct is negligent if it creates an objectively unreasonable risk of harm" (*Ryan v. City of Victoria*, 1999, para. 28). Furthermore, "to avoid liability, a person must exercise the standard of care that would be expected of

[11] There are statutory rules that prevent government bodies from being sued in negligence under certain circumstances under a general principle of sovereign immunity. However, this principle does not prevent negligence actions in all circumstances. See, for example, the *Crown Liability and Proceedings Act* (1985), which enables liability to be imposed on the Canadian government for the actions of its employees in some circumstances.

an ordinary, reasonable and prudent person in the same circumstances" (para. 28).

The measure of what is reasonable depends on the facts of each case, including the likelihood of a known or foreseeable harm, the gravity of that harm, and the burden or cost that would be incurred to prevent the injury (*Ryan v. City of Victoria*, 1999, para. 28). The particular type of negligence and the subsequent class of relationships that could give rise to a duty of care is open-ended and constantly evolving (*Cooper v. Hobart*, 2001, paras. 31, 35). Categories of relationships that have been found to have sufficient proximity to give rise to a duty of care include where the defendant's act foreseeably causes physical harm to the plaintiff or to the plaintiff's property (*Alcock v. Chief Constable of South Yorkshire Police*, 1991), negligent misstatements (*Hedley Byrne & Co. v. Heller & Partners Ltd.*, 1963), and failing to warn of the risk of danger (*Rivtow Marine Ltd. v. Washington Iron Works*, 1974). Courts consider how close the relationship is between the parties and how fair it is to impose a duty on the defendant in the circumstances of the relationship (Feldthusen, 2017; *Cooper v. Hobart*, 2001).

There are policy debates as to whether governments should be held liable in negligence for actions that harm citizens, with those in favour emphasizing that governments should be under the same law that applies to private citizens, and those against emphasizing that large damage awards could drain public resources away from other positive initiatives and could make governments liable for discretionary and subjective policy decisions (Phegan, 1976; Feldthusen, 2013; Siebrasse, 2007; Cohen & Smith, 1986). Public authority liability has been limited to claims of negligence in relation to operational negligence only (Hogg et al., 2011; Daly, 2014; Klar, 2012). Governments cannot be liable in negligence in relation to higher-level government policy decisions. Actions in public authority liability are an important tool to address the impact of government activity on individuals where the government negligently provides services (Linden, 1973; Feldthusen, 2012).

For negligence to apply to activities arising from open data, a duty of care by government to citizens must first be shown (*Cooper v. Hobart*, 2001, para. 15; Linden & Feldthusen, 2011, p. 292). Courts have found that governments can owe a duty of care to citizens in some contexts (*Swinamer v. NS*, 1994), with examples including municipalities having a duty to prospective buyers of real estate to inspect housing developments (*Kamloops [City of] v. Nielsen*, 1984) and municipalities having a duty to maintain roads in a non-negligent manner (*Just v. British Columbia*, 1989). Whether there could be a duty of care by government bodies that release open data and maintain open data portals to users of open data is currently unknown. Potential plaintiffs include parties that use the data for commercial activities, private-sector parties involved in public–private partnerships, interest groups that use open data in advocacy, software creators that rely on open data in hackathons, and those who use open data for reporting purposes (Robinson & Johnson, 2016; Johnson & Robinson, 2014).

In the current data-driven climate, there are many types of activities in which parties use open data. Ascertaining relationships between people in a possible act of negligence would be complicated, but analyzing complicated relationships and the related duty of care is something that courts often do, and especially so when negligence relates to a new activity. As an analogy, examples of relationships that courts have found are close enough (proximate) to give rise to a duty of care include a duty by police to victims in criminal investigations (*Hill v. Hamilton-Wentworth Regional Police Services Board*, 2007), and a duty by government safety inspectors to protect workers from criminal conduct perpetrated by others (*Fullowka v. Pinkerton's of Canada*, 2010). Conversely, there are examples in which the judiciary has *not* adopted new relationships as giving rise to a duty of care. For example, the courts have not recognized an action for negligent breach of a provincial government's statutory duty to enforce a statutory decree (*Holland v. Saskatchewan*, 2008).

Assessing the types of activities for which a government may be found negligent in its activities turns on the distinction between policy decisions and operational decisions. If something is considered a policy decision, then there is no possibility of bringing an action in public authority liability. If, however, an action is negligent because of *how* it is done, then there is the possibility of bringing an action (Hogg et al., 2011, pp. 226–227). Policy decisions refer to high-level government decisions, such as allocation of budgets or the creation of government programming, while operational decisions refer to the day-to-day implementation of government policy (*R. v. Imperial Tobacco*, 2011, para. 90). The reasoning behind this distinction is largely based on efforts to keep political decision-making in the hands of government and to prevent second-guessing of each decision by individual citizens. A government body will have the technical expertise to establish their policy objectives and implement them, and will be better positioned to have information about their financial resources and staff capacity (*R. v. Imperial Tobacco*, 2011, para. 90). The prohibition on imposing public authority liability for discretionary policy-making allows government the freedom to make subjective decisions within the limits of their power without the risk of liability or harm (Hogg et al., 2011, p. 226). This is particularly important for the complex give and take involved in budget prioritization.

In the context of open data, a municipal government may be liable in negligence for the management of data, depending on whether the manner in which a dataset is managed is considered to be an operational decision (*Just v. British Columbia*, 1989, pp. 1237–1238). Alternatively, a government may have immunity if "open data" is characterized as a discretionary governmental decision-making process and a policy choice. However, given the complexity of data frameworks, it is difficult to imagine that every decision made would be a matter of policy. It is more likely that decisions about open data portals contain a mixture of policy decisions made to create the system, which are then implemented through a series of operational decisions (following the analysis in *Just v. British Columbia*, 1989). In that case, governments would not be immune from liability for all their actions that arise from open data. The requirements for a successful action in public authority liability have simply not been tested thus far for government handling of open data. The public authority liability criteria do, however, underscore the uncertainty of liability concerns as they apply to open data, and support the idea that liability uncertainty might be stalling open data efforts. If governments are worried about liability costs from bad decisions around open data, they might "rationally" act by not making a decision or by not releasing open data. This is counterproductive for the government bodies, as well as for the broader community that has an interest in open data. If open data adds value, then all sides should be in favour of mechanisms that facilitate release of "good" open data.

6. Government Strategies: Shields from Liability

Liability avoidance and mitigation tactics by government are in some respects a logical response for governments to adopt in the face of concerns about both real and perceived liability risks arising from open data. Liability could indeed arise where data lead to infringements of privacy, intellectual property, defamation, product liability, or cybersecurity, or where there is negligent handling of data. Whether, and to what degree, governments may be liable for open data activities is uncertain. Government open data activities have not been the subject of litigation in Canada, and hence the likelihood of governments being found liable and the assessment of damages are difficult to quantify. However, a perception of liability can nonetheless result in governments taking more conservative positions on open data implementation, with the idea that it is better from a liability perspective to go slow and release fewer datasets that are less controversial.

Thus far, governments have adopted licences almost as the sole mitigation strategy to the perceived and uncertain liability risk for open data. Standard licence agreements detail the terms and conditions under which a dataset may be accessed and used by downstream users. Licence agreements contain waivers concerning the veracity of the data, and often are accessible through click-wrap agreements (Judge & Scassa, 2010). For example, the Government of Canada open data licence contains a "no warranty" section. This confirms that "information is licensed 'as is,' and the Information Provider excludes all representations, warranties, obligations, and liabilities, whether express or implied, to the maximum extent permitted by law" (GoC, 2017). In relation to activities of third parties, the licence further clarifies that "the Government of Canada is not liable for any damage caused by the use of the data, nor for how the data is used" (GoC, n.d.b). Similar terms and conditions are found in municipal government open data portals throughout Canada.

However, data licences do not address all the issues around liability. The European Commission report, which recommends that government adopt licences to limit liability, also acknowledges that a contractual model does not allow the government to exonerate itself from all potential liabilities (de Vries, 2012, p. 11). For example, contract laws may incorporate threshold good faith and fairness terms, or consumer protections, which can in turn limit the applicability of terms and conditions contained in a contract (de Vries, 2012, p. 11).[12] Urging that governments release datasets through the blanket use of

[12] De Vries is referring to the 1993 Unfair Contract Terms Directive, Council Directive 93/13/EEC of 5 April 1993 on unfair terms in consumer contracts. (1993). Official Journal of the European Union, L 095, pp. 0029–0034.

licences addresses the most obvious risks arising from data that are released. It does not, however, cover all potential harms, including notably harms from *not* releasing data in a timely manner or not releasing comprehensive datasets. Licence restrictions do not capture the opportunities lost to the public in economic, cultural, and innovative value. A licence-based liability approach is also not sensitive to the possibility that liability fears can result in fewer datasets, or even in no open data program existing at all when there is no open data mandate to proactively release open data. For that, a comprehensive statutory scheme addressing the objectives, rights, and responsibilities for open data would better support the public interest and would clarify liability.

7. Advocate Strategies: Liability as a Sword

While governments may react to liability by adopting defensive strategies that deter open data activity, advocates for open data may react to liability by using it as a sword to initiate greater activity. Civil-society advocates potentially could use a range of public-interest strategies to spur government to action. For example, open data advocates could file court actions based in negligence as part of a broader effort to get an ever-greater number of meaningful datasets in open data format and better-quality data, which allege that government did not exercise reasonable care in the creation of open data portals. Public-interest strategies aimed at promoting open data may include advocacy groups requesting specific open datasets from government to draw attention to the limited nature of the datasets and to shift the cost-benefit analysis to favour wider proactive release of open data. Ground-up advocacy strategies by NGOs that focus on municipal governments might be particularly effective for garnering public support and media attention, as the datasets held by cities most directly affect people's daily activities, from recreation to commutes. Civil-society advocates could track the added value from the release of specific open datasets and use that information to build economic arguments that more open data would be worth the cost to government of creating and maintaining open data portals. By establishing the breadth of users' reliance on open datasets, civil-society advocates could strategically deploy general principles of negligence to argue that government has a duty of care to improve the quality and quantity of open data.

An action in negligence could also be filed directly by an individual who has suffered harm relating to open data—for example, due to negligent release of private personal information, negligent release of copyrighted material, or negligent release of data that were submitted to government under a non-disclosure agreement. In addition, there is the possibility of an individual who has a compelling claim in negligence receiving support from interest groups, such as NGOs, who wish to bring a test case against the government. Such test cases are commonly brought to clarify existing issues in relation to new situations or to address emerging legal issues. A test case could provide an opportunity to test the strength of a negligence action in relation to open data. It would require a strong set of facts, which show that harm has been caused by the release of open data. In addition to individual claims of negligence, public-interest groups or law firms could bring a class-action lawsuit, in which a large number of people have the same complaint against the same defendant—in this case, those who claim injuries arising from negligent handling of open data by the government. For a class action to proceed, the class of claimants must be ascertainable and have similar issues. The benefit of bringing a class-action suit is that it provides an opportunity to address a legal harm that has been suffered by many people, but where the transaction costs would make it prohibitively expensive and time consuming for individuals to bring hundreds of individual lawsuits—for example, where the harm suffered by any one person is of low monetary value. Class actions can also be helpful where the litigation involves highly technical issues that might be cost-prohibitive for one party to cover the legal expenses.

These processes allow claimants to use the law of negligence as a sword in advocacy strategies. This is an important opportunity for considering rights and responsibilities in the complex open data environment, which involves different types of open data, many different circumstances according to which open data are released and utilized, and many actors involved in open data processes. However, there are also drawbacks to individuals or civil society groups using negligence as a vehicle for obtaining government action. Negligence actions are based in the common law, where courts decide cases based on the parties before them and their particular facts. Negligence actions will be shaped by the interests of the plaintiffs bringing the claims and may not be responsive to the myriad issues that interest the larger public. A negligence action may not be sensitive to all the policy considerations that governments face and to government's finite resources. A more detailed, holistic, and nuanced approach for open data should reflect the complex relationship of duties and responsibilities between government and citizens. It may take a long time for the application of negligence principles to open data to be established, as courts may take different approaches or reach different conclusions about government liability for open data. A statutory framework, hence, might be better suited than a common law negligence approach to setting and implementing open data priorities.

One overlooked aspect of the growing interest in open data is the potential for negligence based on a *failure* by government to act. As citizens become more aware of open data, have positive experiences with the open data that are available, and more open data portals are developed, it is foreseeable that there will also be an increase in expectations for expanded open data availability. The principle of public authority liability provides a tool for individuals or civil-society groups to bring an action against a government body for negligently acting, and also for negligently failing to act. A possible case based on public authority liability for an omission might argue that datasets of a certain type ought to be available, and that it was negligent for the government not to release them.

Another avenue for advocates is to argue that governments are liable for releasing, or failing to release, open data because they cause *future* harm (Porat & Stein, 2011). For example, a plaintiff could argue that open data containing personal information causes injury with respect to the future harm of possible identity theft even where there is no evidence now of identity theft (Solove & Citron, 2018).

8. Statutory Scheme for Open Data Clarity

Public authority liability requires that operational (not policy) choices of government negligently impact a claimant and that a government failure to act causes harm. This avenue for litigation is unexplored for open data, and hence it is uncertain whether and how public authority liability would apply to open data activities. In particular, it is not known whether open data activities would give rise to a duty of care owed from government to the user of open data. Additionally, it is not known how a court would assess the nature of open data and the various choices made by government and administrative officials, and at what points the steps that government took are policy choices (which would be immune) or operational (which could be subject to liability). Further, it is unclear what liability the government might incur for failing to act with respect to open data.

The Canadian government has already adopted an open data policy, as have some provinces and many municipalities across the country. The federal Directive on Open Government affirms Canada's commitment to open government, and one of the core aspects of that is open data (GoC, 2014). These open data policies are welcome and have enabled growth in the release and use of open data. The rhetorical commitment to a policy supporting open data is strong and well established in Canada. As a legal right or obligation, however, the scope of open data remains uncertain, and which activity (or inactivity) might incur liability for the government is unpredictable. It is certain that liability laws are applicable in some manner to open data activities. This may be through actions in negligence as public authority liability or through specific torts such as defamation, privacy, or intellectual property infringements. Common law negligence is designed to be flexible and applicable to new situations, so its general principles should adapt to apply to open data activities. However, there are still many open questions around the extent of government liability, namely which open data activities by government might incur liability, whether government could incur liability for failures to act with respect to open data, whether government activities would be characterized as "policy decisions" that are immune, and the degree to which licences will protect government from negligence arising from open data actions or omissions. Common law principles over time will clarify these questions as case law develops, but that process is incremental, fact-specific, and shaped by the interests of the parties.

Accordingly, in order to better manage open data and to provide greater predictability around the application of liability principles, we recommend that open data statutes be enacted at all levels of government to specify open data duties and rights for both government and citizens. The statutes, directives, and executive orders from jurisdictions such as the EU and US that have mandated government information be made available in open format, although laudable in policy, lack clear liability provisions and fall short of being comprehensive schemes outlining the rights and responsibilities of various actors. By developing a framework that assigns rights and responsibilities in open data and clarifies liability issues, a statutory scheme will encourage thoughtful open data release and spur governments to develop a robust open data framework.

A statutory framework for open data could also serve many other public policy goals beyond liability. A statutory scheme would have the impact of clarifying data activities broadly. It could specify what constitutes "open" (e.g., whether a Canadian-specific policy would allow user registration requirements, waivers, or downstream obligations to be imposed), how intellectual property and privacy will be balanced and protected, the criteria for data quality, specifications for which data will be made open and which data will presumptively not be made open, details for how data will be presented, which governmental body will be in charge, what licensing will be used, how often data will be updated, and third-party data rights. A statutory scheme could also support public–private partnerships through processes of crowdsourcing to create more open datasets. Since open data is, by definition, not confidential, historic datasets could be made available to private partners for data entry and digitization. A statutory scheme could also aid in the broader development of open data processes by implementing a shared resource bank of information.

Of course, for many of the statutory provisions we suggest below, civil society groups or open data consortia have already put forth detailed schemes—for example, definitions of "open data" and the criteria for satisfying an "open" release. The definition of "open data" from Open Knowledge International, for instance, requires that data be "freely used, modified, and shared by anyone for any purpose" (Open Knowledge International, n.d.b). These existing definitions and guidelines are important contributions and should be strongly considered when legislatures are debating an open data statute. However, there may be instances where a comprehensive and Canadian-focused scheme for open data will select different requirements for openness and different pathways to "open." A model open data statute should consider the following criteria.

An open data statute should detail governmental responsibilities with respect to open data, such as detailing the types of datasets that ought to be released and processes for citizens to request datasets. It should delineate that governments can incur liability by negligently releasing data *and* by negligently failing to release open data in a timely manner where release of open data is in the public interest. Liability for omissions would obviate risk-averse governments falling back on inaction as a safe haven from liability and a litigation-avoidance strategy. A statutory framework should define a clear statutory duty to affirmatively create open data portals and proactively release open data. It should define open data principles and objectives and define "open data" broadly by setting out the types of data that must be included and the format in which data should be generated and published. The statute should set out mandatory timelines for the release of historic datasets and timelines for the release of newly created data. It should establish a framework for creating and maintaining open data portals, including technical requirements, administrative processes, maintenance schedules, and control processes to ensure data quality. The statute should also provide a framework for intra- and inter-governmental sharing of data to facilitate user-friendly access to complete datasets, and it should prioritize centralized open data repositories.

For the public, a statutory scheme should provide a clear framework of rights and responsibilities that would describe how people can access and use open data, while also reflecting an understanding of government processes in this area. Oversight and monitoring for open data could follow a similar approach to privacy and access-to-information schemes by creating an office of an open data commissioner or ombudsperson. However, the statute should also incorporate an individual right of action against the government for negligent activity with open data. This will be beneficial for individuals, public-interest groups, and class actions, as a clear right to litigation will allow these groups to monitor and to sue government for failure to release open data or for release of infringing or poor-quality data. The statutory framework would both provide tools for citizens to monitor open data activities through a commissioner or ombudsperson and accord a legal recourse if administrative avenues are ineffective.

As the statutory framework will provide greater certainty in the rights that citizens hold in this area, it will also reciprocally detail their responsibilities. For example, for volunteered information where citizens can upload data, they should have a responsibility to ensure that copyright or privacy rights have not been infringed and that up-to-date and good-quality data are used. The statutory framework could encourage users of open data to report on downstream uses to better capture this added value for the public. Users could be required to acknowledge the government as the original data source whenever there is Crown-sourced data use. A statute could require that open data users share alike by requiring that further uses developed from government open data are likewise shared in an open format, under the model of a "Crown Commons licence" (Judge, 2010).

The rationale for a statutory scheme is that, if explicit statutory directives for open data are enacted, then governments will more readily implement comprehensive open data schemes. A statutory scheme could take a carrot-and-stick approach by setting out limits on government liability where there have been good-faith efforts to release open data or, conversely, good-faith efforts to protect data from disclosure that is infringing, but pairing that with a right of action so individuals or civil-society groups could enforce these rights in court.

9. Conclusion: Incentives to Open

Recent years have seen an explosion in public interest in open data, and overwhelming support for it. These calls for open data are predicated on assumptions about open data as part of a democratic process. Public availability of data held by public bodies is understood to increase the transparency and accountability of the public sector and enable public participation. It increases communication flows across sectors and helps citizens to identify where information gaps may exist. There is a growing need for an increased use of open data and a broadening of the variety of open data available to obtain these benefits. Yet, uncertainty about the scope of liability that governments might incur for open data activities and the general failure to account for potential liability that governments might incur for open data inactivity may stall further progress by governments on open data. The development of a statutory framework to support open data efforts can provide a structure for rights and obligations and can provide clarity for government bodies that may otherwise behave conservatively in order to mitigate risk.

We have focused on a statutory open data scheme to address liability incentives and disincentives. As we have argued, an open data statute would reduce uncertainty for both government and individuals around open data obligations and expectations, which could be unnecessarily deterring governments at all levels from making more data open. With greater predictability and certainty on the scope of liability, and on which activities will incur liability, it is hoped that governments would release open data more thoughtfully, more comprehensively, more proactively, and faster. A statutory framework would not provide immunity. Instead, it would provide a clear limitation on the liability risks so governments that are imagining a worst-case scenario of unending liability will have their liability fears sufficiently allayed to begin working on the higher-hanging fruit on the open data tree. Arguably, open data efforts have stalled now, after the low-hanging open data fruit has been picked, as governments seek cover in inactivity to avoid real and perceived liability risks. A statutory liability provision could help get efforts going on the harder cases of open data release.

References

Statutes and Case Law

Alcock v. Chief Constable of the South Yorkshire Police, (1991) 4 All ER 907 H.L.
Cooper v. Hobart, 2001 SCC 79, (2001) 3 S.C.R. 537.
Crown Liability and Proceedings Act, R.S.C., 1985, c. C-50.
Donoghue v. Stevenson, (1932) AC 562.
Fullowka v. Pinkerton's of Canada Ltd., (2010) SCC 5, (2010) 1 S.C.R. 132.
Hedley Byrne & Co. v. Heller & Partners Ltd., (1963) 2 All ER 575 H.L.
Hill v. Hamilton-Wentworth Regional Police Services Board, (2007) SCC 41, (2007) 3 S.C.R. 129.
Holland v. Saskatchewan, 2008 SCC 42, (2008) 2 S.C.R. 551.
Just v. British Columbia, (1989) 2 SCR 1228.
Kamloops (City of) v. Nielsen, (1984) CanLII 21 (SCC), (1984) 2 S.C.R. 2.
Open, Public, Electronic, and Necessary (OPEN) Government Data Act. Title II of Foundations for Evidence-Based Policymaking Act of 2018. P.L. 115-435. United States. (2019). https://www.congress.gov/115/bills/hr4174/BILLS-115hr4174enr.pdf
R. v. Imperial Tobacco Co Ltd., (2011) 3 SCR 45, 2011 SCC 42.
Rivtow Marine Ltd. v. Washington Iron Works, (1974) S.C.R. 1189.
Ryan v. Victoria (City), (1999) 1 SCR 201, 1999 CanLII 706 (SCC).
Simpler, Faster, Better Services Act, 2019, S.O. 2019, c. 7, Sched. 56.
Swinamer v. Nova Scotia (Attorney General) (1994) 1 S.C.R. 445.
U.S. v. Carroll Towing Co., 159 F.2d 169, 174 (2nd Circuit 1947).

Secondary

Bhusan A., & Bond, R. (2013). *Open data, transparency and international development.* The North-South Institute. http://www.nsi-ins.ca/wp-content/uploads/2013/11/2013-Open-Data-Summary-Report.pdf

Black's Law Dictionary. (1979). Tort. In *Black's Law Dictionary* (5th ed.). West Publishing Company.

Blackman, L. (2009). Omniveillance, Google, privacy in public, and the right to your digital identity: A tort for recording and disseminating an individual's image over the Internet. *Santa Clara Law Review, 49*(2), 313–392.

Blagg, A. (2008). Has the interactivity of the Internet opened the door to tort liability? An analysis of the potential tort liability for viral video contests. *Florida State University Law Review, 35*(4), 1041–1068.

Borgesius, F. Z., van Eechoud, M., & Gray, J. (2015). Open data, privacy, and fair information principles: Towards a balancing framework. *Berkeley Technology Law Journal, 30*(3), 2073–2131.

Cerrillo-i-Martinez, A. (2012). Fundamental interests and open data for re-use. *International Journal of Law & Information Technology, 20*(3), 203–222.

Chandler, J. A., & Levitt, K. (2011). Spatial data quality: The duty to warn users of risks associated with using spatial data. *Alberta Law Review, 49*(1), 79–106.

Chayes, A., Fisher, W., Horwitz, M., Michelman, F., Minow, M., Nesson, C., & Rakoff, T. (n.d.). *Economic analysis of alternative standards of liability in accident law.* https://cyber.harvard.edu/bridge/LawEconomics/neg-liab.htm

City of Ottawa. (n.d.). *Open data.* https://traffic.ottawa.ca/map/opendata_info

Cohen, D., & Smith, J. C. (1986). Entitlement and the body politic: Rethinking negligence in public law. *Canadian Bar Review, 64*(1), 1–57.

Conroy, A., & Scassa, T. (2015). Promoting transparency while protecting privacy in open government in Canada. *Alberta Law Review, 53*(1), 175–206.

Daly, P. (2015). The policy/operational distinction–A view from administrative law. In M. Harrington (Ed.), *Compensation and the common law.* LexisNexis. Available at SSRN: https://ssrn.com/abstract=2515742.

de Vries, M. (2012). *Topic report No 2012/13: Open data and liability.* European Public Sector Information Platform. https://data.europa.eu/sites/default/files/report/2012_open_data_and_liability.pdf

European Union (EU). (2003). *Directive on the re-use of public sector information, Directive 2003/98/EC.* Revised July 17, 2013, as *Directive 2013/37/EU.*

Finch, K., & Tene, O. (2014). Welcome to the Metropticon: Protecting privacy in a hyperconnected town. *Fordham Urban Law Journal, 41*(5), 1581–1616.

Feldthusen, B. (2012). Simplifying Canadian negligence actions against public authorities—or maybe not. *Tort Law Review, 20*, 176–184.

Feldthusen, B. (2013). Public authority immunity from negligence liability: Uncertain, unnecessary, and unjustified. *Canadian Bar Review, 92*, 211–234.

Feldthusen, B. (2017). Bungled policy emergency calls and the problems with unique duties of care. *University of New Brunswick Law Journal, 68*, 169–201.

Foong, C. (2010). Open content licensing of public sector information and the risk of tortious liability for Australian governments. *Murdoch University Law Review, eLaw Journal, 17*(2), 23–49.

Furnas, A. (2013). *How open data can engage civil society and improve procurement oversight*. Sunlight Foundation. https://sunlightfoundation.com/2013/10/16/how-open-data-can-engage-civil-society-and-improve-procurement-oversight/

Garner, B. A. (1995). Tort. In *A Dictionary of Modern Legal Usage* (2nd ed.). Oxford University Press.

Government of Canada (GoC). (2014). *Directive on open government*. https://www.tbs-sct.gc.ca/pol/doc-eng.aspx?id=28108.

Government of Canada (GoC). (2017). *Open government licence–Canada*. http://open.canada.ca/en/open-government-licence-canada

Government of Canada (GoC). (n.d.a). *Open government portal*. https://open.canada.ca/data/en/dataset

Government of Canada (GoC). (n.d.b). *Open government–frequently asked questions*. https://open.canada.ca/en/frequently-asked-questions.

Government of Ontario. (2021). *Digital and data directive*, 2021. https://www.ontario.ca/page/ontarios-digital-and-data-directive-2021.

Hardcastle, L. (2012). Government tort liability for negligence in the health sector: A critique of the Canadian jurisprudence. *Queen's Law Journal, 37*(2), 525–576.

Hogg, P., Monahan, P., & Wright, W. (2011). *Liability of the Crown* (4th ed.). Carswell.

Johnson, P., & Robinson, P. (2014). Civic hackathons: Innovation, procurement, or civic engagement? *Review of Policy Research, 31*, 349–357.

Johnson, P. A., & Sieber, R. E. (2012). Motivations driving government adoption of the geoweb. *GeoJournal, 77*, 667–680.

Judge, E. F. (2006). Cybertorts in Canada: Trends and themes in cyber-libel and other online torts. In T. Archibald & M. G. Cochrane (Eds.), *Annual Review of Civil Litigation 2005* (pp. 149–188). Carswell.

Judge, E. F. (2010). Enabling access and reuse of public sector information in Canada: Crown commons licenses, copyright, and public sector information. In M. Geist (Ed.), *From "radical extremism" to "balanced copyright": Canadian copyright and the digital agenda* (pp. 568–642). Irwin Law.

Judge, E. F., & Scassa, T. (2010). Intellectual property and the licensing of Canadian government geospatial data: An examination of GeoConnections' recommendations for best practices and template licences. *Canadian Geographer, 54*(3), 366–374.

Kaczorowski, R. J. (1990). The common-law background of nineteenth-century tort law. *Ohio State Law Journal, 51*(5), 1127–1200.

Kesan, J. P., & Hayes, C. M. (2019). Liability for data injuries. *University of Illinois Law Review, 2019*(1), 295–362.

Klar, L. N. (2012). *R. v. Imperial Tobacco Ltd.*: More restrictions on public authority tort liability. *Alberta Law Review, 50*(1), 157–170.

Linden, A. M. (1973). Tort law as ombudsman. *Canadian Bar Review, 51*, 155–168.

Linden, A. M. (1995). Tort liability of governments for negligence. *The Advocate, 53*(4), 535–548.

Linden, A. M., & Feldthusen, B. (2011). *Canadian tort law.* LexisNexis Butterworths.

McKinney, J., Guidoin S., & Marczak, P. (n.d.). *Gaps and opportunities for standardization in OGP members' open data catalogs.* Open North. https://drive.google.com/file/d/0B739vUevKlPgUlZrcDlkd3QwdGc/view

Morris, C. (1967). Negligence in tort law. With emphasis on automobile accidents and unsound products. *Virginia Law Review, 53*(4), 899–910.

National Conference of State Legislatures. (2021). *State open data laws and policies.* https://www.ncsl.org/research/telecommunications-and-information-technology/state-open-data-laws-and-policies.aspx

Open Government Partnership. (2019). *What is the Open Government Partnership?* http://www.opengovpartnership.org

Open Knowledge International. (n.d.a). *Terms of use.* https://okfn.org/terms-of-use/

Open Knowledge International. (n.d.b). *Open definition 2.1.* http://opendefinition.org/od/2.1/en/

Osborne, P. H. (2015). *The law of torts* (5th ed.). Irwin Law.

Ostrom, V. (1975). Public choice theory: A new approach to institutional economics. *American Journal of Agricultural Economics, 57*(5), 844–850.

Phegan, C. S. (1976). Public authority liability in negligence. *McGill Law Journal, 22*(4), 605–629.

Peixoto, T. (2012). The uncertain relationship between open data and accountability: A response to Yu and Robinson's *The New Ambiguity of "Open Government." UCLA Law Review Discourse, 60*, 200–213.

Porat, A., & Stein, A. (2011). Liability for future harm. In R. S. Goldberg (Ed.), *Perspectives on causation* (pp. 221–239). Hart Publishing.

Posner, R. A. (1972). A theory of negligence. *Journal of Legal Studies, 1*(1), 29–96.

Powered by Data. (2015). *Towards a data strategy for the Ontario nonprofit sector.* https://theonn.ca/wp-content/uploads/2015/07/Towards-a-Data-Strategy-for-Ontario-Nonprofit-Sector_ONN_Final_2015-07-13.pdf

Robinson, P., & Johnson, P. (2016). Civic hackathons: New terrain for local government-citizen interaction? *Urban Planning, 1*(2), 65–74.

Rosenthal, L. (2007). A theory of government damages liability: Torts, constitutional torts, and takings. *Journal of Constitutional Law, 9*(3), 797–870.

Rustad, M. L., & Koenig, T. H. (2004). Cybertorts and legal lag: An empirical analysis. *Southern California Interdisciplinary Law Journal, 13*(1), 77–140.

Sangiambut, S., Landry, J.-N., Lenczner, M., & Salteret, N. (n.d.). *Canada in the world: Towards Canadian-led open government*. Open North. https://drive.google.com/file/d/1UorayZvFmzgFJsPDgY1rH49JyEopA4g-/view.

Schultz, M. (2014). The responsible web: How tort law can save the Internet. *Journal of European Tort Law, 5*(2), 182–204.

Siebrasse, N. (2007). Liability of public authorities and duties of public action. *University of New Brunswick Law Journal, 57*, 84–101.

Solove, D. J., & Citron, D. K. (2018). Risk and anxiety: A theory of data breach harms. *Texas Law Review, 96*, 737–788.

Strachan, L. A. (2011). Re-mapping privacy law: How the Google maps scandal requires tort law reform. *Richmond Journal of Law & Technology, 17*(4), 1–30.

Sunlight Foundation. (n.d.a). *Open data policies and implementation: Frequently asked questions*. http://sunlightfoundation.com/policy/opendatafaq/#liability

Sunlight Foundation. (n.d.b). *Open data policy guidelines*. https://sunlightfoundation.com/opendataguidelines/

Verhulst, S. (2017). *Why we should care about bad data*. The Gov Lab. http://thegovlab.org/why-we-should-care-about-bad-data/

Warner, S. (1919). Duty of a railway company to care for a person it has without fault rendered helpless. *California Law Review, 7*(5), 312–322.

Yu, H., & Robinson, D. G. (2011). New ambiguity of open government. *UCLA Law Review Discourse, 59*, 178–208.

About the Authors

Elizabeth F. Judge is Professor of Law in the Faculty of Law at the University of Ottawa, where she specializes in intersections of law, technology, and policy. She is a member of the Centre for Law, Technology and Society, an affiliate member of the Institute for Science, Society and Policy, and holds a cross appointment with the Department of English. She is the co-author of the treatise *Intellectual Property: The Law in Canada* (2nd ed., Carswell, 2011) and has published widely on intellectual property rights, privacy, tort liability for new technologies, and the regulation of technology. As a member of several interdisciplinary research teams, Judge has researched law and policy questions arising from smart cities, locational privacy, geospatial information, and open data.

Tenille E. Brown is Assistant Professor in the Bora Laskin Faculty of Law at Lakehead University. Her research examines the intersection between property, technology, and geography, with a focus on spatial theory. She is a member of the Centre for Law, Technology and Society and the Human Rights Research and Education Centre at the University of Ottawa, and a barrister and solicitor at the Bar of Ontario. Brown holds an LLM from the University of Ottawa, in the field of Aboriginal law, and an LLB (Scots law) from the University of Dundee. She publishes in the area of technology, property, and human rights.

PART III

New Landscapes for Open Data

CHAPTER 6

Examining the Value of Geospatial Open Data

SARAH GREENE AND CLAUS RINNER

Abstract

Transparency, accountability, administrative efficiency, and economic development are the common motivations for making government datasets publicly available. Open data often include geographic references and may be offered in formats ready to be processed in geographic information systems (GIS). The present research contributes to assessing the value of these geospatial open data. We focus on the economic-development goal of municipal open data programs, the available file formats, and their innovation potential. In a case study of four major Canadian cities, we analyze the thematic distribution and the prevalence of GIS-ready data files among available open datasets. For the City of Toronto, we also examine access statistics for the most popular open datasets and their use in developing digital products. The results of this research suggest that political, administrative, and public support for the future maintenance and expansion of open data may require strategic releases of datasets that demonstrably support the stated goals of the respective open data initiative.

Acknowledgements

This research was partially funded by the Social Sciences and Humanities Research Council of Canada through the Geothink partnership grant.

1. Research Context

Open data are provided by different levels of government and can be freely used and redistributed by anyone (Sadiq & Indulska, 2017). They are available to private-sector companies, NGOs, journalists, researchers, and citizens through web-based portals (Johnson, 2016). These portals make the data available without delay, usually with no registration required, and in a number of different formats, the selection of which often depends on the resources available to the specific government organization (Johnson, 2016). Common open data file formats include Adobe PDF for reports, Microsoft Excel for spreadsheets, and Esri shapefile or Google KML for geospatial data (Baculi & Rinner, 2014; Wilson & Cong 2020). Location information is estimated to be present in 80% of all government and industry datasets, and open data are no exception (Baculi et al., 2017). Johnson et al. (2017) present a thorough analysis of the implications of open data practices on civic participation, geographic coverage, and private-sector relations, implications that are most pronounced in regard to geospatial datasets. In this chapter, we examine the contribution of geospatial open data to the value of the expanding open data initiatives worldwide. Research on the value of open data is necessary to understand their prospects and guide their development.

The discussion of open data in the scientific literature is linked to the recent evolution of e-governance and Web 2.0. As defined by Deloitte Research (2000, p. 1), e-governance is "the use of technology to enhance the access to and delivery of government services to benefit citizens, business partners and employees." This ties in with the Web 2.0 evolution, which brought about two-way communication and collaboration within and between governments, as well as with the public (Rinner et al., 2008; Sandoval-Almazan & Gil-Garcia, 2012). Open data catalogues are an increasingly popular format for the sharing of data, due to the end user's ability to download the data with ease, quickly, and at no cost (Borzacchiello & Craglia, 2012). Although there are no direct costs involved, there are secondary factors to be considered, such as the need for an Internet connection to view and/or use the data that can exclude some users from being able to access the information (Sieber & Johnson, 2015). Further, there are additional barriers toward accessing open data, which may exclude some users due to a lack of knowledge of available datasets or how the data can be used. This is particularly true for geospatial open data that require specialized geographic information system (GIS) software to be processed (Baculi et al., 2017). In this context, Coetzee et al. (2020) note that open data are often integrated with other components of open information sharing, including open source software, open hardware, open standards, open education, and open science. Of the three types of open geospatial data distinguished by Coetzee et al. (2020, p. 1), "collaboratively contributed, authoritative and scientific," we focus on authoritative datasets in this chapter—that is, those generated by or for public administration.

In theory, open data can provide significant benefits to government and citizens through a number of avenues. By providing data openly, government agencies aim to increase transparency, enhance administrative efficiency, and promote economic development (Pereira et al., 2017; Zeleti & Ojo, 2017). Transparency and accountability are among the most widely discussed goals of open data (Robinson & Johnson, 2016; Martin & Begany, 2017). These goals focus on enhancing the relationship between government and citizens, including an emphasis on sharing information before being asked (Scassa, 2015)—the "open by default" approach. Drawing economic benefits from open data involves creating innovative applications, which can be used to help solve everyday problems (Graves & Hendler, 2013; Scassa, 2015). These applications then contribute to the common good through two possible pathways: (1) increasing government efficiency and innovation at the local level, and/or (2) creating monetary gains through the sales of applications, which increases tax revenues (Scassa, 2015).

Municipalities are introducing open data programs with the promise of increased resident engagement, which can then be combined with innovative activities to create new opportunities for residents and government. A cyclical process is usually described, where governments hope that residents will engage with open data, downloading them to further manipulate and reuse (Scassa, 2015). However, many municipalities have discovered that having an open data portal may not be sufficient to engage residents in using the data (Johnson, 2016). This is where civic hackathons have played an important role in connecting residents and private-sector companies more closely to the open data (Johnson & Robinson, 2014). Civic hackathons are events run by governments, which encourage the public to use open data to create different products, mainly under the category of mobile or web-based applications (Johnson & Robinson, 2014; Sieber &

Johnson, 2015; Robinson & Johnson, 2016). These hackathons encourage residents and private-sector companies to download and use open data, increasing the popularity of open data portals. They usually focus on solving everyday problems to improve residents' lives, and can result in applications that provide the creators with monetary gains (Robinson & Johnson, 2016).

The diverse benefits that drive open data programs should be considered in determining whether such programs are successful (Sieber & Johnson, 2015; Thorsby et al., 2017). Among these factors, promoting economic development is arguably the easiest to quantify. Open data create opportunities for citizens, private-sector companies, and NGOs to create innovative products and encourage them to be involved in entrepreneurial activities, which can help the local community as a whole (Sieber & Johnson, 2015). The emerging economic benefits are then brought back to government through taxes, job creation, and service improvements (Janssen et al., 2012). The broader theme of economic development focuses on driving innovation. This has been outlined as an important aspect of open data by both the Cities of Toronto and Edmonton (City of Edmonton, 2017; City of Toronto, 2017). Increasing opportunities for innovation is therefore seen as an important focus within municipal governments, while open data programs are seen as a way to achieve this goal.

Throughout the literature, there are a number of varying opinions on the value of certain open data file formats over others. Some claim that data provided in a spatial format are less "open" as their use requires a specific skill set and more expensive software (Janssen et al., 2012; Chan et al., 2016; Thorsby et al., 2017). Others argue that geospatial file formats are more valuable, as they can be used to visualize data in an interesting and captivating way, leading to potential economic development through the creation of map-based applications (Janssen & Zuiderwijk, 2014; Robinson & Johnson, 2016). As for non-spatial open data, they have been found to serve an important role in increasing accountability and transparency between governments and residents, building trust, and leading to greater participation and collaboration (Thorsby et al., 2017).

The present research contributes to the objective of assessing the value of open data. We surmise that attempts to assign a financial or social value to open data must consider the goals of an open data program, and the usability and de facto usage of published datasets. We therefore focus on the stated economic-development goal of many open data programs and the role of geospatial data. Using a case study of four major Canadian cities, we analyze the thematic distribution and the prevalence of geospatial data among available open datasets. For the City of Toronto, specifically, we were also able to assess access to its most popular open datasets and their use in developing digital products.

2. Data and Methods

2.1 Study Area

In Canada, open data became prominent following its success in countries such as the United States and the United Kingdom (Vogel, 2011). The momentum toward open data here picked up great speed, however, after the federal government developed an open government strategy, in March of 2011, and through the development of a national action plan on open government, in 2012, which encourages and supports governments of all levels in providing data openly to their citizens (Government of Canada, 2016; Gill & Corbett, 2017). Both of these plans outlined the importance of open data as a whole, including improving the availability of information, encouraging citizen participation in government, increasing professional and public integrity, improving public services, and improving efficiency throughout government operations (Government of Canada, 2016). As open data has continued to develop in Canada, there has been a focus at the municipal level, perhaps because local government is in the best position to connect and engage with residents. The pioneers of open data at the municipal level in Canada formed a working group, titled the G4, focused on sharing successes and ongoing problems with open data releases and supporting each other, as well as other municipalities considering the development of open data programs (Giggey, 2012). The G4 cities are Vancouver, Edmonton, Toronto, and Ottawa, and constitute the study area for this research. Their open data websites were started in either 2009 or 2010, and at the time of this survey, the sites were located at the following URLs (as at summer 2017):

- http://vancouver.ca/your-government/open data-catalogue.aspx
- https://data.edmonton.ca
- http://toronto.ca/open
- http://data.ottawa.ca

2.2 Data Collection for the G4 Cities

The open data catalogues of the G4 cities were reviewed by visiting their individual web portals and collecting two distinct statistics about the dataset themes and data file formats. This included the count of datasets by the nine thematic categories shown in Table 6.1. These were derived from the literature (Roy, 2014; Dong et al., 2017; Thorsby et al., 2017) and each dataset was represented once, through the theme that best described it.

Theme	Examples
Business	Food truck locations, business permits
Planning and Development	Ward boundaries, neighbourhood names, building permits
Parks, Recreation and Culture	Parks, recreation schedules, outdoor pool locations
Health, Public Safety and Legal	Crime statistics, parking tickets, food safety
Educational, Community and Social Services	School locations, 311 data, homeless shelters
Governmental Data	Meeting minutes, budgetary data, census data
Environmental	Garbage and recycling schedules, water main breaks
Transportation	Bus schedules
Infrastructure	Street network

Table 6.1. Open Data Themes and Examples of Corresponding Datasets. *Source*: Sarah Greene.

In terms of file formats, we understand "dataset" as an individual catalogue item, while a "data file" is the unit through which a dataset can be downloaded. A dataset will have at least one data file associated with it. The file formats available for each dataset were collected. The list of file formats included 35 entries, though the eight most frequently recorded formats were relatively consistent across the catalogues: CSV (comma-separated values file), DWG (Autodesk drawing format), GeoJSON (Geographic JSON), JSON (JavaScript Object Notation), KML/KMZ (keyhole markup language), SHP (Esri shapefile), XLS (Microsoft Excel spreadsheet), and XML (extensible markup language).

An important distinction for the purpose of this research is between spatial and non-spatial data files. More specifically, we classified the DEM (digital elevation model), DGN (design), DWG, ECW (enhanced compression wavelet), GeoJSON, GeoRSS (Web feed including geographic features), GeoTIFF (georeferenced TIFF), GTFS (general transit feed specification), IMG/IGE (ERDAS IMAGINE image file format), KML/KMZ, LAS (lidar data), MrSID (georeferenced raster images), MultiPatch (Esri 3D format), SHP, SketchUp (3D model), and TIFF (tagged image file format) file formats as "GIS-ready" (Baculi et al., 2017), or ready to be loaded in GIS software and to be mapped and spatially analyzed. These data files include points such as school locations, lines such as road networks, or areas such as parks (Currie, 2013), as well as remotely sensed photos and images. In contrast, examples of other data files, offered in formats such as CSV, XLS, or XML, include budgetary information, annual reports, and event schedules. Geographic references are also often found in these spreadsheets and other formats, such as when addresses or latitude and longitude coordinates are included as text (Currie, 2013). However, those datasets were not considered GIS-ready for the purpose of this research, as they require further manipulation to be visualized and analyzed spatially.

2.3 Additional Data Collection and Analysis for the City of Toronto

To further assess the contribution of open data and the role of GIS-ready data files, a case study of the City of Toronto was undertaken. An evaluation index was created that focused on answering a number of questions related to the program goal of economic development. Based on the methodology used by the global Open Data Barometer (ODB, 2016), five of the above thematic categories are most closely associated with the ODB's "innovation" impact group:

- planning and development;
- transportation;
- infrastructure;
- crime; and
- business data.

These themes contribute to economic development because the data are being "commonly used in open data applications by entrepreneurs, or with significant value to enterprise" (ODB, 2016, p. 12). We used these groups to identify the potential contribution of GIS-ready open data to economic development in the City of Toronto.

A questionnaire-style set of criteria with evaluation scores was developed, as shown in Table 6.2.

Question	Response Score
1. What is the percentage of GIS-ready data files in the category of Innovation?	Less than 25% - 0 Between 25-50% - 3 Between 50-75% - 7 Greater than 75% - 10
2. Are innovation-related GIS-ready data files downloaded more often on average?	Below Average - 0 Average - 5 Above Average - 10
3. Are the webpages of innovation-related GIS-ready data files visited more often on average?	Below Average - 0 Average - 5 Above Average - 10
4. Of the products created by third-party users, how many can be considered a spatial product?	Less than 25% - 0 Between 25-50% - 3 Between 50-75% - 7 Greater than 75% - 10
Total Score	/40

Table 6.2. Evaluation of Potential Contribution of GIS-ready Open Data to Economic Development.
Source: Sarah Greene.

Question 1 of the evaluation was answered by calculating the total number of GIS-ready data files and dividing it by the total number of data files available within the City of Toronto's open data portal as at summer 2017. Questions 2 and 3 were answered by using web logs provided by the city. We obtained web-access statistics for the top 100 downloaded data files from the time period between January 1 and May 28, 2017. These data were reduced to 75 data files that fell under the innovation impact group defined by the ODB (2016). The data were provided in a spreadsheet that included each data file name, a description, and the number of times the file was visited and downloaded, as a data file could be viewed without being downloaded. Question 4 was answered by examining the gallery of products created by third-party users, which is included on the City of Toronto's open data portal. The products were provided as URLs to web pages, which either shared the product in question or linked to a page from where the product could be downloaded. These products were examined for spatial components, such as maps.

3. Analysis and Results

3.1 Data Formats and Themes in the G4 Cities' Open Data Catalogues

Across the G4 cities, each dataset had an average of over four associated data files, with great variation between the City of Toronto, with an average of just 1.3 files per dataset, and the City of Edmonton, with 5.8 files per dataset (see Table 6.3). The City of Vancouver provided the majority of their datasets in at least two different file formats. If a dataset was provided in a spreadsheet format, it was usually provided in both CSV and XLS format, while GIS-ready data were primarily provided in DWG, KML, and SHP format. Other common data formats included XML and JSON. Toronto's and the City of Ottawa's datasets varied significantly in the number of data files provided, ranging from only one to five or more different data files, including both GIS-ready and other data formats. Edmonton provided multiple data formats for each dataset uniformly throughout their catalogue. All non-spatial data were provided in eight different formats, which included spreadsheets and web-based services, while their spatial data were provided in GeoJSON, KML, and SHP, as well as spreadsheets (though the latter were not included in the GIS-ready category in this research).

City	Number of Datasets	Number of Data Files	Files per Dataset
Vancouver	284	597	2.1
Edmonton	774	4487	5.8
Toronto	248	312	1.3
Ottawa	129	460	3.6
TOTAL	1435	5856	4.1

Table 6.3. Counts of Datasets and Data Files for the G4 Cities.
Source: Sarah Greene.

Figure 6.1 provides an overview of the number of data files found within the nine identified themes described in the methodology. Overall, the category with the largest number of data files was government data. This included an array of topics, ranging from census data, budget information, and government staff-related details. The theme of education, community, and social services had the second largest count of data files. These included community-based surveys, social services, and school-related information. The business category had the smallest number of data files, with business-related data being quite sparse across the municipalities.

In terms of the spatial categorization of open data by theme for the G4 cities, there were 1,103 GIS-ready data files, making up about 19% of the total number of data files. Conversely, data files that were not GIS-ready numbered 4,770, or over 80% of all data files. Across the G4 cities, only two themes had more GIS-ready data files than other formats: infrastructure (58%) and planning and development (just over 50%). In addition, three themes—recreation and culture (35%), environmental (25%), and transportation (20%)—had non-negligible proportions of GIS-ready data files. There were, however, at least some GIS-ready data files available in each of the nine themes.

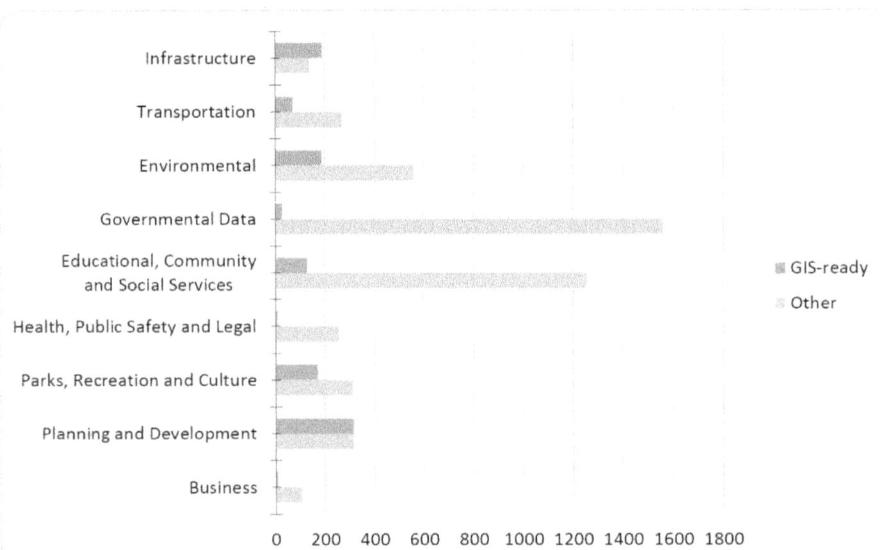

Figure 6.1. Number of GIS-ready Data Files compared to other Data Files by Theme.
Source: Sarah Greene.

Interestingly, innovation-related themes tended to have higher percentages of GIS-ready data files, with 35% of all innovation-related data being GIS-ready. There were 590 GIS-ready files in the innovation category, compared to 1,083 files that were not GIS-ready. In other words, innovation-related data files that were GIS-ready made up more than half of all GIS-ready files (590 out of 1,103). The GIS-ready data formats were clearly associated with innovation in the G4 open data catalogues.

3.2 The City of Toronto's GIS-Ready Open Data

Within the City of Toronto's open data catalogue, 123 of 312 data files were classified within the category of innovation. While the percentage of GIS-ready data files among all Toronto's open data files was 28% (86 of 312), the percentage of GIS-ready data files within the innovation category was larger, at 33% (41 of 123). This led to a score of 3 for the first question of the evaluation.

To answer evaluation questions 2 and 3, the popularity of GIS-ready data files within the innovation category was assessed using the selection of 75 innovation-related files among Toronto's top 100 open data downloads. A large number, 45 of 75 data files (60%), were GIS-ready. Table 6.4 outlines the average number of downloads and webpage visits for the 75 data files, broken down by GIS-ready versus other data files. The average number of downloads per file during the study period was 387. The average number of downloads for GIS-ready data files was higher, at 436. This led to a score of 10 for question 2 of the evaluation. The number of downloads per data file ranged from 137 to 3,369. The five most-downloaded data files, as well as eight of the top 10, were classified as GIS-ready. The number of webpage visits for each data file ranged from 230 to 9,785 views. The overall average number of webpage visits was 1,992, while GIS-ready data files had a higher average of 2,238 views. This led to a score of 10 for question 3 of the evaluation.

	Average Downloads	Average Webpage Visits
Total Data Files	387	1992
Spatial Data Files	436	2238
Non-Spatial Data Files	318	1621

Table 6.4. Average Number of Downloads and Webpage visits per Innovation-related Toronto Data File over a six-month Period.
Source: Sarah Greene.

Some of the products created using the city's open data were presented in an online gallery within Toronto's open data website. This gallery contained 51 different products as at summer 2017. Each product was examined to determine if it included a spatial component. This included products that used web maps and/or static maps to show information based on the dataset. We found that 33 out of 51 products could be considered as spatial. These included a number of mobile applications focused on transportation, a game, and online webpages providing analysis of a number of different topics. The non-spatial products totalled 18 out of 51 and mainly consisted of applications related to garbage and recycling schedules and/or reminders, along with applications highlighting upcoming events. The spatial products outweighed the non-spatial products, making up 65% of all those presented in the gallery. This led to a score of 7 for question 4 of the evaluation. A summary of this evaluation is shown in Table 6.5.

Question	Response Score
1. What is the percentage of GIS-ready data files in the category of Innovation?	Between 25-50% - 3 points
2. Are innovation-related GIS-ready data files downloaded more often on average?	Above Average - 10 points
3. Are the webpages of innovation-related GIS-ready data files visited more often on average?	Above Average - 10 points
4. Of the products created by third party users, how many can be considered a spatial product?	Between 50-75% - 7 points
Total Score	30/40 points

Table 6.5. Summary of Evaluation of the Potential Contribution of GIS-ready Open Data to Economic Development in Toronto.
Source: Sarah Greene.

Based on the results of the individual evaluation questions, GIS-ready open data are more prevalent within the theme of innovation. Further, the GIS-ready data files were downloaded and viewed at a higher rate than other data files. Additionally, the majority of the third-party products showcased by the City of Toronto included a spatial component.

4. Recommendations

4.1 Open Data in the G4 Cities

Between the G4 cities, there were significant differences in terms of the number of open datasets and their associated data files. However, there also were consistent patterns in the types of data files released with certain themes, and in the frequency of spatial versus non-spatial open data. Within the total number of datasets in the G4 catalogues, the categories of government data and education and of community and social services were most populated, and also consistently had more non-spatial data files. This may be related to the goal of government transparency and accountability, which many cities cite as the original purpose of creating an open data portal. The most common themes for GIS-ready open data were infrastructure, along with planning and development. These datasets revolve around technical information related to geography, such as political and administrative boundaries, roads, and building permits. Those who access these files will most likely wish to view them in a GIS environment. Further, many of these datasets can serve as base data, to be used with additional information to provide a bigger picture, such as when analyzing the location of child-care centres, while using roads as a point of reference to evaluate accessibility. It is clear that the value of spatial versus non-spatial data is heavily dependent on the individual end user's purpose in using the data.

When considering the high prevalence of non-GIS open data files in the G4 cities, it is important to note that even though many of these files included geographic references, such as latitude and longitude coordinates, they were not necessarily provided in a GIS-ready format. This can, for example, be the case for some of the CSV and JSON files present in the G4 data portals. In fact, Baculi et al. (2017) found that about 80% of open data files across Canadian municipalities included geographic references. These files can be used to produce valuable spatial products but may need to be further manipulated by a technical user in the appropriate software. A trade-off therefore occurs in the case of non-GIS data files that include spatial information, by potentially increasing the audience of a data file due to it being a less technical file type, while preventing some users from leveraging the full value of the dataset.

This trade-off ties back to the availability of different data files across datasets and between portals. There does not seem to be a standard in terms of the number or type of data files that should be released with a certain type of dataset. As the four open data programs examined in this study began at roughly the same time, the stage of development of an open data portal did not seem to have an impact on the data files available. The City of Edmonton's approach of uniformly releasing datasets in a fixed number and type of data files may help in terms of providing open data to meet the needs of all potential end users, but it does bring up the issue of staff resources needed for producing and uploading the various data files, as well as the storage space and network bandwidth needed to maintain the portal. By considering which data themes are more valuable in a spatial versus non-spatial format, along with considering which data files may complement one another, such as by providing CSV and SHP files for the same dataset, open data could be more strategically released to meet the needs of all end users.

4.2 The Contribution of GIS-Ready Open Data to Toronto's Economic Development

Based on the results of the evaluation, GIS-ready open data were found to have a higher prevalence within the theme of innovation for the City of Toronto's goal of economic development. The evaluation showed that GIS-ready data files were visited and downloaded at a higher rate than their frequency in the catalogue suggests. Interestingly, among the top data files, many of the non-GIS data files initially found in the list were accompanying files, such as "readme" files or other metadata, which were removed for the analysis. This further demonstrates the popularity of GIS-ready data files among open data end users. Additionally, the products created with the open data also tended to feature a spatial component, further proving the greater impact of geospatial open data. As the goal of economic development focuses on encouraging residents and private-sector companies to use the open data to create applications and other products, the data that are available to these end users should focus on content useful for creating applications, and also should be in a format that allows for these products to be created with ease.

By creating a gallery of products, the City of Toronto creates a connection with their open data users. Connecting with the end user can allow government staff to better understand which data are being used and how they are used. The city may expect a dataset to be most valuable in one format, while the end users most inclined to interact with that dataset may find it valuable in formats not previously considered. By having an open and ongoing discussion with the public relating to their wants and needs, an open data program can focus on providing the right data in the most-needed file format(s). This research was shared with staff in the City of Toronto's Information & Technology Division in April 2018, while the city was in the process of developing a new open data portal to replace the open data catalogue accessed during this research. The new portal aims to "meet the unique needs of our users," with features including "flexible data formats" and "designed for technical and non-technical audiences" (City of Toronto, 2018a), which are supported by the results of this research.

Using the results of this study could help develop general guidelines toward releasing municipal information related to specific themes in certain data formats. Some effort could be undertaken in releasing existing data files in GIS-ready formats, where this is not already done systematically. More importantly, future releases of new datasets should be targeted to user needs. This may include, for example, releasing datasets within similar themes or taking a uniform approach to releasing data in a set number of file formats that complement one another. Generally, the proposed evaluation index can be used to help cities create strategic plans toward releasing open data, with a focus on geospatial open data, which have proven to support Toronto's economic-development goal.

4.3 Limitations of the Study

Based on the study area and the methodology used in this study, there are some limitations. Firstly, we only included the G4 cities, which have highly developed open data catalogues and, therefore, may yield different results compared to newer portals. Additionally, the results may have varied if a greater number of catalogues were assessed. In particular, the City of Edmonton had significantly more datasets and associated data files than the other three catalogues, which may have skewed the summary results. Further, municipalities may have varying responsibilities under different provincial regulations and procedures. For example, Ontario has numerous municipal-level electricity-distribution companies, while other provinces have few or no utilities operating at the local level. The administrative unit within each city that operationalizes the open data program can also affect the focus of the program and the types of data released. This can lead to great variation between open data catalogues within a province or country.

Further limitations may be associated with the choice of criteria to assess the value of open data. The evaluation included only four survey questions. This was due to a lack of control over the data provided by the City of Toronto. The criteria provided robust questions for the limited sample data but this would be enhanced by more in-depth usage data. For example, there is a lack of knowledge of who is downloading or viewing open data, and what the data are used for. The City of Toronto has made some progress on the latter through showcasing some products in their online gallery, but this is likely only a small, non-representative sample of the products created with their data. This study is, therefore, a preliminary analysis of geospatial open data in the context of economic development, and has the potential to be further enhanced with additional data and evaluation criteria.

Finally, this research provides a snapshot as of summer 2017. Since then, the City of Toronto has developed an Open Data Master Plan and Roadmap (City of Toronto, 2018b), which guides the 2018–2022 development of their open data portal and related policies. Many aspects of the plan mesh with our findings, such as collaborating with potential end users in developing open data policies, pursuing an open by default principle, and strategically prioritizing dataset releases. In contrast to this research, economic development and facilitating "market opportunities" for the local economy (City of Toronto, 2018b, p. 26) appears as a secondary goal compared to a stated "focus on datasets to solve civic issues" and improving "City efficiency" (p. 5). While not mutually exclusive, the emphasis on civic society versus private-sector support will be subject to the political orientation of future city councils in Toronto and elsewhere.

5. Conclusions and Outlook

The consistent and ongoing evaluation of open data programs is key to maintaining existing programs and achieving the future success of open data. Further analysis of the value provided by geospatial versus non-spatial data files should be undertaken at the municipal level, as well as for higher jurisdictions. Canada is composed of provinces and territories, each publishing their own open data. With its vast land mass, Canada is home to the first geographic information system ever created, the Canada GIS, established in the late 1960s to better manage the country's natural resources and agricultural lands (e.g., Goodchild, 2018). Geospatial data are particularly sensitive in the context of First Nations land management. The adoption of GIS to negotiate land allocations between First Nations in northern Canada was discussed by Duerden (1996) in the context of the Yukon land claims. (Issues of data sovereignty and Crown–First Nations relationships with respect to open data are discussed by Lauriault in Chapter 1 of this volume.)

A consistent approach to dealing with metadata, feeds, APIs, and data visualizations within government open data portals will be needed for replicable research. The proposed open data evaluation index should be refined as more comprehensive and detailed usage data become available in collaboration with municipalities. Qualitative, case-by-case research could investigate the circumstances under which apps and other open data-based products become successful, and how success should be defined in this context. It appears that municipal open data is becoming an established service, which is starting to go through improvement and reconceptualization cycles. The possible convergence of community-based open data such as OpenStreetMap with government open data such as road network files will further enrich open data ecosystems. We hope that this research will contribute to making open data programs even more valuable for users and, therefore, more sustainable in times of scarce government resources.

References

Baculi, E., & Rinner, C. (2014). A geographic content analysis of municipal open data catalogues across Canada. *Cartouche, Newsletter of the Canadian Cartographic Association, 88,* Winter/Spring 2014, 8–9.

Baculi, E., Fast, V., & Rinner, C. (2017). The geospatial contents of municipal and regional open data catalogs in Canada. *Journal of the Urban and Regional Information Systems Association, 28*(1), 39–48.

Borzacchiello, M. T., & Craglia, M. (2012). The impact of innovation of open access to spatial environmental information: A research strategy. *International Journal of Technology Management, 60*(1/2), 114–129.

Chan, M., Johnson, P. A., & Shookner, M. (2016). Assessing the use of government open data and the role of data infomediaries: The case of Nova Scotia's community counts program. *eJournal of eDemocracy and Open Government, 8*(1), 1–27.

City of Edmonton. (2017). *What is open data?* https://www.edmonton.ca/city_government/initiatives_innovation/open data.aspx

City of Toronto. (2017). *Open data master plan—update report.* http://www.toronto.ca/legdocs/mmis/2017/ex/bgrd/backgroundfile-102582.pdf

City of Toronto. (2018a). *The new open data portal.* https://www.toronto.ca/city-government/data-research-maps/open data/open data-portal/

City of Toronto. (2018b). *Open data master plan 2018–2022.* City council item EX30.12, Attachment 1. http://www.toronto.ca/legdocs/mmis/2018/ex/bgrd/backgroundfile-110740.pdf

Coetzee, S., Ivánová, I., Mitasova, H., & Brovelli, M. A. (2020). Open geospatial software and data: A review of the current state and a perspective into the future. *ISPRS International Journal of Geo-Information, 9*(2), 90. https://doi.org/10.3390/ijgi9020090

Currie, L. J. (2013). *The role of Canadian municipal open data initiatives: A multi-city evaluation.* [Unpublished master's thesis]. Queen's University. https://datalibre.ca/2013/09/25/master-thesis-the-role-of-canadian-municipal-open data-initiatives-a-multi-city-evaluation/

Deloitte Research. (2000). *At the dawn of e-government: The citizen as customer* (A global public sector study). Deloitte Consulting.

Dong, H., Singh, G., Attri, A., & El Saddik, A. (2017). Open data-set of seven Canadian cities. *IEEE Access, 5*, 530–543.

Duerden, F. (1996). Land allocation in comprehensive land claim agreements: The case of the Yukon land claim. *Applied Geography, 16*(4), 279–288.

Giggey, R. (2012) *The G4: Setting city data free.* http://canadiangovernmentexecutive.ca/the-g4-setting-city-data-free/

Gill, M., & Corbett, J. (2017). Downscaling: Understanding the influence of open data initiatives in smaller and mid-sized cities in British Columbia, Canada. *The Canadian Geographer, 61*(3), 346–359.

Goodchild, M. F. (2018). Reimagining the history of GIS. *Annals of GIS, 24*(1), 1–8.

Government of Canada. (2016). *Canada's action plan on open government 2012-2014.* http://open.canada.ca/en/canadas-action-plan-open government

Graves, A., & Hendler, J. (2013). *Visualization tools for open government data* [Conference paper]. *Proceedings of the 14th Annual International Conference on Digital Government Research* (pp. 136–145). Association of Computing Machinery.

Janssen, M., Charalabidis, Y., & Zuiderwijk, A. (2012). Benefits, adoption barriers and myths of open data and open government. *Information Systems Management, 29*(4), 258–268.

Janssen, M., & Zuiderwijk, A. (2014). Infomediary business models for connecting open data providers and users. *Social Science Computer Review, 32*(5), 694–711.

Johnson, P. A., Sieber, R., Scassa, T., Stephens, M., & Robinson, P. (2017). The cost(s) of geospatial open data. *Transactions in GIS, 21*(3), 434–445.

Johnson, P. (2016). Reflecting on the success of open data: How municipal government evaluates their open data programs. *International Journal of E-Planning Research, 5*(3), 1–12.

Johnson, P., & Robinson, P. (2014). Civic hackathons: Innovation, procurement, or civic engagement? *Review of Policy Research, 31*(4), 349–357.

Martin, E. G., & Begany, G. M. (2017). Opening government health data to the public: Benefits, challenges, and lessons learned from early innovators. *Journal of the American Medical Informatics Association, 24*(2), 345–351.

Open Data Barometer (ODB). (2016). *ODB 4th edition methodology - v1.0.* World Wide Web Foundation. https://opendatabarometer.org/doc/4thEdition/ODB-4thEdition-Methodology.pdf

Pereira, G. V., Macadar, M. A., Luciano, E. M., & Testa, M. G. (2017). Delivering public value through open government data initiatives in a smart city context. *Information Systems Frontiers, 19*(2), 213–229.

Rinner, C., Keßler, C., & Andrulis, S. (2008). The use of web 2.0 concepts to support deliberation in spatial decision-making. *Computers, Environment and Urban Systems, 32*(5), 386–395.

Robinson, P. J., & Johnson, P. A. (2016). Civic hackathons: New terrain for local government-citizen interaction? *Urban Planning, 1*(2), 65–74.

Roy, J. (2014). Open data and open governance in Canada: A critical examination of new opportunities and old tensions. *Future Internet, 6*(3), 414–432.

Sadiq, S., & Indulska, M. (2017). Open data: Quality over quantity. *International Journal of Information Management, 37*(3), 150–154.

Sandoval-Almazan, R., & Gil-Garcia, J. R. (2012). Are government Internet portals evolving towards more interaction, participation, and collaboration? Revisiting the rhetoric of e-government among municipalities. *Government Information Quarterly, 29*(S1), S72–S81.

Scassa, T. (2015). Public transit data through an intellectual property lens: Lessons about open data. *Fordham Urban Law Journal, 41*(5), 1759–1810.

Sieber, R. E., & Johnson, P. A. (2015). Civic open data at a crossroads: Dominant models and current challenges. *Government Information Quarterly, 32*(3), 308–315.

Thorsby, J., Stowers, G. N. L., Wolslegel, K., & Tumbuan, E. (2017). Understanding the content and features of open data portals in American cities. *Government Information Quarterly, 34*(1), 53–61.

Vogel, L. (2011). The secret's in: Open data is a foreign concept in Canada. *Canadian Medical Association Journal, 183*(7), E375–376.

Wilson, B., & Cong, C. (2020). A survey of municipal open data repositories in the U.S. *International Journal of E-Planning Research, 9*(4), 1–22. http://doi.org/10.4018/IJEPR.2020100101

Zeleti, F. A., & Ojo, A. (2017). Open data value capability architecture. *Information Systems Frontiers, 19*(2), 337–360.

About the Authors

Sarah Greene completed a bachelor's degree in Environmental Studies at the University of Waterloo and a master's degree in Spatial Analysis (MSA) at Ryerson University. Both her undergraduate co-op placement and her master's research dealt with open data in Canada. This chapter is based on her major research paper in the MSA program. She completed her MSA practicum placement as a Data Development intern at Environics Analytics, where she is now a Senior Research Associate.

Claus Rinner is a Professor in the Department of Geography and Environmental Studies at Ryerson University. His research expertise within geographic information science includes participatory GIS and spatial decision support. More recently, he became interested in open geospatial data and 3D-printed geographies. He teaches in Ryerson's BA in Geographic Analysis and Master of Spatial Analysis programs.

CHAPTER 7

Data for Development: Exploring Connections between Open Data, Big Data, and Data Privacy in the Global South

TERESA SCASSA AND FERNANDO PERINI

Abstract

This chapter considers the interrelated themes of open and big data in the Global South, with a particular emphasis on privacy concerns. Open data and big data are examined together, in part because of the emerging view that open government data alone cannot meet the data needs of developing countries. We examine the potential uses and applications of big data analytics to inform evidence-based policy-making, mostly around sustainable development, as well as some of the associated challenges. We also identify and address data-protection and privacy concerns that arise from the use of open and big data, with a particular focus on the experience of countries of the Global South. The chapter concludes with some suggestions about the kind of research needed to shape the future of open data in the Global South.

Acknowledgements

This chapter was prepared with funding support from the International Development Research Centre. An earlier version was presented as part of a workshop at the International Open Data Conference in Buenos Aires, Argentina, in September 2018.

The so-called data revolution has profoundly changed the role of data in society and the economy. Data, data analytics, and data-fuelled technologies offer new ways to identify and address problems, and promise greater efficiency in processes and decision-making for the public and private sector alike. Data-related innovation is also driving economic prosperity. The data revolution has, in turn, motivated research about data and associated technologies, their promise, benefits, and risks. Most of this research comes from the Global North and focuses on these benefits, risks, and challenges in that context.

This chapter considers the interrelated themes of big data and open data in the Global South, with a particular emphasis on certain key concerns, such as privacy. Open data and big data are considered together since they are, in many ways, becoming inextricably linked as the data revolution continues to unfold. We review a body of research primarily produced in the Global South that has been funded entirely or in part by the International Development Research Centre (IDRC), a Canadian Crown corporation. In total, we considered thirty publications wholly or partially funded by the IDRC. This literature explores the relevance of data for development and the dimensions of data opportunities, particularly in relation to sustainable development goals (SDGs). At the same time, it identifies and explores data harms and the need for better data governance.

The chapter features three broad themes: open data, big data, and data protection/privacy. Although there are issues that cut across all three, each theme reveals a core set of concerns. The first part of the chapter examines each of the themes and identifies these core issues. Under the first theme, open data, we address the work of the global community that has pushed for the disclosure of primarily government data as a means to increase transparency, accountability, and innovation. Given that resource and capacity issues sometimes limit the scope of available government data, we also explore the potential for other sources of open data, including private-sector and research data. For big data, we examine the potential uses and applications of big data analytics to inform evidence-based policy-making, mostly around sustainable development, as well as some of the associated challenges. Materials under the third theme, data protection and privacy, explore the use and misuse of personal data and related challenges for privacy protection.

There are clearly important overlaps between the three themes. In Part 2 of this chapter, we identify and elaborate upon a series of cross-cutting themes. In our conclusion, we identify gaps in the research and sketch out some of the work needed to shape the future of open data in the Global South.

1. Open Data, Big Data, and Data Privacy

1.1 Open Data

Open data generally requires "that a dataset be accessible (usually by being online) at no cost, and with no technical restrictions to prevent its re-use" (Davies & Perini, 2013, p. 3). According to commitments made through the Open Government Partnership, a majority of countries worldwide are now publishing "some or all of their data" (Davies & Perini, 2016, p. 149). Open government data are generally seen to have the potential to support three goals: transparency and accountability; innovation and economic development; and inclusion and empowerment (Open Data for Development, 2016), although Davies and Perini (2016) argue that a fourth area—the use of open data to support internal government reforms—is also important in the development context.

In the Global North, "open data" has generally been used interchangeably with "open government data." Davies and Perini (2016) note that most open data research focuses on government as the primary data source. However, they observe that "in developing countries a wide range of government, NGOs, international agency and private actors may be involved [in] creating and holding relevant data" (Davies & Perini, 2016, p. 153). This point is also emphasized in the African context, where a report suggests that open data communities look to "data from non-governmental actors, such as oil, mining and gas companies (open extractives), aid agencies (open aid), government procurement (open contracting), and scientific publications (open access)" (UNECA, 2017, p. 27). Crowdsourced data can also be another source of open data (UNECA, 2017).

According to Davies and Perini, research is also required in order to better understand open data used for decision making. They identified four priority areas for open data research that looked at the flow of open data to users through a variety of intermediaries; understanding how the broader context affects open data initiatives; understanding how "global standards, platforms, infrastructures and 'eco-systems' of open data affect local contexts"; and understanding how benefits of open data initiatives are distributed (Davies & Perini, 2013, p. 7). Davies and Perini later (2016) refined their research framework. They argued that open data research should consider not only the kinds of decisions being made using open data but the governance settings in which those decisions are made. They suggest that research should focus on "emerging outcomes," and should consider not only the different outcomes sought through open data but the relationship between how data are supplied and the realization of outcomes. They propose a research framework for open data case studies, with a view to grouping research into key areas and supporting cross-case comparisons.

Overall, there are a number of open data challenges in the Global South. One is the sustainability of open data initiatives in some countries. In some cases, there is a need to broaden efforts to build open data capacity, including bringing in and expanding the expertise of national statistical offices (UNECA, 2017). At the same time, the literature identifies developing regional hubs and creating links across countries as a way of providing coherence and coordination to national efforts to develop open data programs (Open Data Institute, 2016). Drawing on the experiences and expertise of leaders in open data in the Global South is another way to support such movements, and the Open Data Leaders Network, convened by the Open Data Initiative, offers different stories of open data success (Open Data Institute, 2016). It emphasizes the role of open data leaders in championing open data projects, and bringing them to fruition, but recognizes as well the need for strong peer networks within and across jurisdictions (Open Data Institute, 2016, p. 8).

There is a growing awareness that open data may create new privacy challenges, as well as concerns that privacy may become an excuse not to open and share data (Open Data Research Network, 2013), even though privacy and openness are not antithetical concepts (Gurumurthy & Chami, 2016). There is a need for engagement around the balance between open data and privacy, recognizing that there may be national and culture-specific views of how best to achieve this balance (Open Data Research Network, 2013).

Open data is generally recognized as important for providing a supply of useful data for many purposes, for building capacity within governments, and for encouraging innovation in government. However, the *Africa Data Revolution Report 2016* (UNECA, 2017), prepared by the African Centre for Statistics at the United Nations Economic Commission for Africa, questions whether its potential is over-promised, suggesting that evidence of the utility of open data is mostly anecdotal. There is also a possibility that in some countries the focus may be on providing open data as an end goal rather than on the potential applications for open data. Two phenomena—"open washing" (where data appear to be open but are not readily available for unrestricted reuse) and "open wishing" (where the benefits of open data are over-promised)—are described as pervasive (Open Data for Development, 2016). There are also concerns that unless attention is also paid to capacity building among potential user communities for open data, greater use of open data will be made, rather, by those who are privileged, reinforcing social and economic divides (UNECA, 2017, p. 30). Open Data for Development (2016), in particular, recognizes a need to address gender issues in open data but acknowledges that this remains challenging.

1.2 Big Data for Development: Leveraging the Private Sector

Although government open data programs involve governments making their own data more broadly available, many governments in the Global South face data deficits—where they lack the data they need for their own planning and decision-making processes. There is, therefore, a considerable interest in the potential of big data analytics to meet informational and data gaps in countries of the Global South. Gaps may arise where national statistical agencies lack the capacity to collect sufficient data (Gurumurthy & Chami, 2018; LIRNEasia, 2017b; UNECA, 2017). Such data are usually only collected at intervals of up to 10 years, which makes them less useful than big data for assessing progress toward SDGs or for identifying and responding quickly to new trends or situations (LIRNEasia, 2017a; Surendra et al., 2017; Lokanathan et al., 2017). There may, therefore, be a particular need to supplement state statistical data, particularly with respect to SDGs (LIRNEasia, 2017a, 2017b; UNECA, 2017). Nevertheless, the capacity of the public sector to access, use, store, and secure big data is an important issue (LIRNEasia, 2017a). Some problems relate to the lack of interoperability between available data sources, as well as the lack of country-level plans and processes for big data (Manoj, 2017). Further, some administrative data may either be lacking or difficult to use (UNECA, 2017; Manoj, 2017).

Big data analytics require large volumes of data, and the quantity of available government data may not be sufficient—certainly not for all purposes (Gurumurthy & Chami, 2018; Lokanathan et al., 2017). As a result, there is a general recognition of a need to look to other sources. The external big data source most often referenced in the literature is mobile-communications data from telecommunications service providers (UNECA, 2017; Lokanathan et al., 2017; LIRNEasia, 2018, 2017a, 2017b). Other important sources are satellite data and social media data (LIRNEasia, 2017b; Lokanathan et al., 2017; UNECA, 2017). The *Africa Data Revolution Report* (UNECA, 2017, p. 22) identified a need for systematic efforts "to harness data held by private-sector communities for sustainable development in Africa." Some mention is also made of using data from civil-society actors as well as citizen-generated data (UNECA, 2017; Lokanathan et al., 2017).

Sourcing big data from the private sector can raise challenges around obtaining access and permission to use these data (Lokanathan et al., 2017; Gurumurthy & Chami 2016, 2018; IT for Change, 2017). The use of intermediaries is a possible solution. Intermediaries could "gain access to (privately held) data, conduct the analyses and share insights with government institutions" (LIRNEasia, 2017a, p. 10). Such a solution might also help overcome the lack of capacity for in-house public-sector big data analytics (Lokanathan et al., 2017). By contrast, a "data as a public good" approach might see states mandate the disclosure of "critical data" by private-sector companies for use by government (Gurumurthy & Chami, 2018; IT for Change, 2017).

A number of studies demonstrate how big data analytics have been used to address issues in countries within the Global South. Some studies looked at specific applications, including national identity cards, predictive policing, credit scoring, and smart meters (Hickok et al., 2017). One case study looked at using call detail records or "telephony metadata" to predict socio-economic characteristics of the Sri Lankan population as a means of supplementing census data (Surendra et al., 2017). Big data have also been used to predict outbreaks of disease (LIRNEasia, 2017a), in intelligent transportation systems (Hickok et al., 2017), or to monitor the performance of new programs or initiatives (UNECA, 2017). One report considered how big data could be specifically used to support SDGs (Lokanathan et al., 2017).

Each of the case studies identifies both benefits and harms flowing from big data analytics. While the benefits are often quite specific to the problems sought to be addressed by the adoption of the technology, the harms tend to be similar across applications and relate to issues such as abuse of the results of the analytics; biased results; overreliance on analyzing data for decision-making while ignoring other considerations; privacy invasion and surveillance; lack of ethical frameworks; and lack of algorithmic transparency (Hickok et al., 2017; LIRNEasia, 2018; Samarajiva & Perera-Gomez, 2018; Lokanathan et al., 2017).

Gurumurthy and Chami (2018) suggest that in the rush to embrace big data solutionism there is a "side-stepping" of ethical and privacy concerns. While some work has been done on providing normative frameworks for the use of big data (LIRNEasia, 2018), there is a general recognition of significant gaps in legal and ethical frameworks (UNECA, 2017). LIRNEasia identified a need for networking and the sharing of best practices around the use of big data analytics (LIRNEasia, 2017b). A number of authors identify gaps in governance (UNECA, 2017; Gurumurthy & Chami, 2018; Manoj, 2017). Governance can be broadly understood to include methods, procedures, data management, and analysis (Manoj, 2017), as well as governance in terms of privacy, access, and transparency concerns. In their report from a workshop on big data for development, Lokanathan and Perera-Gomez (2016) flagged a need for more research on the harms of big data. There was a concern that actual harms, and not just theoretical harms, need to be identified and studied. More concrete examples could lead to strategies to prevent such harms or to limit their impact (Lokanathan & Perera-Gomez, 2016). LIRNEasia (2017a, p. 12) argues that "regulatory frameworks need to evolve in parallel with big data in development." Lokanathan et al. (2016) have suggested that developing codes of practice, built upon professional standards, might provide guidance to those engaged in big data analytics.

The completeness and quality of data available for big data analytics are also an issue (Manoj, 2017; Lokanathan et al., 2017; IT for Change, 2017). There are concerns about who is counted and who is excluded from big data (Lokanathan & Perera-Gomez, 2016), as well as about "the marginalisation of women's ways of knowing and an undermining of democratic life in general," for example, in contexts in which political decision-making becomes data-driven (Gurumurthy & Chami, 2016). Gender inclusivity in datasets is identified as a problem, particularly given the nature of some of the data that might be used, and the "structural inequalities and entrenched prejudices in many societies" that may limit the inclusion of data about women (van der Spuy & Aavriti, 2017, p. 30). For example, social media data are collected only from those who have access to and use social media; similarly, mobile-phone data can only be collected from those with mobile phones (LIRNEasia, 2017b).

There are also concerns that the limits of big data analytics are not well understood. Big data analytics deal with correlation and not causality (Lokanathan et al., 2017; IT for Change, 2017). Not only does this mean that big data analytics cannot replace deductive reasoning, some have also suggested that they might not be well-suited to dealing with many of the complex issues facing the Global South (Lokanathan et al., 2017; IT for Change, 2017).

Large datasets are also important for uses in other emerging technologies. The use of artificial intelligence (AI) will require significant amounts of training data. On the positive side, AI could lead to "innovative, data-driven, technical innovations to help address pressing social problems" (Smith, 2018, p. 9). At the same time, many of the risks of AI in the Global South mirror those discussed in relation to big data, including surveillance and loss of privacy, as well as bias and discrimination in decision-making caused by non-representative datasets, and other biases present in AI algorithms. Smith (2018, p. 13) expresses concerns over "how our current set of institutions and cultures shapes the evolution of technologies, and how, in turn, these technologies shape these institutions and cultures." He identifies a need for policy and regulatory frameworks, as well as further research to understand both potential applications and impacts of AI.

1.3 Data Protection and Privacy

The nature and volume of personal information being collected in the big data society are concerning. The literature on the Global South identifies a lack of adequate legal and normative infrastructure to protect privacy rights, particularly with rapidly evolving technologies (Hosein, 2011; Hosein & Nyst, 2013). Although in some cases there are simply no effective privacy laws in place, even in those instances where laws are in place the proper funding and staffing of oversight bodies must be ensured (ADC, 2014). There are also concerns that technologies rejected as privacy invasive in the Global

North are being "dumped" in the Global South (Hosein & Nyst, 2013; Hosein, 2011). Hosein (2011) notes that development funds from the Global North may even be used to purchase these technologies for countries in the Global South. National ID systems that incorporate biometrics, communications-surveillance technologies, electronic health registries, and DNA databases are examples of adopted technologies that have significant privacy implications. In some cases, the privacy issues flow in part from poor security measures around digital data.

Specific technologies adopted by governments may have significant privacy implications. One of these is biometrics, often adopted in conjunction with national identification systems (Hosein, 2011; Hosein & Nyst, 2013; ADC, 2017). The most commonly used form of biometrics in the Global South appears to be fingerprinting. There are concerns about the lack of adequate privacy frameworks for government adoption of biometrics systems (Hosein & Nyst, 2013; ADC, 2017). For example, there is considerable risk of abuse if specific legal frameworks are lacking to set the parameters for when and in what circumstances law-enforcement officials can access biometric databases (ADC, 2017). Biometric-identification systems also raise issues that go beyond privacy. For example, such systems can exclude individuals or segments of the population from programs and services where biometric data cannot be collected, or where the technologies used to collect data are not suited to local conditions (ADC, 2017).

Some technologies are specifically oriented toward law enforcement and national security. These tend to raise significant privacy concerns. Communications surveillance and predictive policing are examples (Hosein & Nyst, 2013; Cortés, 2015; Hickok et al., 2017). A number of potential harms flow from data-based surveillance, including the use of such technologies to track protestors and suppress civil liberties; the risk of data breaches; and the fact that algorithms used may lack transparency, making it difficult to understand how individuals are singled out within the bulk data (Samarajiva & Perera-Gomez, 2018; Hosein, 2011; Hosein & Nyst, 2013). The effect of constant surveillance on a population is also a concern, particularly as it may lead to behaviour modification that both limits autonomy and that may undermine the usefulness of the data analysis being carried out (Samarajiva & Perera-Gomez, 2018). Van der Spuy and Aavriti (2017) suggest that behaviour modification due to surveillance is also likely to disproportionately affect women. Predictive policing can lead to unjustified surveillance and discrimination (Hickok et al., 2017). Its methods may also be opaque (Hickok et al., 2017). Scott-Railton et al. (2017) cite the use of spyware by state officials to infect targets' phones or computers. Not only are such technologies highly invasive, they could potentially be used to target opponents or those critical of government. This highlights that privacy issues are closely intertwined with human-rights issues; poor privacy-protective frameworks can contribute to the misuse of personal information in ways that adversely affect privacy and other human rights and civil liberties.

More general privacy concerns include the potential for state surveillance that is exacerbated where large volumes of data are collected about individuals (Hosein & Nyst, 2013; Hosein, 2011; Samarajiva & Perera-Gomez, 2018). Mobile-communications data are of particular concern. As noted above, these data are identified as being a particularly useful category of data for supplementing open data in big data analytics. From a privacy perspective, such data raise problems of bulk surveillance (Samarajiva & Perera-Gomez, 2018; Hosein & Nyst, 2013). Data-minimization principles and data-retention limits are required. Lokanathan and Perera-Gomez (2016) suggest that for big data it is important to develop privacy frameworks on the front end—in other words, some form of privacy by design, rather than relying upon concepts of notice and consent. One study considered the role of information intermediaries in ensuring the privacy of Internet users by adopting appropriate protocols and safeguards for managing subscriber information. Manoj (2017) suggests that international ethical standards may be required to address privacy issues in big data.

In a study from Argentina, the Asociación por los Derechos Civiles (ADC, 2014) looked at whether citizens' personal data was adequately protected by the state. It found problems, including excessively broad exceptions for the use of personal information by state actors. It also noted that the oversight body was under-resourced to the point of being ineffective. Another case study by the same organization looked at the impact of the introduction of a national biometric-identification system on human rights (ADC, 2017). The report noted that this system is not easily reconcilable with constitutional guarantees, raising important human-rights issues. It also identified concerns about the potential of biometric systems to be used as tools to target particular segments of the population. Another study on communications-surveillance practices in Columbia identified significant deficiencies in the legal protections for privacy and civil liberties, and suggests that the laws are not well adapted to emerging technologies (Cortés, 2015). A study on the protection of personal information in public databases in Paraguay found problems that flowed from inconsistent application of the existing law, which itself was out of date with respect to rapidly evolving technologies (Acuña, et al., 2017).

While privacy is most often considered in terms of individuals, there was also concern about the potential of privacy-invasive technologies to facilitate the identification, profiling, and targeting of minority communities (Gurumurthy & Chami, 2018). Hosein (2011) warns of the secondary effects of national registry systems, including those for health data, noting that such systems can "reveal ethnic origin or religious affiliation in a systematic manner," raising fears of data misuse. Collective, not just individual, approaches to privacy are therefore required.

2. Cross-Cutting Themes

There is clearly a demand for open and big data in the Global South, notwithstanding the potential risks and concerns. In this data landscape, a number of sub-themes emerge that cut across the three areas of big data, open data, and data protection/privacy. These are outlined below.

2.1 A Need for Improved Legal Frameworks for Data Governance

The need for improved legal frameworks and governance emerges from the literature. In the open data context, deficits in legal governance infrastructure were linked to the fragility of open data commitments and to concerns about the overall sustainability of open data programs. In the context of big data, there were concerns that the necessary legal and governance frameworks to ensure appropriate use of big data were absent. There are calls for better privacy laws, as well as for the reform of such laws, in response to rapidly evolving technologies. In some cases, there were recommendations that existing institutions (e.g., national statistical agencies, privacy commissions) be better supported in order to enable more effective governance. Overall, there was preoccupation that governance generally lags behind the adoption of digital technologies, and that "the world's poorest" are the last to be heard in conversations about digital governance (Hampson, 2018).

2.2 Shifting Public- and Private-Sector Roles Raise New Challenges

Data and their associated technologies can affect the traditional roles of public- and private-sector actors. For example, in the open data context, the private sector is emerging as a source of open data. There is also potential for open government data to stimulate private-sector innovation. In the big data context, the private sector could be an important source of data for government data analytics, particularly in relation to meeting SDGs or in assessing progress towards meeting them. Mobile-communications data, remote-sensing data, and social-media data are identified as important big data sources, although it is not always clear how governments will be able to reliably access and use such data. Notwithstanding the perceived importance of private-sector data, there seems to be a consensus that national statistical offices remain important sources of data, and require financial support, capacity building, and independence. Changing public- and private-sector roles are also evident in relation to privacy. The considerable risks to privacy of massive quantities of data collected by the private sector are exacerbated when government can access these data for investigative purposes without adequate transparency and oversight.

2.3 The Development Context Raises Different Issues than in the Global North

Some open data issues may play out differently in the Global South than they do in the Global North. This can require different strategies and approaches. For example, in the Global South, achieving greater transparency through open data might be more likely to lead to the gaming of government data (Davies & Perini, 2016). And while open data in the Global North are often touted as a vehicle for stimulating innovation in the private sector, in the development context there are suggestions that it might be more appropriate for open data programs to focus on using open data for innovation in government.

Particular issues for big data include the challenges for countries of the Global South in gaining access to important and adequate data sources. This is particularly a concern since flawed data can produce flawed analytics. Concerns were raised about the potential that certain people and/or communities might be excluded from datasets relied upon in analytics. While bias and exclusion are also issues in the Global North, the relative paucity of data sources, as well as conditions that might lead to considerable unevenness in the data, make these issues more acute in the Global South. Gurumurthy and Chami (2018) also note that the "complexity of development requires knowledge that is contextual, requiring conventional theory-building that uses causation-based models, rather than merely correlation-based ones most often employed in big data techniques."

The adoption and use of technologies may also play out differently in the Global North and South. For example, it was observed that some technologies with significant privacy implications are rejected by governments in the Global North, but are purchased with aid dollars for adoption and use in the Global South (Hosein, 2011). In addition to the privacy risks posed by such practices, the technologies may also not be well-adapted to local conditions, leading to the collection of incomplete or flawed data, and exacerbating issues of exclusion and disenfranchisement.

2.4 Capacity Building is Essential

Capacity building is seen as a serious need across all areas. In the open data context, capacity building was identified as a need within national statistical offices, within government (not only in operationalizing open data programs, but in learning to make use of open data), and within civil society in order to develop the skills to use open data effectively. Capacity building for big data was identified as a need for governments in order to make effective use of big data (Lokanathan & Perera-Gomez, 2016). There is a broad need for data scientists in the public-, private- and non-state-actor sectors (Lokanathan et al., 2017). There are also gender issues in capacity building (van der Spuy & Aavriti, 2017), with a "significantly lower number of females in the big data for development space" (LIRNEasia, 2017b, p. 8). Capacity building to address privacy issues is also important. The literature identifies a need for greater education and awareness around privacy issues, a need for capacity to understand, identify, and address privacy issues arising from the use of big data and other emerging technologies, and a need for greater state resources for developing and maintaining privacy protection and oversight. The *Africa Data*

Revolution Report (UNECA, 2017, p. 20) noted that there was a need for both reforms and investment if Africa "is to harness the data revolution for accelerated sustainable development."

Capacity issues also arise in relation to gaining access to data and research that may be unavailable because it lies behind paywalls (LIRNEasia, 2017a; UNECA, 2017; van der Spuy & Aavriti, 2017). A number of papers emphasized the need for open access to research publications and research data. In addition, there were calls for more research to be carried out across each of the three themes discussed here— open data, big data, data protection/privacy—with an emphasis on the needs of the Global South. A number of papers proposed specific research agendas or identified research priorities (UNECA, 2017; van der Spuy & Aavriti, 2017; Davies & Perini, 2013, 2016; Hampson, 2018; Lokanathan & Perera-Gomez, 2016).

2.5 Data have a Complex Relationship with Sustainable Development Goals

The SDGs are closely linked to data issues, since data will be an important tool to measure progress toward meeting them (Manoj, 2017). In the context of open data, greater transparency and increased capacity to use open data within government and civil society are seen as benefits. Open data is described as "a vital part of ensuring effective monitoring of the SDG agenda, as well as improving the achievement of targets within the goals" (Open Data for Development, 2016, p. 36). Big data are seen as a means not just of measuring progress but of identifying areas where changes could be made to policy or practices in order to help meet SDGs (Lokanathan et al., 2017). A major challenge is finding sufficient sources of big data (Manoj, 2017), as well as ensuring those data sources are suitable for the purposes to which they will be put. One source notes that because the SDGs require data for assessment, they may drive a push toward improvement of data sources and an increase in supply (UNECA, 2017). The SDGs may also help shape approaches to who and what is counted, by whom and for whom. This will be crucially important. If a goal of the SDGs is to count the uncounted, then it will be necessary to find ways to ensure that the use of big data analytics does not compound the problem. It will be necessary to ensure that datasets are sufficiently inclusive so that they do not contribute to marginalization (LIRNEasia, 2017b).

In spite of the potential for data to help meet SDGs, there are reasons to be cautious. Lokanathan et al. (2017) note that using big data to address some SDGs may come at a cost. For example, the use of big data in policing may help reduce crime but may create issues around surveillance and privacy. There is also concern that if governments turn to the private sector as a source of big data, this could create new dependencies (Gurumurthy & Chami, 2018). Van der Spuy and Aavriti (2017) suggest that pressure to adopt technologies to meet SDGs can lead to adoption without adequate protection for privacy and human rights.

2.6 Gender Dimensions are Important and Insufficiently Addressed

There are important gender dimensions to data. In the open data context, for example, it is necessary to consider who gets counted in official data, as well as what subset of that data is made available as open data (Open Data for Development, 2016). Addressing gender gaps will require significant time and resources, as there are many systemic barriers. This includes a "lack of understanding of the relationship between open data and gender, and limited capacity on gender-related programming and analysis" (Open Data for Development, 2016, p. 38). Lokanathan and Perera-Gomez (2016), as noted, also raise concerns about addressing gender in big data research where women are absent from the data. For example, mobile-communications data—an important source for big data in the Global South—may be significantly under-inclusive of data about women, particularly where households share a single phone and the phone is controlled by a patriarch. The enthusiastic embrace of technology-based research methods, such as big data analytics, also carries with it the risk of marginalizing women's ways of knowing—substituting automated analyses for experience-based and traditional knowledge (Gurumurthy & Chami, 2016). Van der Spuy and Aavriti (2017) emphasize that information communication technologies (ICTs) are not gender neutral. They suggest that although the adoption of ICTs is often linked to increased empowerment and agency, such systems can reinforce existing hierarchies. They observe that "surveillance is never gender-neutral, and reflects asymmetries in power" (2017, p. 46).

2.7 Aspects of the Data Revolution Threaten Human Rights and Civil Liberties

The literature reveals considerable concerns about the risk that under-inclusiveness in open data and in big datasets will lead to further marginalization and exclusion of certain segments of the population, including not only women but also ethnic minorities and those living in rural and remote communities. For example, the *Africa Data Revolution Report* (UNECA, 2017, p. 15) notes: "Official statistics can be and have been used as a tool for social inclusion, integration and development, but equally for social exclusion, economic extraction, exploitation and political exclusion." As a result, it is important to keep asking the questions: "Data for whom? Controlled by whom? And to what end?" (Gurumurthy & Chami, 2018; see also UNECA, 2017; IT for Change, 2017). Nascent concepts of data sovereignty may also lead some communities to insist upon rights to their own data (Gurumurthy & Chami, 2018; IT for Change, 2017). There was some critique of techno-solutionism, and of an evolving data context in which "algorithms determine (and even replace) deliberation and discussion" (Gurumurthy & Chami, 2016). There is also the risk that participation in an increasingly automated society becomes impossible for those without technological access.

The lack of adequate legal frameworks for technology governance was clearly a concern for the protection of privacy and other human rights. A study on a biometric-identification system in Argentina raised concerns that there was insufficient transparency and oversight frameworks to ensure that the database was not used for improper purposes that could include targeting groups and individuals for discriminatory purposes, infringing their civil liberties (ADC, 2017).

Human rights that become particularly important in the big data environment include the right to be counted; the right of access to information; the right to participate in the collection, production, and dissemination of data; the right to privacy, non-discrimination, and equality; and the right to freedom of expression (UNECA, 2017).

3. Conclusion: Moving Forward—Research for the Data Society

Although there is a growing body of quality research undertaken across a range of data-related issues in the Global South, there remains room for much more. This is an area where both technology and its local adoption are evolving rapidly. As a result, there are always new issues that require consideration. The novelty of the technology, the complexity of the challenges it raises, and the diversity of its impacts across different social and economic divides means that there is an ongoing need for research into data and the Global South.

Particularly in the early days of the development and adoption of new technologies, there is a need for broad-based research that identifies key issues, whether they relate to potential applications, advantages of adoption, impacts, or governance. Such research can lay the foundation for future work by identifying key questions or unresolved issues. Broad themes that need to be further developed in future research include data sovereignty (the right of states and/or communities to control data about them), the shifting relationship of private and public sectors with respect to data, and emerging rights of individuals to control data about them. Such rights include privacy, but may go beyond conventional understandings of privacy to include concepts such as data portability.

While broad-ranging studies can fill important knowledge gaps, there is also a distinct need for research in the form of context- or technology-specific case studies. Such case studies may be particularly important in understanding successes or failures in the use of data, in identifying unanticipated problems, and in attempting to address any challenges. Case studies from the Global South will reveal and identify challenges that are particular to that context. Case studies, however, must be more than just exercises to champion or tout the successes of particular technology adoptions; they must be both rigorous and critical, enabling the identification of benefits and harms, as well as potential solutions.

In addition to case studies that focus on particular technologies, there is need for further research on governance. It is clear that data-related technologies raise significant privacy and human rights concerns. The pressure to adopt technologies that promise solutions to pressing problems may often lead to a neglect of governance issues. Research is needed to identify and examine privacy and human rights issues in the abstract, but it must also do so in the context of concrete case studies. Governance issues include the need for effective laws and the resources to support the administration of those laws. However, there is also a need for case studies of particular governance options. The concept of data trusts, for example, is gaining ground in the Global North as a potential data governance mechanism. This might be a fruitful area of research for data governance in the Global South. In addition, research on tools other than legislation, including strategic litigation, the use of incentives, or trust systems, to cite but a few examples, is necessary and important.

References

Acuña, J., Fulchi, L. A., & Sequera, M. (2017). *La protección de datos personales en bases de datos públicas en Paraguay*. Asunción, Paraguay : Technologia & Comunidad. https://www.tedic.org/wp-content/uploads/2017/09/La-protecci%C3%B3n-de-Bases-de-Datos-en-Paraguay_Documento-Final.pdf

Asociación por los Derechos Civiles (ADC). (2017). *La identidad que no podemos cambiar: Cómo la biometría afecta nuestros derechos humanos*. https://adcdigital.org.ar/wp-content/uploads/2017/06/La-identidad-que-no-podemos-cambiar.pdf

Asociación por los Derechos Civiles (ADC). (2014). *The collecting state—A study about Argentina and citizens' personal data*. https://adcdigital.org.ar/portfolio/the-collecting-state/

Cortés, C. (2015). *Communications surveillance in Colombia: The chasm between technological capacity and the legal framework*. Working Paper 3. Dejusticia. https://www.dejusticia.org/wp-content/uploads/2017/04/fi_name_recurso_683.pdf

Davies, T., & Perini, F. (2016). Researching the emerging impacts of open data: Revisiting the ODDC conceptual framework. *The Journal of Community Informatics, 12*(2), 148–178. http://ci-journal.org/index.php/ciej/article/view/1281

Davies, T., & Perini, F. (2013). *Researching the emerging impacts of open data: ODDC conceptual framework* (ODDC Working Papers No. 1). http://www.opendataresearch.org/sites/default/files/posts/Researching%20the%20emerging%20impacts%20of%20open%20data.pdf

Gurumurthy, A., & Chami, N. (2018). *Data frameworks for a right to development*. United Nations Research Institute for Social Development. http://www.unrisd.org/TechAndHumanRights-Gurumurthy-Chami

Gurumurthy, A., & Chami, N. (2016). *Data: The new four-letter word for feminism*. GenderIT. https://www.genderit.org/articles/data-new-four-letter-word-feminism

Hampson, F. (2018). *Improving Internet governance: Support to the global commission on Internet governance*. IDRC Digital Library. https://idl-bnc-idrc.dspacedirect.org/handle/10625/56925

Hickok, E., Chattapadhyay, S., & Abraham, S. (Eds.). (2017). *Big data in governance in India: Case studies*. Centre for Internet & Society. https://cis-india.org/internet-governance/files/big-data-compilation.pdf

Hosein, G. (2011). *Privacy and developing countries*. Office of the Privacy Commissioner of Canada. https://priv.gc.ca/en/opc-actions-and-decisions/research/explore-privacy-research/2011/hosein_201109/

Hosein, G., & Nyst, C. (2014). *Aiding surveillance: An exploration of how development and humanitarian aid initiatives are enabling surveillance in developing countries*. IDRC Digital Library. https://idl-bnc-idrc.dspacedirect.org/handle/10625/52191

IT for Change. (2017). *Policy frameworks for digital platforms: Moving from openness to inclusion* [Background paper]. http://itforchange.net/sites/default/files/1377/Background%20Paper_Platform%20Policies_August%202017.pdf

LIRNEasia. (2017a). *Big data and SDGs: The state of play in Sri Lanka and India*. IDRC Digital Library. https://idl-bnc-idrc.dspacedirect.org/bitstream/handle/10625/56907/IDL-56907.pdf

LIRNEasia. (2017b). *Mapping big data for development and the global goals*. IDRC Digital Library. https://idl-bnc-idrc.dspacedirect.org/bitstream/handle/10625/56905/IDL-56905.pdf

LIRNEasia. (2018). *Annex 19: Code of practice for the secondary use of mobile network big data*. IDRC Digital Library. https://idl-bnc-idrc.dspacedirect.org/bitstream/handle/10625/56918/56976.pdf

Lokanathan, S., & Perera-Gomez, T. (2016). *Workshop report on shaping a research and policy agenda on big data for development in the global south*. IDRC Digital Library. https://idl-bnc-idrc.dspacedirect.org/handle/10625/56910

Lokanathan, S., Perera-Gomez, T., & Zuhyle, S. (2017). *Mapping big data solutions for the Sustainable Development Goals (Draft)*. IDRC Digital Library. https://idl-bnc-idrc.dspacedirect.org/handle/10625/56906

Manoj, M. (2017). *Big data governance frameworks for "Data Revolution for Sustainable Development."* Centre for Internet & Society. https://idl-bnc-idrc.dspacedirect.org/handle/10625/56914

Open Data for Development. (2016). *Open data for development: Building an inclusive data revolution*. IDRC. http://od4d.net/result/od4d-annual-report-2016/

Open Data Institute. (2016). *Open data leaders network digest*. Open Data Institute. Available at: http://od4d.net/wp-content/uploads/2017/05/Open-Data-Leaders-Network-Digest.pdf

Open Data Research Network. (2013). *Open data and privacy: Discussion notes*. http://www.opendataresearch.org/content/2013/501/open-data-privacy-discussion-notes.html

Samarajiva, R., & Perera-Gomez, T. (2018). *Bulk data: Policy implications (Draft)*. IDRC Digital Library. https://idl-bnc-idrc.dspacedirect.org/handle/10625/56922

Scott-Railton, J., Marczak, B., Abdul Razzak, B., Crete-Nishihata, M., & Deibert, R. (2017). *Reckless V: Director of Mexican anti-corruption group targeted with NSO group's spyware*. The Citizen Lab. https://citizenlab.ca/2017/08/nso-spyware-mexico-corruption/

Smith, M. L. (2018). *Artificial intelligence and human development* [White paper]. Ottawa: IDRC. Available at: https://www.idrc.ca/sites/default/files/ai_en.pdf

Surendra, A., Lokanathan, S., Lasantha, F., & Gomez, T. (2017). *Predicting socio-economic characteristics of the Sri Lankan population using call detail records (CDRs)* [Policy brief]. IDRC Digital Library. https://idl-bnc-idrc.dspacedirect.org/handle/10625/58172

United Nations Economic Commission for Africa (UNECA). (2017). *The Africa data revolution report 2016: Highlighting developments in African data ecosystems*. Prepared by the UNECA, the United Nations Development Programme, the International Development Research Centre of Canada, and the World Wide Web Foundation. https://www.africa.undp.org/content/dam/rba/docs/africa-data-revolution-report-2016.pdf

Van der Spuy, A., & Aavriti, N. (2018). *Mapping research in gender and digital technology*. Association for Professional Communications. https://www.apc.org/sites/default/files/IDRC_Mapping_0323_0.pdf

About the Authors

Teresa Scassa is Canada Research Chair in Information Law and Policy at the University of Ottawa, Faculty of Law. She is the author or co-author of several books, including *Digital Commerce in Canada* (LexisNexis, 2020), *Canadian Trademark Law* (LexisNexis, 2015, 2nd ed.), and *Law Beyond Borders* (Irwin Law, 2014); is co-editor of *Artificial Intelligence and the Law in Canada* (LexisNexis, 2021) and *Law and the Sharing Economy* (University of Ottawa Press, 2018); and has written widely in the areas of intellectual-property law, law and technology, and privacy. Scassa is a member of the Canadian Advisory Council on Artificial Intelligence and of the Geothink research partnership. She is also Senior Fellow with the Centre for International Governance Innovation's International Law Research Program.

Fernando Perini is Senior Program Specialist at the International Development Research Centre. Part of the Democratic and Inclusive

Governance Division, he coordinates a range of efforts on data for development, including open data, feminist open government, digital rights, and artificial intelligence for development. With 12 years of experience in programs and acting as the IDRC Regional Director for Latin America and the Caribbean, he has led a large global portfolio and donor partnerships. He has written extensively in the topics of data, management, governance, technology, and development, including co-editing *The State of Open Data: Histories and Horizons* (African Minds and IDRC, 2019) and serving as technical advisor for the *World Development Report 2021: Data for Better Lives* (World Bank, 2021). Perini has extensive international experience as a researcher, consultant, and lecturer, and holds a PhD from the University of Sussex (Science Policy Research Unit) in the management of technology and innovation.

CHAPTER 8

The Future of Open Data is Rural

Renee Sieber and Ian Parfitt

Abstract

Open data advocates and businesses looking to capitalize on open government data envision a seamless data layer interoperable across subnational levels of government. Most research into open data has focused on urban centres because cities represent significant sources of government data. That same research is not conducted in rural areas. We argue that an urban vision of open data has shaped rural open data and look at four areas of urban–rural difference regarding open data: technical capacity (from relatively fewer government resources and availability of local skills), motivations (e.g., related to hazards and emergency preparedness), datasets and analysis (largely due to remotely sensed imagery), and jurisdictionality. A better understanding of issues would allow rural communities to anticipate challenges and opportunities. By advancing the conversation around open data, we can increase the likelihood that rural communities, and those interested in rural issues, can access open data to similar extents as in urban areas.

Acknowledgements

We thank Tom Dool; the Social Sciences and Humanities Research Council's Community and College Social Innovation Fund grant, "Open Data for Open Government in Rural BC" (no. 890-2015-2016); and the SSHRC Partnership Grant, "How the geospatial web 2.0 is reshaping government-citizen interactions" (no. 895-2012-1023).

We are enmeshed in an "open" culture, whether applied to science, software, or government data. Open government data promise to spur economic development, ensure accountability of government practices, and induce government-to-government collaboration (Sieber & Johnson, 2015). The rhetoric is also seamlessly geographic. In other words, government data should be available across the entirety of the landscape whether federal or municipal, urban or rural.

Most research into open data has focused on large urban centres because cities represent significant sources of government data and because cities claim the largest concentrations of populations. That same research is not conducted in rural areas; the notion of open data, then, has been shaped by how we know urban data. This means we have a particular lens through which we understand technical capacity, motivations for opening data, required datasets and analysis, as well as the role of local vis-à-vis other levels of government. As the European Data Portal Consortium (2020, p. 6) reminds us, we need to resist the perception that all that is required is to transplant urban open data practices to rural areas. An urban open data lens may be inappropriate for rural areas.

Canada is ideal for exploring the differences in a developed economy in terms of rural and urban open data provision because of the country's large size and steep population gradient. When compared to Canadian urban centres, rural and remote communities have a much lower population density, with mountains, forests, and farmland taking the place of buildings and tightly packed road networks. Rural is defined by Statistics Canada as those parts of the country "that remain after the delineation of population centres using current population data" (du Plessis et al., 2002; cf. Statistics Canada, 2019). Aside from those gaps compared to the urban or metropolitan region "fabric," lower population densities in rural jurisdictions result in fewer resources financed through taxes, which in turn make it difficult to adopt the same level of data-management technology as found in large, densely populated communities, such as metro Vancouver or Toronto. We argue that, whereas some layers of spatial data used for planning or decision-making are common to rural communities and larger urban regions such as parcel fabric data or road network data, a much more significant non-residential part of rural regions requires different types of data than urban areas. This includes data about resources, including ecosystems, fish and wildlife, forests, soils, and minerals; it also includes data about threats, including terrain hazards and forest fuel loads (Schaffers et al., 2011). Although some Canada-wide datasets exist in open formats, the data often cover the entire country at a coarse spatial scale: smaller (i.e., higher) resolution data are required for local decision-making or research within rural towns or regions.

Relative to rural areas, urban centres often have the resources and capacity to experiment with different methods for providing open data (Gurstein, 2011; Ruijer & Meijer, 2020). By understanding which issues may be specific to making data open in rural communities, rural government/agencies can better anticipate issues when following urban models and develop successful and efficient data-collection and -sharing platforms. Rural open data policies and programs are not yet well developed, and little information is available on the successes and challenges of communities that have taken on this task. By advancing the conversation around open data, supporting the development of a governance structure and finding ways to reduce costs of open data delivery through standardization and process optimization, we can increase the likelihood that rural communities can one day have access to open data in the same way that citizens in larger urban centres do today.

We will discuss how differences between rural and urban places lead to differences in how open data are produced and consumed. This in turn challenges government policy that seeks to provide equivalent levels of service across the nation or province/state. Since most people in Canada live in urban areas, these differences may be overlooked in assessments of open data policy or practice. For instance, most research into open data has focused on the national, subnational, or large metropolitan levels of government, with little consideration of the unique characteristics of rural areas like those in Canada. In this chapter we will introduce important rurally specific issues to the future of open data, with examples drawn from experiences in rural British Columbia.

1. Explicating the Assumptions of Open Data

Before we begin unearthing the assumptions of urban open data and their impacts on rural open data, it is important to affirm the difficulty in arriving at a single definition of rural. The delineation between urban and rural areas in Canada has been defined in many ways, including at least six by Statistics Canada (2015), the organization responsible for statutory national demographic information. Rural areas can be defined by distance from a population centre, population size or density, and also sociologically, for instance, by people or places that have a rural culture. According to a more recent Statistics Canada (2019) definition, rural includes small towns and villages with a population of fewer than one thousand, agricultural lands, wilderness, and remote areas. "Rural" even includes relatively unpopulated regions within metropolitan areas and census agglomerations. Statistical definitions of rural effectively can be antonymic: rural becomes the opposite of urban and we discuss the effects of this framing later. Rurality can also be expressed as a site of imagination, "connected with all types of cultural meanings, ranging from the idyllic to the oppressive, and as a material object of lifestyle desire for some people—a place to move to, farm in, visit for a vacation, encounter different forms of nature, and generally practise alternatives to the city" (Cloke, 2006, p. 18).

Rural areas can be distinguished from urban areas by their landscape. Whereas the urban landscape is dominated by the built environment, such as road networks, buildings, and utility lines, the rural landscape is dominated by relatively natural features, like fields, forests, lakes, and mountains. A rural region may have cities or towns embedded within it, and most people may live in these centres; however, it is the matrix around and between these communities that for the most part defines rurality. This is reflected in the English term "countryside" for rural areas (McCarthy, 2008). Rural communities require similar data as larger urban centres for community planning and service delivery but also need information about the matrix around communities, for instance about natural resources.

Rurality suggests a dormant or static resource-based economy like agriculture or forestry. However, rural areas have experienced considerable economic restructuring (Ryser & Halseth, 2010; Halseth & Ryser, 2018). Restructuring has been led by increased mobility of capital and diseconomies of scale that penalize large industries (e.g., with rising energy costs), labour-shedding technologies that enable short-term or "on demand" work, and upskilling of resource jobs (for "tech-enabled resource industries"). Halseth and Ryser (2018) argue that this restructuring has led to a declining tax base and a decline in responsiveness to innovation and change more generally, precisely what is required to create the infrastructures necessary for open data.

Rural governments also rely heavily on government revenue. This "reliance on government support can create inefficiencies and dependence . . . as well as false expectations surrounding the viability of some rural economies" (Ryser & Halseth, 2010, p. 514). All this, as we will argue, does not bode well for rural open data.

Ultimately, where it concerns rurality, we find du Plessis et al.'s (2002, p. 4) argument persuasive. Rural-policy analysts often start with the question: "What is the size of the rural population?" We suggest that an appropriate response is: "The answer depends upon the issue you are addressing. Why are you asking?" This is supported by research using several open data sources in Tanzania to define "rural" that showed different definitions could change the value of economic-development indicators for some places and, consequently, affect policy decisions (Wineman et al., 2020).

For us, the "why are you asking" provokes three questions specific to open data. Do the characterizations of rurality align with open data? Do the assumptions, which largely originate within urban areas, fit with rural experiences? And can the conditions of rural areas support and benefit from open data?

1.1 Technical Capacity Limits Rural Open Data Development and Sustainability

Open data is recognized for its potential to create new jobs as part of the knowledge economy and increase data literacy. Probably the most evident difference between rural and urban areas concerns access to technical capacity. Lack of technical capacity represents a long-standing problem in rural areas, characterized by stark income differentials, lack of formal education, comparatively lower literacy and numeracy levels, out-migration of individuals with skills, inability of governments to match salaries for jobs requiring technical expertise, the lack of specialization and professionalization (which may mean governments must hire non-professionals in these roles), and the workload on government employees that may limit time for training in new technologies (Brown, 1980; Zarifa et al., 2019). Contrast the gaps with an increasing digitization of government services, a development for which rural people are disadvantaged relative to the skills and access required to use tools such as e-government. Conversely, technological innovations can reduce physical travel time, isolation, and lack of awareness, which historically have been barriers to ICTs

(Huggins & Izushi, 2002; Spicer et al., 2021). Rural areas are realizing that they need to overcome this technical divide and become digital. Open data is one pathway to this transformation.

It is possible for rural areas to marshal the skills necessary to open up data. The county of North Frontenac, Ontario, with a population of fewer than 2,000 people as of Canada's 2016 census, implemented an open data portal. Should a region acquire the skills necessary for implementation, they may still lack the skills for sustainability. North Frontenac's portal went through a period of two years without updates, although the site was revived in 2020. Timeliness (or the lack of) of open data updates represents an important indicator of the viability of a government's open data initiative (Zuiderwijk et al., 2012).

Technical capacity assumes that all the activities involved in opening the data (e.g., data standardization, privacy protection, database handling, portal construction, firewalls, backups) must be handled in-house. Regions can rely on open data-portal firms like Socrata; North Frontenac relies on Esri. Reliance on the private sector could speed up or increase access to rural open data so the demand-side benefits would likely accrue earlier than through developing in-house supply capacity (Johnson et al., 2017). Although this removes technical barriers, it comes at the expense of paying for an ongoing subscription or a supplier's understanding of local regulations.

Prerequisites for open data include not only data handling but the infrastructure needed to support the data, like Internet broadband. Rural access to broadband has long lagged behind urban access, despite being considered a key driver of sustainable economic growth (Lennie et al., 2005; Grimes, 1992). Indeed, much of the literature on ICTs in rural economic development continues to focus on broadband access. The rollout of broadband Internet by the private sector has disadvantaged rural communities, since denser populations provide richer paybacks to broadband investors (Salemink et al., 2017). This was recognized and partially addressed in Canada by programs like Industry Canada's "Connecting Canadians" initiative (Government of Canada, 2020); yet as of 2020, 16% of rural Canadians, or approximately 6 million people, still lacked sufficient broadband access (Canadian Internet Registration Authority, 2020). Since the COVID-19 pandemic, when individuals, governments and firms needed greater access, the gap between urban and rural in Canada has widened. Speeds for rural download were 12 times slower compared to urban areas and upload speeds were 10 times slower (Canadian Internet

Registration Authority, 2020; Carra 2020). Like many others, Malecki (2003) notes that broadband costs far more in rural areas and methods are lacking to accommodate that cost. In Canada, the minimum price for broadband can be twice as much in rural versus urban areas (CRTC, 2020).

The nature of open data actually makes identifying end users quite difficult. A dataset may be downloaded once from a government data portal yet used in an app by thousands of consumers (Chan et al., 2016). Less is known about rural users of open data. The Regional District of East Kootenay reports that the largest users of their open data catalogue are hunters seeking information on private versus Crown land during the fall hunting season, as hunting is generally only permitted on public land (Nicole Jung, personal communication, 2017). In many cases, these users are coming from more urban places and so their usage is not necessarily indicative of the needs of rural users. Lacking knowledge of users' abilities renders capacity building quite difficult.

Technical capacity for data handling and making sense of the data are not necessarily resolved in urban areas. Information intermediaries, hackathons, and open data "book clubs" have emerged to increase open data literacy (Johnson & Robinson, 2014; Chan et al., 2016; Montes & Slater, 2019). These initiatives, which are often homegrown, also serve to create value from the data by developing applications or performing simple statistics (e.g., bivariate comparisons, averages, and counts). Whether due, for example, to lack of local technical knowledge or sheer lack of numbers of people, these initiatives are far less likely in rural areas. It should be noted that rural areas are not completely bereft of tech innovation and skills. Farming, with its use of drones, precision agriculture, and artificial intelligence for pest and drought detection, certainly challenges our stereotypes of technology deficits in rural areas (Shearmur et al., 2020).

A neoliberal strain runs through the rhetoric of technical capacity, which urban areas may be better equipped than rural areas to accommodate. Namely, digital literacy is the responsibility of the citizen or is downloaded from higher to lower levels of government. Open data embeds assumptions of the citizen as do-it-yourself technical entrepreneur, where digital divides suggest these might be lacking. It also suggests a method for higher levels of governments to relieve themselves of responsibility for capacity development. As Ryser and Halseth (2010, p. 518) report:

> Once grounded in top-down planning and support, bottom-up approaches to rural economic development have emerged since the 1980s. . . . A concern about the shift to bottom-up approaches is that they are driven by government preferences to off-load responsibilities to rural places with limited capacity and inadequate funding.

This is accompanied by similar neoliberal goals of replacing government functions with the private sector. Rural areas may be more vulnerable to corporate capture than urban areas.

Finally, we often forget that open data assumes an abstraction of government data as an end in itself and not merely a means to an end (e.g., in support of a specific policy). Pinto and Onsrud (1995) wrote about the evolution in thinking about government data produced by geographic information systems (GIS). Increasingly, valuation of that data shifted from evidentiary material to support decision-making to an end product that could be sold or repurposed. Cities, in their GIS departments, likely have greater awareness that they are creating data-as-product because they have customers for that data; for example, other municipal departments or the private sector. A rural community may encounter this abstraction less often; instead, the focus may be on the production of reports limited to a single instance. This may explain the higher percentage of less usable formats such as PDF files in rural open data portals compared to urban data portals (European Data Portal Consortium, 2020). It is not until data are realized as an end product that they can be reused or revalued to become the basis for a new-economy value chain.

1.2 Motivations/Goals Underlying Opening Data Are Different for Rural Areas

In this chapter, we primarily consider open data for rural areas in the Global North. Most literature on open data for rural areas covers the developing world—the Global South (e.g., Davies & Perini, 2016; Schaap et. al., 2019). That literature begins with the assumption that open data is a natural good, where the primary motivations for open data emphasize greater transparency, with the goal of improving the lives of people and reducing corruption (Leone, 2015; Verhulst & Young, 2017). In this regard, the literature reflects some degree of paternalism and colonialism, in the sense that open data proponents in the Global North (e.g., developers of open data standards and apps) believe that transparency of data in the Global South can both reveal and reduce rampant corruption (Serwadda et al., 2018). For rural areas in the Global North, the motivation for open data is less focused on detecting corruption and more on addressing power imbalances between citizen groups and extractive industries, or on economic development. Rather than lofty rhetoric linking open data to democratic principles of transparency or government accountability, the goals tend toward evening the playing field in land-use decisions or the transactional on the economic-development side. Motivations also include assisting other levels of government, like provincial agencies to enhance forestry management, ensure emergency preparedness, increase biological conservation, improve agricultural practices. A goal of open data could also be in assisting international firms to decide on, for example mining operations.

Our research on Canadian cities found that internal business intelligence is listed as an important motivation for opening up urban data (Sieber & Johnson, 2015). That is, data structured to be available to the private sector and the general public can be just as easily used by units within the public sector. Use by units in government, however, implies a certain degree of extant professionalization, including knowledge of privacy protection—especially as data fusion allows for considerable opportunities for reidentification. Utility by other governmental units implies understanding of licensing, use of standardized classification systems, and even file-naming and data organization. Huggins and Izushi (2002, p. 113) argue that "[t]his leaves most [rural] employees reliant upon 'teach-yourself' practices," an ad hoc and fragmented form of professionalization. Open data as business intelligence could help identify needs for data-handling expertise elsewhere in the organization. Open data becomes an entree for rural areas to conversations about data management and improved opportunities for data-driven or evidence-based policy.

The motivation for open data on the supply side can be as simple as efficiency and effectiveness gains, which are particularly crucial for low-resource rural governments. This could be reducing workloads in answering information requests at regional government offices or developing spatial data handling capacity at smaller municipalities (Tom Dool, personal communication, 2017). Initiatives aimed at building capacity in small communities can help identify whether the regional government should become the central service provider.

Tom Dool, a rural GIS expert, spoke about the multiple roles played by small community staff. The same person may be chief administrative officer, chief financial officer, and also be the entire Department of Public Works. He was concerned about the ability of individual communities to build capacity for GIS and other data systems while performing mission-critical activities like addressing aging roads and water infrastructure. Standardized open data across the region represents an additional hurdle for rural communities; at the same time, it can enhance regional integration of administrative effort, capacity building at all levels, and delivery of shared services.

Economic development represents a strong motivation in urban areas but the rhetoric plays out differently; in the case of urban areas, it is often driven by firms developing new data products, processes, or services. By contrast, rural open data seems to be a means to an end—the data serves a thematic purpose. The adoption (i.e., the usage) of open data we have seen in urban areas is driven in part by hackathons, where entrepreneurial individuals with the time, energy, and passion to play with data chase an end result that can be a product, like an app. Rural areas may see the hackathon as a luxury: economic development via entrepreneurs may be an existential need for rural areas. Malecki (2001, p. 61) recognized that "[s]uccess in the digital economy will depend on the role of entrepreneurs. . . . We cannot look at entrepreneurship in isolation from the demographics of rural America. In essence, it is a human capital issue—and a social capital issue."

1.3 Rural Areas Require a Different Mix of Data Sources and Different Methods of Analyses

Rural areas require a different mix of data from urban areas. Some data needs are common in all areas, including transportation, cadastre (parcel boundaries), flood, fire and debris-flow hazards, air and water quality, and utility data. Rural areas may rely even more than urban areas on these types of data––for example, bus or ride-sharing information—due to the infrequency of rural transit and the distance between home and services (Skerratt, 2018). In contrast to urban areas, rural areas show a greater need for environmental data, including rare and endangered biota, agriculture, and extractive resources, like timber, minerals, and oil and gas. Urban areas have been associated with increased rates of faunal and floral extinction (McKinney, 2002);

however, relatively natural rural and remote areas are identified as sites for conservation (Samson et al., 2004; Light, 2004). Jobs urban to rural differ as well: resource extraction, resource-based manufacturing, and resource trade comprise most rural employment in Canada (Bollman, 2000; Zarifa et al., 2019).

As we have indicated throughout the chapter, compared to urban areas, rural areas have less open data. Remote-sensing technologies like high-resolution multi- or hyper-spectral imagery, and lidar (light detection and ranging remote sensing) can be used along with image processing software to fill this gap. Lidar, in particular, has revolutionized terrain hazard mapping, forest-development planning, and forest inventories. The Internet of Things (IoT), a predominant feature of smart cities (Zanella et al., 2014), could play a role in improving rural information; for example, in generating more comprehensive data about climate, streamflow, or snowpack. A significant barrier to implementation of IoT in rural regions, especially mountainous regions, is connectivity. Data from IoT and lidar are often patchwork (e.g., when collected with drone- or airplane-based rather than satellite-based sensors). Adding to this patchwork is spatial scale (i.e., resolution). Data often cover the entire rural region at a coarse resolution; higher resolution data are required for local decision-making or research within towns and villages. The difference with urban-rural contexts is that data for urban areas tend to be offered at the same resolution ("scale"). In rural areas, a patchwork of data collected at different scales is more common, thereby increasing analysis costs.

Policy-making relies on multiple sources of data, like remote sensing and IoT, which suggests the need for open data originating from private sources, especially those datasets funded by government or captured on public land (in commonwealth countries, Crown lands). Even data originally collected by government, which have been the domain of national-level public-sector organizations like NASA for satellite imagery, are increasingly being produced by numerous private companies. Davies and Perini (2016, p. 153) observe that there is an

> embedded assumption … that the kinds of data that might be used to deliver on the promise of open data will be held by governments. Whilst strong and well-resourced states may have historically played an important role as nodal powers, with a

> monopoly on comprehensive data collection ... a wide range of government, NGOs, international agency and private actors may be involved creating and holding relevant data.

The patchwork of potential rural open data persists even as more data becomes plentiful because imagery and IoT data are collected by firms for their own strategic purposes, are likely sold under restrictive data licences, or are simply too expensive to acquire.

Discussions of open data increasingly include data that are crowdsourced unofficially by non-experts. There is growing interest in harnessing the field knowledge and experience of hunters, ranchers, and other rural people to collect data about species (Boyce, 2017), ecosystems (Launspach & Bolgrien, 2016), or land use (Fritz et al., 2017). Given low population densities in rural areas, however, volunteer data monitoring and non-government-led data portals may not be sustainable over the long term. Conversely, crowdsourcing, especially if it is paid, is seen as attractive to rural residents because crowdsourcing can provide extra income, afford flexible hours, and allow for continued maintenance of a healthy work–life balance (Vasantha et al., 2014).

Skills related to open data provisioning emphasize analytics, standards, and data handling geared toward types of datasets used in cities or at national levels. Remote sensing poses very different data-handling requirements from urban data. These high-resolution point-cloud and pixel-based datasets generate very large files. By contrast, city datasets (e.g., budgeting, parks) tend to be quite compact (Currie, 2013). A rural region may necessitate hundreds of terabytes of lidar, for instance, which involve large data storage and high bandwidth transmission rates. Rural geographic datasets often require spatial simulation modelling and big data and machine-learning techniques to extract value. This data handling differs from the suite of technical skills typically acquired by open data staff. If they have any prior training, they likely have learned spreadsheets, markup languages (e.g., HTML, XML), or data-science techniques. Overall, the open data community focuses on these methods over remote sensing and pixel-based methods.

Differing motivations and data needs emerge when one examines types of portals for rural areas compared to urban areas. The Mackenzie Data Stream (https://mackenziedatastream.ca/) is an example of an open data portal developed around the theme of water quality rather than developed around a jurisdiction like a city or province. This portal includes open data for the Northwest Territories as well as parts of northern British Columbia. Government standards and protocols like those from the Canadian Aquatic Biomonitoring Network (Environment Canada, 2021) help non-experts contribute to monitoring; the water portal then aggregates this standardized data so researchers or agencies can compare water quality across large areas and identify water-quality concerns. Rural sites rarely offer services beyond data aggregation. Edmonton's Citizen Dashboard is an instance of a portal now combined with analytics: their urban tool provides a range of real-time analytics related to the city's services (https://dashboard.edmonton.ca/). We anticipate that rural portals will take a trajectory similar to Edmonton's in expanding capacity.

1.4 Rural Open Data is More Likely to be Trans-Jurisdictional

We argue that rural open data is much more likely to be trans-jurisdictional than in urban areas. The concept of trans-jurisdictionality refers to activities that consistently engage multiple levels of government. These are situations in which the boundary between jurisdictions is blurred, for example in terms of responsibility of shared resources. Issues do not solely reside within a single jurisdictional boundary but cross "physical, administrative, discipline, social and political boundaries at all levels" (Gray et al., 2016, p. 4).

Much of the data used by urban areas are generated by those same urban areas, whether from surveys or other forms of data collection (cf. Currie, 2013). Even as urban areas in the developed world are considered the epitome of open data, there can still be variations across and within jurisdictions (e.g., in poor urban neighbourhoods; see Stephens, 2017). Compared to urban areas, rural areas depend upon an aggregation of data from multiple levels of government. This reflects interactions that are more likely to be vertical—unincorporated areas interacting with villages; villages with regional/municipal councils, provincial, and federal levels of government. In the Canadian province of British Columbia, rural regional councils rely on the province to supply datasets on, for example, land cover and "desirable or useful" amenities (e.g., libraries, schools, and hospitals). Outside of small, urbanized centres in rural areas, data required for planning are generated by other jurisdictions. Data control (e.g., in terms of licensing, standards, and updates) is retained by other jurisdictions.

Rural areas also are sites where the countryside occupies much more of the overall land base, and plays a larger role in economics, recreation, and in an identity more rooted in nature (Haartsen et al., 2003; Bell, 1992). Individuals regularly interact with other governmental levels, so rural areas need data from other levels of government. Rural jurisdictions tend to be physically large, and they often lack the resources to collect the data themselves; the data they need, of natural resources, say, are under the regulatory control of the province or the federal government.

Trans-jurisdictionality can benefit a rural community. Trans-jurisdictionality recognizes distinct roles for government data collection, including differential resources needed to collect those datasets; it reduces unnecessary duplication in data collection and publishing (Parfitt, 2017). Benefits are coupled with concerns. Open data is predicated on the principle that the data are open irrespective of their use and users. However, there is no guarantee that, for example, multiple jurisdictions share the same open data licence or terms of service. The Canadian Chamber of Commerce (2017) proposed that subnational governments (i.e., provinces, cities, villages) adopt a common open data licence because "the current landscape is marred by a patchwork of different and non-interoperable licenses, inconsistent adoption, and jurisdictional open data policies that, ironically, violate the key principles of open data." The patchwork will impede rural areas reliant on vertical trans-jurisdictionality. As stated above, even knowing the licences does not guarantee a dataset's release; a government may control the data but not own them, inducing "not only uncertainty as to the applicability of the license, but also ambiguity as to who has the final word in releasing the data" (Conradie & Choenniab, 2014, p. S14).

Beyond negotiating licensing agreements, a higher level of government may not wish to cede control. Ryser and Halseth (2010, p. 519) review the research that finds quite durable concentrations of power at higher levels of government: "Many senior governments seem reluctant to decentralize power to rural regions, and governments at a number of levels." To that end, "some governing bodies have removed the legislative tools that provided rural communities leverage to negotiate with corporations over local benefits or diversification opportunities" (Ryser & Halseth, 2010, p. 519). This questions the assumption among open data proponents that a locality has control over all the data it needs to function (e.g., for emergency preparedness or for natural-resources planning). The comparable example in urban areas is with public-transportation data, which is held by a separate administrative entity or, increasingly, privately held by ride-sharing entities like Uber. Compared to rural areas, if data are necessary then the city collects and manages those data.

Parker (2000) wrote about rural broadband but the findings could just as easily apply to rural open data. As Parker (2000, pp. 286–287) observed: "Many Federal and state government agencies have data networks that reach into rural communities, but are dedicated exclusively to government use.... Those networks do serious harm to the economic health of rural communities." This suggests federal and state/provincial entities could consume any local capacities built for rural open data; for example, by hiring away skilled employees.

Simultaneously with limits imposed on rural communities' authority to tap into technical and other resources (Brown, 1980), cost-cutting at the federal and state/provincial levels since the 1980s has resulted in a downloading of responsibilities to the local level. In British Columbia, for instance, "wildland–urban interface" (where homes are built next to wilderness) wildfire planning now resides with local and regional government. The second author has experienced situations of jurisdictional confusion that were life-threatening: in one case of flooding, regional government looked to the province's river forecast centre to issue evacuation orders while the province argued that issuing evacuation orders was not its responsibility. Trans-jurisdictionality can also effect a delegation without resources to manage these new responsibilities, a situation that urban areas might be better equipped to absorb or counter.

A related challenge is one of "distantiation," in which decision-making, data production, and publishing are removed from the locality. This makes sense from a fiscal and expertise perspective—ICTs coupled with broadband can make centralized decision-making cheaper and more attractive (Halseth & Ryser, 2018). Centralization is promoted as a key metric of success in open data publishing in the Global South (Linders, 2013). While distantiation can reflect efficiency, it also can allow higher levels of government to divert resources more effectively to populous urban areas, for instance in an emergency. Even if individuals from different jurisdictional levels work alongside each other in an emergency, they are still subject to different organizational cultures, career trajectories, and reporting hierarchies. If local engagement and control of open data are prioritized, then open data production should not be distantiated.

Horizontal trans-jurisdictionality—relations among adjacent entities of approximately the same level of authority (e.g., city–city, city–village)—occurs in both urban and rural areas. Horizontal integration, where communities of similar size coordinate data provision and publishing, is especially crucial in rural areas due to extensive fragmentation of local authorities. It has long been noted that rural communities exhibit considerable fragmentation of authority, with the proliferation of non-school special districts, boards, commissions, and bureaus (Brown, 1980; Dolan, 1990; Carter, 2008). Presumably each is collecting its own data. Regional governance to support and maintain a regional open data portal may benefit each community. Trans-jurisdictionality requires new policy and management structures, but they "will only be effective if they are accompanied by sufficient resources to conduct their tasks and allowed sufficient time to develop mature leadership, trust, and structures" (Ryser & Halseth, 2010, p. 518).

The Kootenays region exemplifies the complicated web of relations and services in rural areas that can impact open data provision. The Kootenays have an à la carte service provision reflected in taxation in unincorporated rural areas, where one rural electoral district, town, hamlet, or subdivision can choose from a menu of services, ranging from official community planning or wildfire planning to libraries or recreation facilities, street lighting, or sidewalks (Tom Dool, personal communication, 2018). Each proposed new service or facility is typically approved via a referendum rather than imposed by a regional government. This fragmentation of services can present considerable challenges to regional or other authorities wishing to create seamless and interoperable open datasets.

Complicating trans-jurisdictionality is that, in countries like Canada, Australia, New Zealand, and the United States, nations exist within nations. In Canada, First Nations fall under the jurisdiction of the federal government, creating vertical trans-jurisdictionality where horizontal trans-jurisdictionality may be more efficient (e.g., collaborating on local economic development). Town interactions with Indigenous communities may require the former interact with the federal government, which then interacts with the First Nation(s). Indigenous Peoples regard open data quite differently and view their data as a matter of sovereignty, toward protecting community and cultural information (Phillips, 2015; Kukutai & Taylor, 2016). Data about Indigenous Peoples have historically been collected to "primarily servic[e] government requirements rather than support... indigenous peoples' development agendas" (Kukutai & Taylor, 2016, p. 3). Consequently, Indigenous Peoples may resist definitions that, according to the Open Knowledge Foundation (n.d.), open their community data so that they are "free to use, re-use and redistribute, without any legal, technological or social restrictions." Additionally, Indigenous communities may still be in land-claims/treaty processes so opening data may run counter to their interests. Open data in the aforementioned countries therefore resembles government-to-government data sharing, not open data publishing.

2. Conclusion and Recommendations

Rural open data exists at the intersection of population density, human capital, ICTs, and socio-economic goals. These features interact with one another. A low population density over a large spatial extent correlates with a lack of government resources. Lower government resources combined with lower levels of technical skills equals a human-capital gap; low population density combined with lower incomes can generate less market incentive to develop services like broadband or open data. Rural is also defined by the goals to which open data will be directed. Unlike urban applications (e.g., sidewalks and urban trees), rural open data often focus on land usage for recreation, resource extraction and agriculture, and landscape-level hazards like wildfire, flooding, and landslides. Overlapping jurisdictions among the province/state, the regional district, and the municipality also present a problem. Crown land furthers this complex matrix of ownership. Crown land is the responsibility of the province/federal government and often comprises natural resources so it represents a significant part of rural economy and identity.

In response to these challenges, building capacity in rural areas is frequently considered a national priority, including building broadband and data-handling infrastructures and developing human capital through education, employment, and entrepreneurial opportunities (e.g., Skerratt, 2018). Developing human capital is challenging when few guideposts exist in urban contexts, with out-migration of skills and young people, and with the need to create or recruit new leaders comfortable with technological change. Digital literacy, including the ability to use software, to code, and to build computerized devices, should be an important outcome for the primary and post-secondary education system or in extra-curricular clubs and maker spaces. Many remote areas do not have post-secondary institutions; however, distance education or self-directed learning via forums can partially fill this gap where broadband is available. Dabson (2001) argues that, for success in rural areas, an entire entrepreneurial infrastructure of intermediaries, trade associations, and resource networks (e.g., training, targeted financing) must be built. As suggested above, rural areas could take advantage of infomediaries like libraries (cf. Robinson & Ward Mather, 2017) to strengthen open data capacity and literacy.

The need to diversify rural economies through developing the service sector is aligned with building technology capacity, so many policy interventions are likely to include building capacity for open data. Developing open data capacity can strengthen community resilience in the face of macro-economic trends like globalization, climate change, and urbanization (Roberts et al., 2017). Beyond education, community-development approaches that include participatory action research and participatory evaluation methodologies can offer effective methods for building community capacities and increasing the sustainability of rural ICT projects (Lennie et al., 2005). Ruijer and Meijer (2020) used a living-labs approach to argue for an intensive support system to teach rural users on various aspects of open data handling: their interventions revealed that significant managerial resources and data standards were needed for open data use to meet its potential. Leadership in the adoption of new technologies is critical (Murray & Dunn, 1995). Empowering women, in particular, is key as women play significant leadership roles in rural community development and as women use many forms of technology more often than men (Hay & Pearce, 2014). Conversely, technology leaders can entrench existing power dynamics or inequalities (Ashman et al., 2017). Overall, collaboration across communities—horizontal trans-jurisdictionality—plays an important role (Eastwood et al., 2017); for instance, by enabling the development of a threshold level of standardized data or by pooling resources in regional offices to provide services for smaller communities.

Entrenchment of power can hide a form of a paternalism, as suggested from an evaluation of rural open data within the EU (European Data Portal Consortium, 2020, p. 21): "Our interviewees agreed that the greatest potential of rural open data was to impact rural rather than have rural users. This is because the skills, knowledge and connections to ideas and innovation were most often found in urban areas with exposure to the quadruple helix of business, government, academia and citizenry."

The EU findings imply that, while information about rural areas may increase in availability, skill building and other resources can occur outside rural areas. As long as availability improves, there may be less motivation to develop capacity to create, sustain, and make use of open data within rural areas. Ruijer and Meijer (2020) characterize open data usage as a process of innovation; continued exogenous production can limit the opportunity to internalize innovation. Ultimately, we can have increasing amounts of rural open data; we can even have increasing use of rural open data. Open data may be "innovated" *for* rural people but not created or used *by* rural people to the same degree as urban.

To embed innovation, place-based economic development is recommended by many investigators (Markey et al., 2012; Markey et al., 2008; Gadsby & Samson, 2016). Their approaches focus on the unique resources, assets, and amenities of each place. This may result in a development road map customized for each community, although open data provision may not be a top priority in every case. Place-based economic development suggests that a one-size solution for rural open data or "smart tech" issues is unlikely (Spicer et al., 2021). Instead, approaches that link specific actors with local resources, amenities, and development priorities at the community level are recommended (Markey et al., 2012; Ashman et al., 2017; Ruijer & Meijer, 2020). These in turn reinforce the need for fine-resolution open data that are useful for local decision-making.

Tools developed for urban open data applications could benefit rural areas as well. Urban areas have extensive best (and worst) practices regarding open data standards, licences, and web portals that provide search-and-discover tools as well as free downloading. Some are directly transferable to rural communities where capacity and funding exist. Cities have harnessed the entrepreneurial spirit through hackathons; for rural places to create a critical mass of interoperable data, it is necessary to attract application development. However, agreement among more jurisdictions would be required. When Canadian cities like Vancouver or Montréal create a data standard, a developer can build a tool with a large potential market. In a rural region, agreement must be reached by several communities to create similar business opportunities. Standards adopted by the province or the nation for its purposes may not suit local needs, especially when jurisdictional scale and data update schedule are considered. This issue is amplified in rural settings, where much more of the land is managed by other jurisdictions. A committed and responsive regional governance structure is required to develop and adopt standards.

Emerging technologies may help or hinder rural open data production and use. Affordable satellite communications could solve issues with broadband access. When we consider satellites as data sources, satellite imagery is increasingly offered at finer spatial resolutions. This could improve the spatial resolution of a region while decreasing the cost of data collection over large rural areas. Cloud-based services could largely eliminate the need for in-house ICT capacity. Conversely, even large changes in the availability of rural open data may fail to produce significant changes on the ground. Indeed, they may lead to more labour-shedding for the tech-intensive industries, say in terms of optimization or scaling-up services. Increased efficiency as a result of available open data may come at the cost of increased employment and upskilling of employees.

Our investigation of the rural dimensions of open data suggests open data practice exhibits both similarity and difference vis-à-vis urban open data. Rural agencies should evaluate each urban practice for local use before adoption. If the goal of open data policy is to benefit all citizens equally, then different interventions may be required in urban and rural contexts. Current market forces tend to favour the development of urban open data capacity, so compensatory public investments should be made in rural capacity. Participatory and place-based rural economic development that accounts for specific characteristics and community assets offers the greatest hope in equipping small towns and rural areas with the skills and tools needed to open up data. Shearmur et al. (2020, p. 311) reveal a paradox (here translated from the French) should rural areas choose to adopt technologies that make them smart: "The intelligent rural area therefore begins to be considered, even if, paradoxically, it forms part of a contest that promotes the smart city. That is, the rural world will become intelligent only if it urbanizes." Rural areas should not have to sacrifice their uniqueness, their rurality, to create, sustain, and find productive uses for open data.

References

Ashman, F. H., & Farrington, J. H., & Skerratt, S. (2017). Community-led broadband in rural digital infrastructure development: Implications for resilience. *Journal of Rural Studies, 54*, 408–425.

Bell, M. M. (1992). The fruit of difference: The rural-urban continuum as a system of identity. *Rural Sociology, 57*(1), 65–82.

Bollman, R. D. (Ed). (2000). *Rural and small town Canada analysis bulletin 2*(6). 21-006-XIE. Statistics Canada.

Boyce, M. S. (2017). Moose survey app for population monitoring. *Wildlife Society Bulletin, 41*(1), 125–128.

Brown, A. (1980). Technical assistance to rural communities: Stopgap or capacity building? *Public Administration Review, 40*(1), 18–23.

Canadian Internet Registration Authority. (2020). *Canada's Internet factbook 2020*. Retrieved May 8, 2021, from https://www.cira.ca/resources/factbook/canadas-internet-factbook-2020

Canadian Radio-television and Telecommunications Commission (CRTC). (2020). *Communications Monitoring Report 2019*. CRTC. Retrieved May 8, 2021, from https://crtc.gc.ca/pubs/cmr2020-en.pdf

Carra, B. (2020, April 2). *Opinion: It's time to act on rural internet access*. CBC News. Retrieved May 9, 2021, from https://www.cbc.ca/news/canada/calgary/covid-19-rural-internet-access-cybera-1.5517643

Carter, D. C. (2008). *Governmental fragmentation and rural sprawl: Case studies examining governmental structure and limited public choice* [Doctoral dissertation, University of Tennessee]. Retrieved May 9, 2021, from http://trace.tennessee.edu/utk_graddiss/417

Chamber of Commerce. (2017). *Policy resolutions 2017*. Archived May 9, 2021, from https://www.kelownachamber.org/files/CCC%20Policy%20Resolution%20Manual%202017.pdf

Chan, M., Johnson, P. A., & Shookner, M. (2016). Assessing the use of government open data and the role of data infomediaries: The case of Nova Scotia's community counts program. *Journal of electronic Democracy, 8*(1), 1–27.

Cloke, P. (2006). Conceptualizing rurality. In P. Cloke, T. Marsden, & P. Mooney (Eds.), *Handbook of rural studies* (pp. 18–28). Sage.

Conradie, P., & Choenniab, S. (2014). On the barriers for local government releasing open data. *Government Information Quarterly, 31* (Suppl. 1), S10–S17.

Currie, L. (2013). *The role of Canadian municipal open data: A multi-city evaluation* [Master's thesis]. Queen's University. http://hdl.handle.net/1974/8159

Dabson, B. (2001). Supporting rural entrepreneurship. In M. Drabenstott & K. H. Sheaff (Eds.), *Exploring policy options for a new rural America* (pp. 35–47). National Science Foundation.

Davies, T., & Perini, F. (2016). Researching the emerging impacts of open data: Revisiting the ODDC conceptual framework. *The Journal of Community Informatics, 12*(2), 148–178.

Dolan, D. A. (1990). Local government fragmentation: Does it drive up the cost of government? *Urban Affairs Quarterly 26*(1), 28–45.

du Plessis, V., Beshiri, R., Bollman, R. D., & Clemenson, H. (2002). Definitions of rural. *Agriculture and Rural Working Paper Series*. Statistics Canada.

Eastwood, C., Klerkx, L., & Nettle, R. (2017). Dynamics and distribution of public and private research and extension roles for technological innovation and diffusion: Case studies of the implementation and adaptation of precision farming technologies. *Journal of Rural Studies, 49*, 1–12.

Environment Canada. (2021). *Resources for conducting aquatic biomonitoring*. Retrieved May 9, 2021, from https://www.canada.ca/en/environment-climate-change/services/canadian-aquatic-biomonitoring-network/resources.html

European Data Portal Consortium. (2020). *Analytical report 14: Enabling smart rural: The open data gap*. Publications Office of the European Union. Retrieved May 15, 2021, from https://data.europa.eu/sites/default/files/analytical_report_14_enabling_smart_rural.pdf

Fritz, S., See, L., Perger, C., McCallum, I., Schill, C., Schepaschenko, D., Duerauer, M., Karner, M., Dresel, C., Laso-Bayas, J. C., Lesiv, M., Moorthy, I., Salk, C. F., Danylo, O., Sturn, T., Albrecht, F., You, L., Kraxner, F., & Obersteiner, M. (2017). A global dataset of crowdsourced land cover and land use reference data. *Scientific Data, 4*, 170075.

Gadsby, L., & Samson, R. (2016). *Strengthening rural Canada: Why place matters in rural communities*. Decoda Literary Solutions.

Government of Canada. (2020). *Extending and enhancing broadband*. Connecting Canadians. Science and Economic Development Canada. Retrieved May 9, 2021, from https://www.ic.gc.ca/eic/site/028.nsf/eng/h_00587.html

Gray, J., Holley, C., & Rayfuse, R. (2016). The challenge of trans-jurisdictional water law and governance. In J. Gray, C. Holley, & R. Rayfuse (Eds.), *Trans-jurisdictional water law and governance* (pp. 3–18). Earthscan, Routledge.

Grimes, S. (1992). Exploiting information and communication technologies for rural development. *Journal of Rural Studies, 8*(3), 269–278.

Gurstein, M. B. (2011). Open data: Empowering the empowered or effective data use for everyone? *First Monday, 16*(2).

Haartsen, T., Huigen, P. P. & Groote, P. (2003). Rural areas in the Netherlands. *Tijdschrift voor economische en sociale geografie*, 94, 129–136.

Halseth, G., & Ryser, L. (2018). *Towards a political economy of resource-dependent regions*. Routledge.

Hay, R., & Pearce, P. (2014). Technology adoption by rural women in Queensland, Australia: Women driving technology from the homestead for the paddock. *Journal of Rural Studies, 36*, 318–327.

Huggins, R., & Izushi, H. (2002). The digital divide and ICT learning in rural communities: Examples of good practice service delivery. *Local Economy, 17*(2), 111–122.

Johnson, P., Sieber, R., Scassa, T., Stephens, M., & Robinson, P. (2017). The Cost(s) of Geospatial Open Data. *Transactions in GIS, 21*, 434–445.

Johnson, P., & Robinson, P. (2014). Civic hackathons: Innovation, procurement, or civic engagement? *Review of Policy Research, 31*(4), 349–357.

Kukutai, T., & Taylor, J. (2016). Data sovereignty for Indigenous peoples: Current practice and future needs. In T. Kukutai & J. Taylor (Eds.), *Indigenous data sovereignty: Toward an agenda* (pp. 1–22). ANU Press.

Launspach, J. J., & Bolgrien, D. W. (2016). *Crowdsourcing as a novel approach to mapping ecosystem services in a Great Lakes area of concern.* Minnesota GIS/LIS Conference, October 26–28, 2016, Duluth, Min., United States.

Lennie, J., Hearn, G., Simpson, L., & Kimber, M. (2005). Building community capacities in evaluating rural IT projects: Success strategies from the Learners Project. *International Journal of Education and Development using Information and Communication Technology, 1*(1), 13–31.

Leone, L. (2015). Open data and food law in the digital era: Empowering citizens through ICT technology. *European Food and Feed Law Review, 10*(5), 356–363.

Light, S. S. (Ed.) (2004). *The role of biodiversity conservation in the transition to rural sustainability.* IOS Press.

Linders, D. (2013). Towards open development: Leveraging open data to improve the planning and coordination of international aid. *Government Information Quarterly, 30*(4), 426–434.

Malecki, E. J. (2003). Digital development in rural areas: Potentials and pitfalls. *Journal of Rural Studies, 19*(2), 201–214.

Malecki, E. J. (2001). Going digital in rural America. In M. Drabenstott & K. H. Sheaff (Eds.), *Exploring policy options for a new rural America* (pp. 49–68). National Science Foundation.

Markey, S., Halseth, G., & Manson, D. (2012). *Investing in place: Economic renewal in northern British Columbia.* UBC Press.

Markey, S., Halseth, G., & Manson, D. (2008). Closing the implementation gap: A framework for incorporating the context of place in economic development planning. *Local Environment, 13*(4), 337–351.

McCarthy, J. (2008). Rural geography: Globalizing the countryside. *Progress in Human Geography, 32*(1), 129–137.

McKinney, M. L. (2002). Urbanization, biodiversity, and conservation: The impacts of urbanization on native species are poorly studied, but educating a highly urbanized human population about these impacts can greatly improve species conservation in all ecosystems. *BioScience, 52*(10), 883–890.

Montes, M. G., & Slater, D. (2019). Data literacy. In T. Davies, S. Walker, M. Rubinstein, & F. Perini (Eds.), *The state of open data: Histories and horizons* (pp. 274–286). African Minds and International Development Research Centre.

Murray, M., & Dunn, L. (1995). Capacity building for rural development in the United States. *Journal of Rural Studies, 11*(1), 89–97.

Open Knowledge Foundation. (n.d.). *What is open.* Retrieved May 9, 2021, from https://okfn.org/opendata/

Parfitt, I. (2017). *Open data and Canadian rural communities.* GIS Education and Research Conference, University of Toronto, Toronto, Ontario, Canada. Retrieved May 10, 2021, from https://www.dropbox.com/s/dbzu9dmajw8n8p7/GISinEd2017%20abstracts%20and%20presentation%20links.pdf

Parker, E. B. (2000). Closing the digital divide in rural America. *Telecommunications Policy, 24*(4), 281–290.

Phillips, G. (2015). *Indigenous data sovereignty and nation rebuilding.* 3rd International Open Data Conference May 28–29, 2015, Ottawa, Ontario, Canada. Retrieved May 9, 2021, from http://conf3.wpengine.com/webcast/recording-indigenous-data-open-governments/

Pinto, J. K., & Onsrud, H. J. (1995). Sharing geographic information across organizational boundaries. In H. J. Onsrud & G. Rushton (Eds.), *Sharing geographic information* (pp. 44–64). CUPR Press.

Roberts, E., Beel, D., Philip, L., & Townsend, L. (2017). Rural resilience in a digital society. *Journal of Rural Studies, 54*, 355–359.

Robinson, P., & Ward Mather, L. (2017). Open data community maturity: Libraries as civic infomediaries. *Urban and Regional Information Science Association Journal, 28*(1), 31–39.

Ruijer, E. & Meijer, A. (2020). Open government data as an innovation process: Lessons from a living lab experiment. *Public Performance & Management Review, 43*(3), 613–635.

Ryser, L., & Halseth, G. (2010). Rural economic development: A review of the literature from industrialized economies. *Geography Compass, 4*(6), 510–531.

Salemink, K., Strijker, D., & Bosworth, G. (2017). Rural development in the digital age: A systematic literature review on unequal ICT availability, adoption, and use in rural areas. *Journal of Rural Studies, 54*, 360–371.

Samson, F. B., Knopf, F. L., & Ostlie, W. R. (2004). Great plains ecosystems: Past, present and future. *Wildlife Society Bulletin, 32*(1), 6–15.

Schaap, B., Musker, R., Parr, M., & Laperriere, A. (2019). Open data and agriculture. In T. Davies, S. Walker, M. Rubinstein, & F. Perini (Eds.), *The state of open data: Histories and horizons* (pp. 35–50). African Minds and International Development Research Centre.

Schaffers, H., Komninos, N., Pallot, M., Trousse, B., Nilsson, M., & Oliveira, A. (2011). Smart cities and the future Internet: Towards cooperation frameworks for open innovation. In J. Domingue, A. Galis, A. Gavras, T. Zahariadis, D. Lambert, F. Cleary, P. Daras, S. Krco, H. Müller, M. Li, H. Schaffers, V. Lotz, F. Alvarez, B. Stiller, S. Karnouskos, S. Avessta, & M. Nilsson (Eds.), *The future internet assembly* (pp. 431–446). Springer.

Schaffers H., Cordoba, M. G., Kallai, T., Hongisto, P., Merz, C., & Van Rensburg, J. (2007). Exploring business models for open innovation in rural living labs. In K. S. Pawar, K.-D. Thoben, & M. Pallot (Eds.), *Proceedings of the 13th International Conference on Concurrent Enterprising* (pp. 49–56). Centre for Concurrent Enterprise.

Serwadda, D., Ndebele, P., Grabowski, M. K., Bajunirwe, F., & Wanyenze, R. K. (2018). Open data sharing and the global south—who benefits? *Science, 359*(6376), 642–643.

Shearmur, R., Charron, M., & Pajevic, F. (2020). Pourquoi seules les villes sont-elles qualifiées d'intelligentes? Un vocabulaire du biais urbain. *The Canadian Geographer/Le Géographe canadien, 64*(2), 310–322.

Sieber, R. E., & Johnson, P. A. (2015). Civic open data at a crossroads: dominant models and current challenges. *Government Information Quarterly, 32*(3), 308–315.

Skerratt, S. (2018). *Recharging rural: Report to the Prince's Countryside Fund.* Retrieved May 9, 2021, from https://www.princescountrysidefund.org.uk/downloads/research/recharging-rural-full-report-final.pdf

Spicer, Z., Goodman, N., & Olmstead, N. (2021). The frontier of digital opportunity: Smart city implementation in small, rural and remote communities in Canada. *Urban Studies, 58*(3), 535–558.

Statistics Canada. (2015). *Rural area.* Census dictionary, online catalogue no. 98-301-XWE. Statistics Canada. Retrieved June 9, 2018, from https://www12.statcan.gc.ca/census-recensement/2011/ref/dict/geo042-eng.cfm

Statistics Canada. (2019). *Rural area.* Dictionary, census of population, 2016. Retrieved May 7, 2021, from https://www12.statcan.gc.ca/census-recensement/2016/ref/dict/geo042-eng.cfm

Stephens, M. G. (2017). *Hyper-local open data and data democracy across scales.* American Association of Geographers Conference, April 5–9, Boston, MA., United States.

Wineman, A., Alia, D. Y., & Anderson, C. L. (2020). Definitions of "rural" and "urban" and understandings of economic transformation: Evidence from Tanzania. *Journal of Rural Studies, 79*, 254–268.

Vasantha, A., Vijayumar, G., Corney, J., Acur Bakir, N., Lynn, A., Jagadeesan, A. P., Smith, M., & Agarwal, A. (2014). Social implications of crowdsourcing in rural Scotland. *International Journal of Social Science & Human Behavior Study, 1*(3), 47–52.

Verhulst, S. G., & Young, A. (2017). *Open data in developing economies: Toward building an evidence base on what works and how*. African Minds.

Zarifa, D., Seward, B., & Pizarro Milian, R. (2019). Location, location, location: Examining the rural-urban skills gap in Canada. *Journal of Rural Studies, 72*, 252–263.

Zanella, A., Bui, N., Castellani, A., Vangelista, L., & Zorzi, M. (2014). Internet of things for smart cities. *IEEE Internet of Things Journal, 1*(1), 22–32.

Zuiderwijk, A., Janssen, M., Choenni, S., Meijer, R., & Alibaks, R. S. (2012). Socio-technical impediments of open data. *Electronic Journal of e-Government, 10*(2), 156–172.

About the Authors

Renee Sieber is Associate Professor of Geographic Information Science at McGill University, where she is jointly appointed between the Department of Geography and the Bieler School of Environment, and affiliated with the School of Computer Science. She investigates information and communications technologies that better connect citizens to cities. Her current interest includes data science, algorithmic regulation, and the impact of artificial intelligence on cities.

Ian Parfitt is an instructor and Geospatial Research Coordinator at Selkirk College, Castlegar, British Columbia. He conducts research in both human and physical geography: he was the primary investigator of an SSHRC College and Community Social Innovation Fund grant titled "Open Data for Open Government in Rural BC" (www.ruralopendata.ca) and is currently Research Program Manager for the NSERC College and Community Innovation grant "Building an Innovative Forestry Technology Cluster." Parfitt holds MSc (Geography) and BLArch degrees from the University of British Columbia. He is pursuing a PhD in remote sensing and conservation policy at UBC-Okanagan.

PART IV

The Future of Open Data

CHAPTER 9

Reflections on the Future of Open Data

PAMELA ROBINSON AND LISA WARD MATHER

Abstract
This chapter takes the form of an extended postscript, a bridge, rather, between the research conducted and shared by our authors and the future of open data in a world that is currently in a state of rapid flux. The COVID-19 global pandemic, the climate emergency, and our collective efforts to confront systemic racism are among the significant current challenges we face as a society. Each of these challenges, among others, has clear points of connection to data and evidence informing decision-making. These challenges reinforce the pressing nature of the central question of this book: What is the future of open data?

1. Challenges to the Future of Open Data

1.1 Broader Ecosystem Dynamics Impacting the Future of Open Data

The grant that funded the research shared in this book came to an end in early 2019, but this compilation of research was completed in early 2021. During this past year, the ongoing rise of smart cities, machine learning and artificial intelligence, and the COVID-19 pandemic present further challenges to the future of open data that will be explored here.

1.2 The Future of Open Data Needs to Reconcile Tensions with Smart City Efforts

The "smart city" movement continues to gain traction in Canada, despite the term taking on quite different meanings. Key features of a smart city typically include interlinked and networked systems which generate big data that are used to "manage and control urban life in real-time" (Kitchin, 2015). Smart cities generate large amounts of data—from sensors, software, social networking, and surveillance cameras, among other sources—which makes these projects part of the larger debates around open data and open government. As Canadian cities are now beginning to use smart city technologies, this raises questions about what "open" means in the context of a smart city. Many characteristics of a smart city could be designed to be open, such as sensor data that are made publicly available, open-source technology, or progress toward an open government policy. But just because they can be open does not mean they will. There is a huge proprietary advantage to being the "owner" of these large datasets, so the incentive to share the data openly and willingly is low.

Importantly, thus far, municipal governments do not always seem to recognize, or reflect on the significance of, the link between smart cities and open data when developing smart city projects. Round one of Infrastructure Canada's Smart Cities Challenge, which took place from the summer of 2018 to the summer of 2019, provided a window into the ways in which open data could find a place in smart city efforts. The Challenge itself embodied unique aspects of openness; for example, all the applications to the Challenge were required to be posted on municipal government websites at the time of submission (Infrastructure Canada, 2019) and applicants were asked to address the extent to which their projects would include elements of open data (Impact Canada, 2017). But an open challenge does not ensure open data outcomes. It is still early days for evaluating the extent to which "open" is a value the winners actively embrace, but as these projects move from plans into actions, it is an important issue to continue to track.

From the fall of 2017 through the spring of 2020, Waterfront Toronto and Alphabet's Sidewalk Labs began their 29-month interaction exploring a large-scale smart city master plan for 12 acres of land on Toronto's waterfront. Among the many points of contention in this project was the issue of how data—open or not—would be governed (Robinson & Biggar, 2021; Scassa 2020). Data trusts were floated as a new governance framework that might help mitigate the tensions between open data, private data, privacy, and security (McDonald, 2019), but the early discussion around this intervention raised many more questions than answers.

A particular category of data produced in some smart city projects has called into question the benefit of an open-by-default approach to data. This is human behavioural data, which include, as Bianca Wylie (2018, p. 2) notes, "both aggregate and de-identified data about people." She argues that this type of data, "even when anonymous or aggregate, needs a special approach that may be hard to reconcile with openness" (p. 1). Human behavioural data, collected by sensors, cameras, software, and social media, are particularly problematic because they have value not only for governments, but also for the private sector. Wylie points out that there is a "legislative and policy vacuum regarding consumer protection and technology products, in particular in the context of data products" (p. 5). Because of this, open data policies that are meant to democratize data could become more about "commercialization and outsourcing" (p. 11). Wylie concludes that the process of opening up data should not be slowed "where it is working"; rather, "out of caution, some open data should not be published as such," but they could, under the right conditions, be shared with stakeholders (p. 6). This caution would protect the individual, as well as the wider public.

Public space in the smart city is at the centre of this dilemma (Robinson, 2018, 2019). Many vendors have products that gather data in public spaces, raising expectations that these datasets should be open because they are generated in public/open spaces. But corporations that implement smart city projects on behalf of municipalities can claim ownership of the data they collect in public space. This is problematic for three reasons. One, when public surveillance and data collection are permitted, individuals may no longer have a reasonable expectation of privacy. Two, citizens being tracked in public spaces have often not provided informed consent for their data to be collected, yet these data could be used to manipulate their future behaviour. And, three, if corporate interests own data that are of value to governments, it is possible that the data could be sold back to governments as a service. In this case, governments would be data consumers rather than data stewards.

Between the Smart Cities Challenge and Toronto's two-year engagement with Sidewalk Labs on the Quayside project (Robinson &

Coutts, 2019), it is clear that open data is not necessarily fundamentally linked to smart city efforts. The Open Smart City work discussed in Chapter 1 of this volume introduces one approach to better ensure this alignment. The leadership on this approach, coming from Tracey Lauriault, a contributing author to this volume, and Open North (see Lauriault et al. 2019), are now connected to the Smart Cities Challenge through the Community Solutions Network. Will this commitment to open processes and open data continue through other Infrastructure Canada initiatives in the post-COVID era? Will "open" be a fundamental value in future Canadian smart city efforts? Arriving at sensible answers to these questions requires an evaluation of the evolution of how open data figures in new smart city innovation efforts.

1.3 The Future of Open Data Needs a More Nuanced Approach to Whose Data are Gathered and Open

As the open data movement has continued to evolve, a significant tension is emerging. The open data movement's goals of transparent, inclusive, and accountable actions are in contrast to the myriad ways that data can be—and are—readily deployed with the opposite intent or outcomes.

Recent reflections and ongoing research about the potential impacts of artificial intelligence, automated decision-making and machine learning signal cautions for curators and users of open datasets. Poor, equity seeking, and racialized people are subject to more surveillance, and therefore data collection, than people who have more means and political access, and who are white (Eubanks, 2018). From *Weapons of Math Destruction* (O'Neil, 2016) to *Artificial Unintelligence* (Brossard, 2018) to *Black Software* (McIlwain, 2020) to *Data Feminism* (D'Ignazio & Klein, 2020), there is a rapidly expanding scholarship of critical data studies loudly asserting that data-driven efforts, if left unattended or unevaluated, will have a natural tendency to over-serve majority and dominant populations while simultaneously disadvantaging and sometimes harming others. First Nations, Inuit, and Métis Peoples have developed their own governance principles concerning data ownership, control, access, and possession (OCAP) in response to the collection of their data being weaponized against them (FNIGC, 2020).

The late spring of 2020 saw an increase in anti-Black, anti-Asian, and anti-Indigenous racism, leading to large public protests.

The relationships between racialized and equity-seeking communities and the police were central to these protests. While long recognized as problematic, these tensions are connected, in part to the kinds of data gathered about Black, Indigenous, and other racialized people, and how law-enforcement organizations use data (D'Ignazio & Klein, 2020). As the COVID-19 pandemic evolved, public-health disparities in Black, Indigenous, and other racialized communities emerged (Bascaramurty, 2021). The absence of good public-health data in these communities undermined and delayed the delivery of care and support. There is simultaneously too much and not enough data being collected in these communities. The spring of 2020 gave rise to calls for more open, transparent, and accountable data gathering, use, and deployment. So, despite the democratic and inclusive ideals driving the open data movement, the future of open data must attend to these disparities. Open data communities whose membership and leadership do not mirror the diversity of the communities in which they work need to begin building new relationships, with the long-term goal of seeing change over time. Data-driven efforts to address economic, social, spatial, and ecological inequities need to centre the leadership and experiences of the community members experiencing the inequities or these efforts might further entrench persistent settler, colonial, and/or systemically racist systems and practices.

Publishing data often fails to achieve meaningful "awareness" or insight because making sense of data is not easy. As Jean-Noé Landry and Merlin Chatwin describe (2018, p. 4):

> Opening data does not automatically create a data literate public. City officials need to work with potential data users to ensure that they have the right skills to use the data. Officials themselves often require more training to be able to publish and use high quality data. . . . For [many cities], open data has been integrated into their strategy, but it still lacks sufficient human and financial resources to result in meaningful social impact.

One general concern is that, once launched, open data portals seem static and dated, like "abandoned last-minute science fair projects, pie charts sagging because someone didn't use enough glue stick" (Mulholland, 2016). Technology enthusiasts optimistically believe that "if you build it they will come" but research suggests otherwise (Sieber et al., 2016; Sieber & Johnson, 2015; Johnson et al., 2017). The acts of opening the portal or gathering the data are not enough. For an open data ecosystem to thrive, open data advocates and users across public, private, and civil-society sectors continue to see the transformative potential of open data, and continue to work to achieve its many elusive goals.

There is a good deal of agreement across sectors, including among governments, non-profit organizations, and community groups, about what open data initiatives need to do now. Inside government, staff are routinely having to make the business case for further investments in open data (Robinson & Johnson, 2016). Beyond the entrepreneurial use of these datasets, and despite the open data movement's foundational commitment to democratic principles, there is a need for civic infomediaries (Robinson & Ward Mather, 2017) to advocate for open data release that serves public and/or civic intent as well. Non-profit groups, such as Code for Canada, Code for America, and the Open Data Institute, work to improve government, and the use of government data, from the inside by embedding technologists on fellowships inside governments to help bring new thinking and mobilize new ways of working. From civic hackathons (Costanza-Chock, 2020; Johnson & Robinson, 2014; Robinson & Johnson, 2016) to the leadership of public libraries helping community members begin to understand and use data, the work of civic infomediaries continues to hold space for open data use for the public good.

The COVID-19 pandemic presented a new challenge to the open data movement in that, despite the digital nature of open data, the work of open data civic infomediaries has historically relied on people working together in person to mobilize open data use. Civic hackathons tend to gather people in physical locations. Co-working spaces (e.g., WeWork, the Centre for Social Innovation in Toronto) and civic technology hubs including Civic Hall (New York) and Civic Hall Canada (Toronto) have been built around the belief that by gathering like-minded people together, creative combustion can emerge from the collision of ideas and people in shared spaces. Civic technology groups across North America (e.g., Smart Chicago, Civic Tech Toronto) regularly meet in person or virtually, via weekly hack nights, for example. The Code for Canada and Code for America fellowship models have their fellows working inside government offices, side by side with government staff. Public libraries have made significant investments in data-literacy programming and access to shared technology through lending programs and innovation hubs. All these examples have connected digital datasets with physical and material locations aimed at animating their use. If the civic future of open data depends upon civic infomediaries continuing to gather people to share ideas and to collaborate, then the future of open data will, like many other important pursuits, need to evolve new techniques for working together.

2. The Future of Open Data is . . . Emergent and Evolving

Academic research is easier to conduct on static or completed subject matter. Research in real-time in collaboration with partners presents a wide range of challenges. The research conducted here, with its focus on the future of open data, has straddled the opportunity to evaluate the ongoing evolution of open data ecosystems while also tracking a series of conditions that are impacting how that ecosystem may continue to evolve. As open data ecosystems have matured, the research shared here sheds new light on the nuance and texture needed in the kinds of data gathered and deployed, in the governance frameworks to regulate and advance open data use, and as concerns the participation and engagement by open data actors.

Thus far, open data ecosystems have shown their capacity to adapt and respond to these changing dynamics. The persistence of the COVID-19 pandemic, among other significant societal challenges, suggests further turbulence and challenge ahead. Across these challenges it is clear, the work of opening data for private and public good is an asymptotic pursuit that will require ongoing attention, investment, and evaluation, and refinement and revision of actions.

References

Bascaramurty, D. (2021, January 26). Racialized Canadians have some of the highest rates of COVID-19 infections in the country. Who can allay their doubts about taking the vaccine? *Globe and Mail*. https://www.theglobeandmail.com/canada/article-racialized-canadians-need-the-covid-19-vaccine-more-urgently-than-most/

Brossard, M. (2019). *Artificial Unintelligence*. MIT Press.

Costanza-Chock, S. (2020). *Design justice: Community-led practices to build the worlds we need*. MIT Press.

D'Ignazio, C., & Klein, L. (2020). *Data feminism*. MIT Press.

Eubanks, V. (2018). *Automating inequality: How high-tech tools profile, police, and punish the poor.* St. Martin's Press.

First Nations Information Governance Centre (FNIGC). (2020). *Introducing a First Nations data governance strategy.* https://fnigc.ca/news/introducing-first-nations-data-governance-strategy.html

Impact Canada. (2017). *Smart Cities Challenge: Applicant guide.* https://impact.canada.ca/en/challenges/smart-cities/applicant-guide

Infrastructure Canada. (2019). *Smart Cities Challenge.* https://www.infrastructure.gc.ca/cities-villes/index-eng.html

Johnson, P. A., Corbett, J. M., Gore, C., Robinson, P., Allen, P., & Sieber, R. (2015). A web of expectations: Evolving relationships in community participatory geoweb projects. *ACME: An International E-Journal for Critical Geographies, 14*(3), 827–848.

Johnson, P. A., & Robinson, P. (2014). Civic hackathons: Innovation, procurement, or civic engagement? *Review of Policy Research, 31*(4), 349–357. https://doi.org/10.1111/ropr.12074

Kitchin, R. (2015). Making sense of smart cities: Addressing present shortcomings. *Cambridge Journal of Regions, Economy and Society, 8*(1), 131–136. https://doi.org/10.1093/cjres/rsu027

Landry, J. N., & Chatwin, M. (2018). Making cities open by default: Lessons from open data pioneers. Retrieved August 31, 2021, from https://opennorth.ca/publications/2ce88qelsh6m30thifiniy_en

Lauriault, T. P., Bloom, R., & Landry, J.-N. (2019). *The open smart cities guide.* Retrieved May 10, 2019, from https://www.opennorth.ca/publications/#open-smart-cities-guide.

McDonald, S. (2019) *Reclaiming data trusts.* Centre for International Governance Innovation. https://www.cigionline.org/articles/reclaiming-data-trusts

McIlwain, C. D. (2020). *Black software: The Internet and racial justice, from the AfroNet to Black Lives Matter.* Oxford University Press.

Mulholland, J. (2016, March 10). 6 ideas to help government realize open data's transformative power. *Government Technology.* https://www.govtech.com/data/6-Ideas-to-Help-Government-Realize-Open-Datas-Transformative-Power.html

O'Neil, C. (2016). *Weapons of math destruction: How big data increases inequality and threatens democracy.* Crown Publishers.

Robinson, P. (2019). Public space in a smart city. In N. Ahmed, M. Claudel, Z. Ibrahim, C. Pandolfi, & B. Wylie (Eds.), *Some Thoughts* (p. 43). https://some-thoughts.org/

Robinson, P. (2018). Design interventions for a digital venture. *Spacing, 46* (Spring), 30–31.

Robinson, P., & Biggar, J. (2021). Seeing the city as a platform: Is Canada's Smart Cities Challenge a step in that direction? In A. Zwick & Z. Spicer

(Eds.), *The platform economy and the smart city: Technology and the transformation of urban policy*. McGill-Queen's University Press.

Robinson, P., & Coutts, S. (2019). The case of Quayside, Toronto, Canada. In L. Anthopoulos (Ed.), *Smart city emergence: Cases from around the world* (pp. 330–350). Elsevier.

Robinson, P., & Johnson, P. A. (2016). Civic hackathons: New terrain for local government citizen interaction? *Urban Planning, 1*(2), 65. https://doi.org/10.17645/up.v1i2.627

Robinson, P. J., & Ward Mather, L. (2017). Open data community maturity: Libraries as civic intermediaries. *Journal of the Urban and Regional Information Systems Association, 28*, 31–38.

Scassa, T. (2020). Designing data governance for data sharing: Lessons from Sidewalk Toronto. *Technology & Regulation, 2020*, 44–56. https://techreg.org/index.php/techreg/article/view/51

Sieber, R. E., & Johnson, P. A. (2015). Civic open data at a crossroads: dominant models and current challenges. *Government Information Quarterly, 32*(3), 308–315.

Sieber, R. E., Robinson, P., Johnson, P. A., & Corbett, J. M. (2016). Doing public participation on the geospatial web. *Annals of the American Association of Geographers, 106*(5), 1030–1046. https://doi.org/10.1080/24694452.2016.1191325

Simpler, Faster, Better Services Act, 2019, S.O. 2019, c. 7, Sched. 56.

Wylie, B. (2018). *Open data endgame: Countering the digital consensus* (CIGI Paper No. 186). Centre for International Governance Innovation. https://www.cigionline.org/publications/open-data-endgame-countering-digital-consensus

About the Authors

Pamela Robinson is Professor and Director of the School of Urban and Regional Planning at Ryerson University. Throughout her career as a planner, her research and practice have focused on complex, emergent challenges that Canadian communities face. Her current research focuses on the question of who is planning the Canadian smart city? She writes for Spacing.ca about sustainability, technology, and civic engagement in Canadian cities. Robinson was a member of Waterfront Toronto's Digital Strategy Advisory Panel, was an inaugural member of the Multi-Stakeholder Forum for the Government of Canada's Open Government Partnership, and is an advisor on the Toronto Public Library's Innovation Council.

Lisa Ward Mather is an Urban Planner who graduated from Ryerson University's Master of Planning program. She has done research in planning policy and is also interested in the power of new technology to improve planning processes for the public sector, the private sector, and the public. She has worked on projects that explore the role of planning around municipal open data, artificial intelligence, civic technology, and smart cities technology.

Index

Law, Technology, and Media

Series editor: Michael Geist

The *Law, Technology, and Media* series explores emerging technology law issues with an emphasis on a Canadian perspective. It is the first University of Ottawa Press series to be fully published under an open access licence.

Previous titles in *Law, Technology, and Media* Series

Elizabeth Dubois and Florian Martin-Bariteau, eds., *Citizenship in a Connected Canada: A Research and Policy Agenda*, 2020.

Alana Maurushat, *Ethical Hacking*, 2019.

Derek McKee, Finn Makela, and Teresa Scassa, eds., *Law and the "Sharing Economy": Regulating Online Market Platforms*, 2018.

Karim Benyekhlef, Jane Bailey, Jacquelyn Burkell, and Fabie Gélinas, eds., *eAccess to Justice*, 2016.

Michael Geist, *Law, Privacy and Surveillance in Canada in the Post-Snowden Era*, 2015.

Jane Bailey and Valerie Steeves, *eGirls, eCitizens*, 2015.

Michael Geist, ed., *The Copyright Pentalogy: How the Supreme Court of Canada Shook the Foundations of Canadian Copyright Law*, 2013.

For a complete list
of the University of Ottawa Press titles, please visit:
www.press.uOttawa.ca

www.ingramcontent.com/pod-product-compliance
Ingram Content Group UK Ltd.
Pitfield, Milton Keynes, MK11 3LW, UK
UKHW020840290926
15470UKWH00004B/1456

9 780776 629742